Mary Shelley Pechin

The 3-6-5 cook book

Mary Shelley Pechin

The 3-6-5 cook book

ISBN/EAN: 9783744785839

Printed in Europe, USA, Canada, Australia, Japan

Cover: Foto ©Lupo / pixelio.de

More available books at **www.hansebooks.com**

THE 3-6-5 COOK BOOK

For use 365 days in the year

MARY SHELLEY PECHIN

"We live not upon what we eat, but what we digest"

PUBLISHED BY
THE HELMAN-TAYLOR COMPANY
CLEVELAND
1899

Dedication.

In loving memory of one who "looked well to the ways of her household," who spoke with wisdom and kindness and whom all who knew, loved and honored—MY MOTHER.

Preface.

IN THIS BOOK have been gathered a number of recipes: some of which are original, the result of years of house-keeping experience; many old and rare ones are from friends; others have been translated from foreign cook books. It is hoped that they may prove acceptable and be useful to many.

Special attention is asked for the chapter on Food for Invalids, as this contains the results of considerable research, consultation with competent authorities and not a little personal experience.

To all who have so generously and kindly given me their valuable recipes, many of them treasures heretofore carefully guarded as family secrets, I tender my sincere and appreciative thanks.

MARY SHELLEY PECHIN.

ALPHABETICAL INDEX.

AIGRETTES
  Of Parmesan, page 154
ALBERRY PUDDING, 24
ALGONQUIN SAUCE, 96
ALMOND CAKE, 208
ALMONDS, SALTED, 273
ANCHOVY
  Sauce, 96
  Savories, 166
  Straws, 166
  Toast, 166
ANGEL CAKE, 208
ANGELS ON HORSEBACK, 33
APRICOT
  Eggs, 242
  Ice Cream, 227
  Muscovite, 243
  Mousse, 229
  Short Cake, 243
APPLES
  To Bake, 242
  Cheese of, 234
  Dumplings, 242
  Float of, 242
  Fried, 262
  Fritters of, 242
  Jelly of, 262
  Marmalade of, 263
  Pies, 234
  Pudding, 242
  And Tapioca, 242
  Toddy, 298
ARABIAN CHOCOLATE, 298
ARTICHOKE
  Creamed, 320
  Globe, 121
  Jerusalem, 121
  Salad, 114
  Soup, 2

ASH CAKE, 188
ASPARAGUS, 120
  Cream of, 15
  Salad, 114
ASPIC JELLY, 263
BACON, 68
BAKED SOUP, 4
BANANAS
  Fried, 121
  Ice Cream of, 227
BARLEY
  Gruel, 282
  Water, 288
BEARNAISE SAUCE, 97
BECHAMEL SAUCE, 97
BEEF
  A la Mode, 40
  To Boil, 39
  Boulettes, 39
  Broth, 2-275
  Corned, 40
  "   Hash, 40
  "   "   and Cream, 41
  Cold Sandwich, 296
  Dripping, 183
  "   to Prepare, 183
  "   Pastry, 183
  Essence, 277
  Fibrin, 42
  Fillet of, 41
  Frizzled, 178
  Hamburg Steak, 42-279
  Juice, 277
  Mock Duck, 43
  "   Hare, 42
  Olives, 43
  Ox Heart, 43
  Pickle for, 43
  Pot Roast, 43, 44

ALPHABETICAL INDEX.

BEEF—Continued.
  Roast of, 47
  Roll of, 45
  Rolled, 45
  Sirloin of, 47
  Spanish Olla Podrida, 46
  Steak, 46
    " Pie, 44
    " Pudding, 44
    " Rump, 46
  Soup, 2
  Stock, 2
  Stew, Bonnar, 48
    " "Good," 47
  Suet Pastry, 233
  Tongue, Fresh, 47
    " Stewed, 46
    " Salmi of, 189
  Triffles, 48

BEANS, 121

BEETS, 121

BENGAL CHUTNEY, 171

BEVERAGES
  Apple Toddy, 298
  Bonum, 298
  Chocolate, to Prepare, 299
    " Arabian, 298
    " 298
  Claret Cup, 301
  Chablis Cup, 301
  Coffee, Filtered, 299
    " for five persons, 299
  Cocktail a la Sherry, 298
  Cocoa, 300
  Creme de Menthe, 301
  Egg Nog, 300
    " " Very Best, 300
    " Lemonade, 300
  Fishhouse Punch, 300
  Fruit Punch, 300
  Grape Juice Mead, 301
  Ginger Cordial, 302
  Lemon Brandy, 304
  Lemonade, 301
    " Calcutta, 301
  Milk Punch, 302

BEVERAGES
  Orange Brandy, 304
  Peach " 304
  Pineapple Punch, 302
  Rum Punch, 302
  Raspberry Vinegar, 174
  Punch, Very Good, 303
  Shandy Gaff, 302
  Siberian Punch, 303
  Tea, to Make, 303
    " with Flavorings, 303
    " Punch, 304
  Warshaw Punch, 303
  West Point " 363

BISCUITS
  Baking Powder, 193
  Milk 194
  Sour Milk, 194
  Split, 194

BISQUE CLAMS, 4

BLACK BEAN SOUP, 3

BLACKBERRY JAM, 263

BLACK BEETLES, TO KILL, 308

BLACK CAKE, 209

BLACK CURRANT JELLY, 263

BLANKETS, TO WASH, 314

BLANQUETTE OF VEAL, 56

BLUEBERRY CAKE, 210
  Batter Pudding, 244

BOILED CIDER,
  For Tarts, 99

BONES FOR SOUP, 98

BONUM PUNCH, 298

BOSTON BAKED BEANS, 122
  Brown Bread, 191

BOUDINS OF CHICKEN, 75

BOUILLON, 2

BOULETTES, 39

BRAINS
  Calf's, 58
  Croquettes, 58
  Salad, 58
  To Prepare, 58
  Sheep's, 49
  And Tomatoes, 143
  Force Meat Balls, 98

BRAISED BEEF, 39
  Loin of Veal, 63

BRANDY CHERRIES, 265
  " Plums, 266
  " Snaps, 211

BREAD, 191, 193
  Boston Brown, 191
  And Butter Pudding, 244
  Cake, 210
  Coffee, 192
  Corn Meal, 198
  Crackling, 192
  Crumbs, 310
  Cups, 90
  Custard, 199
  Griddle Cakes, 200
  Jelly, 280
  Puffs, 192
  Rye and Indian, 192
  Sauce, 98
  " and Onions, 98
  Soup, 4
  Whole Wheat, 193

BREADING, 309

BREADED SPRING CHICKENS, 175

BREAKFAST DISHES, 177
  A Little Breakfast, 177
  Cold Meat Balls, 177
  Croquettes, 177
  Custard, 177
  Dried Beef and Eggs, 177
  " " Frizzled, 178
  Egg Toast, 178
  Kidney, Stewed, 178
  " "My Devil," 179
  Pork Tenderloins, 179

BREAKFAST DISHES
  Savory Molds, 179
  Toast, Calcutta, 180
  " Tomato, 180
  Veal Sefton, 180
  White Puddings, Virginia, 180

BREAST OF LAMB, 56
  " " Mutton, 56
  " " Turkey, 88
  " " Veal, 55

BRIGHTON PUDDING, 248

BRIOCHE, 196

BROILING, 307

BROTH
  "Sheep Trotters," 278

BROWN BETTY PUDDING, 245
  Flour, 305
  Sauce, 99

BRUSSELS SPROUTS, 121

BUCKWHEAT CAKES, 195

BUNS—
  English, 196
  Good Friday, 196
  Hot Cross, 197
  Karlsbaden, 197

BURNS, 302

BUTTERED CAKES, 195

CABBAGE, 123

CAFE PARFAIT, 227

CAKE, 207
  Almond, 208
  Angel, 208
  Black, to Bake, 209
  Black, 209
  Blueberry, 210
  Bread, 210
  Brandy Snaps, 211
  Caramel, 210
  " Filling for, 210

CAKE—Continued.
　Chocolate, 211
　　" Cookies, 211
　　" Filling for, 211
　　" Custard, 211
　　" " Filling for, 211
　Clove, 212
　Cocoanut, 212
　Cold Water, 213
　Cookies, 213
　Corn Starch, 213
　Crullers, 214
　Cup, 212
　　" Little, 212
　Delicate, 214
　Devil, 214
　Doughnuts, 215
　Drop, 215
　Federal, 216
　Fig, 216
　Fruit, White, 216
　General Directions for, 207
　Ginger Bread, 214
　　" Snaps, 215
　Gold, 215
　Hermits, 217
　Hickory Nut, 217
　Icing Almond, 225
　　" Boiled, 217
　　" Lemon, 215
　　" Royal, 225
　　" Soft, 217
　Imperial, Filling for, 217
　Jelly, 218
　Jumbles, 218
　Lady, 218
　　" Fingers, 218
　Layer, 218
　Little, 219
　Loaf, 219
　Macaroons, 219
　Madelaines, 220
　Maple Sugar, 219
　　" Filling for, 219
　Measurements for, 208
　Nut, 220
　Orange, 220
　Plain, 221

CAKE
　Plum (English), 222
　Plunkets, 224
　Pork, 220
　Pound, 221
　Prince of Wales, 224
　Queen, 222
　Sand Tarts, 225
　Sandwich, 222
　Silver, 224
　Soft, 221
　Spanish Bun, 223
　Sponge, 221, 222
　Sunshine, 223
　Velvet Sponge, 223
　Washington, 223
　White Mountain, 224

CALCUTTA LEMONADE, 301

CALF'S BRAINS, 58
　Brains Salad, 114
　Head, 60
　　" Soup, 10
　　" Terrapin, 60
　Liver, 62

CANNED PEACHES, 261

CAPER SAUCE, 99

CARAMEL, 246
　Cake, 210
　Filling for, 210

CARDOONS, 124

CARROTS
　A la Maitre d'Hotel, 124
　Pudding, 246
　Stewed, 124

CATSUP,
　"Afine," 171
　Bengal Chutney, 171
　Cucumber, 173
　East India, 172
　Grape, 172
　Lemon, 173
　Pepper, 174
　Tomato, 175
　Wine, 176

CAUDLE, 290
CAULIFLOWER, 126
  Salad, 115.
CAVIARE CANAPES, 167
CELERY
  Sauce, 101
  Soup, 5
CHAFING DISH.
  Calf's Head Terrapin, 186
  Cheese Fondue, 185
  Chicken, Creamed, 185
  "   Cold, 185
  Chocolate Caramels, 186
  Cold Beef, 187
  Eggs, "a la Goldenrod," 186
  "   Scrambled, 185
  "   "   and Tomatoes, 186
  Fish Dinner, 186
  Ham, Creamed, 188
  Liver, 187
  Lobster, Creamed, 187
  Macaroni, 188
  Oysters and Celery, 188
  "   Creamed, 188
  "   Panned, 188
  "   and Sherry, 188
  "   Squizzled, 189
  Squabs, Stewed, 189
  Sweet Breads, Creamed, 189
  Tomatoes and Eggs, 190
  Tongue, Salmi of, 189
  Venison Steak, 190
  Welsh Rarebit, 190

CHABLIS CUP, 301

CHEESE
  As Food, 154
  Aigrettes, 154
  Balls, 154
  Cheeselets, 154
  Cottage, 155
  Croquettes, 158
  Curds, 158
  Custards, 155
  Fontainbleau, 321

CHEESE
  Fondue, 155, 185
  Kluskis, 156
  Monkey, 156
  Muff, 156
  Parmesan, 158
  Pudding, 156
  Ramakins, 156
  Roasted, 156
  Salad, 114
  Stewed, 157
  Straws, 157
  Souffle, 157
  Toast, 159
  Welsh Rarebit 159, 190

CHARLOTTE RUSSE, 246

CHESTNUT FILLING, 94

CHICKEN
  Au Casserole, 76
  Broth, 5
  Cream, 290
  Creamed, 88
  Croquettes, 77
  Curry, 77
  Deviled, 78
  Escalloped, 78
  Fried, 79
  Gumbo, 10
  And Green Peppers, 321
  Hash, 79
  "   and Eggs, 80
  "   on Rice, 80
  Hungarian, 79
  Jelly, 80
  Jellied, 80, 81
  Jugged, 322
  Livers, 82
  A la Marengo, 82
  Milk, 286
  Patties, 82
  Pie, 83
  And Poached Eggs, 83
  Pot Pie, 83
  Roasting of, 84
  Roast, 84
  Salad, 115
  Sandwiches, 85, 294

CHICKEN—Continued.
  Souffle. 88
  Soup Bones for, 78
  Soup, 5
  Stewed, 85
  Stuffing for, 89
  Swedish, 84
  Timbales of, 86

CHILI PICKLES, 172

CHOCOLATE, 298
  Cake, 211
  Caramels, 186
  Custard and Cake, 211
  Filling for, 211

CLEANING MIXTURE, 315
  For Carpets, 315
  " Clothing, 315
  " Rugs, 315
  " Woolens, 316

CLOTTED CREAM, 100

CLOVE CAKE, 213

COCOA, 299

COCOANUT CAKE, 213
  " Pudding, 246

COCKTAIL a la Shery, 298
  " Oyster, 35

COD, 21
  Pie, 22

CODFISH
  Balls, 29
  Cakes, 29
  Creamed, 30
  On Toast, 30
  To Freshen, 29

COFFEE
  Bread, 192
  For Fire, 299
  Filtered, 299

COLD MEAT BALLS, 177

COLD ROAST BEEF, 187

COLD WATER CAKE, 213

COLORING FOR SOUP, 7

COMPOSITION OF SOUP, 1

CONSOMME, 6

COOKIES, 213

CORNMEAL BREAD, 190

CORNCAKE, 198, 199
  Muffins, 199
  Pone, 199
  Starch to use, 308
  " Cake, 213
  Green, 124 to 125
  Soup, 6
  " Cream of, 15

CORNED BEEF, 40

COTTAGE CHEESE, 155

CRAB APPLE JELLY, 265

CRACKERS
  And Cream, 291
  And Marmalade, 290
  Soaked, 291

CRACKLING BREAD, 192

CRANBERRIES, 100
  Whipped, 264

CREAM OF CRAB, 20
  Pudding, 247
  Salad Dressing, 115
  " Asparagus Soup, 15
  " Beets Soup, 15
  " Corn Soup, 15
  " Lettuce Soup, 15
  " Green Peas Soup, 15
  " Spinach Soup, 15

CREAMED CHICKEN, 298
  Ham, 188
  Sweetbreads, 189
  Oysters, 188
  Veal, 56

CREAM PIE, 236
  Sauce, 99, 100
  Toast, 259

CRABS
  Deviled, 21
  Soft Shell, 21
  In Season, 21
CRECY SOUP, 7
CROQUETTES,
  Chicken, 77
  Pepper, 132
  Oyster, 35
CROUTONS, 309
CROWN OF LAMB, 50
CRULLERS, 214
CRUMPETS, 199
CRUST COFFEE, 288
CUCUMBERS, 127
  For Fish, 127
  Raw, 126
  Pickles, 171
  Sauce, 100
CUP CAKE, 212
CURRANTS
  To Clean, 305
  Jelly, 264
  " Whipped, 264
  Water, 280
CURRY
  Of Chicken, 77
  " Oysters, 35
CUSTARD, 247
  Bread, 199
  Cake, 212
  Savory, 291
  Souffle, 321
CUTLETS,
  Pork, 68
  Veal, 57
  Lobster, 28
  Oyster, 28
DEVIL CAKE, 214
DEVONSHIRE CREAM, 100

DIPLOMATIC PUDDING, 249
DRAINS, TO CLEAN, 311
DRAWN BUTTER SAUCE, 101
DRIED BEEF, 178
DRIED PEA SOUP, 13
DUCHESS PUDDING, 322
DUCKS
  Broiled Canvas, 91
  Wild, 91
  Roast, 91
  " Tame, 87
  Steamed, 87
DUTCH SAUCE, 101
EAST INDIA CATSUP, 172
  Preserves, 208
EGGS
  Nutriment in, 160
  A la Goldenrod, 186
  Baked, 160
  Balls, 102
  Broth, 278
  And Cheese, 161
  " Cream, 161
  Croquettes, 161
  Deviled, 161
  Fried, 162
  Lemonade, 300
  Milk of, 279
  In a Nest, 162
  Nog, 280, 300
  On Plate, 162
  And Port Wine, 279
  Omelette, 163
  " Celestine, 163
  " Orange, 164
  " Spanish, 164
  Poached, 163
  " and Anchovy, 163
  And Broth, 279
  " Milk, 280
  Scotch, 164
  Scrambled, 185
  " and Tomatoes, 186

ALPHABETICAL INDEX.

EGGS— Continued.
   Stuffed, 164
   Swiss, 165
   A la Tripe, 165
   Tea, 281
   Gruel, 282
   And Orange, 285
   Sauce, 102
   Savory, 167
   Toast, 186

EGG PLANT, 127

ENDIVE, 116

EPICUREAN SAUCE, 162

FAIRY BUTTER, 102

"F. F. V." SALAD, 116

FEDERAL CAKE, 216

FIGS
   In Cream, 250
   Cake, 216
   To Freshen, 308
   Pudding, 250

FISH,
   To Bake, 17
   " Boil, 17
   " " in Court Bouillon, 17
   Chops, 18
   To Cook, 17
   Creamed, 18
   Perch and to Fry, 18
   Pie, 19
   Pudding, 19
   Small, to Fry, 18
   Timbales of, 19
   Brook Trout, 27
   Clams, Cakes, 20
   " Fritters, 20
   " Raw, 20
   " Stuffed, 20
   Cod, Baked, 21
   " Fish Balls, 29
   " " Cakes, 30
   " Creamed, 30
   " to Freshen, 29
   " Pie, 22
   " on toast, 30

FISH
   Crabs, Cream of, 20
   " Deviled, 21
   " Soft Shell, Broiled, 21
   " " Fried, 21
   Frogs Legs, Fried, 22
   " " Stewed, 22
   Finan-Haddie, 31
   For Fish, 110
   Haddock Croutes, 30
   Halibut Pie, 22
   Herrings, Pickled, 31
   " on Toast, 31
   Lobster, to Bake, 23
   " Bisque of, 23
   " to Boil, 22
   " to Broil, 22
   " Creamed, 187
   " Cutlets, 23
   " a la Creole, 24
   " Deviled, 24
   " Newburg, 24
   Mackerel, Fresh, Broiled, 24
   " Salt, Boiled, 31
   " Broiled, 32
   Salmon, Boiled, 25
   " Broiled, 25
   " Kippered, 32
   " Souced, 25
   " Trout, 27
   Salt Fish, to Fry, 30
   Sardines, Deviled, 32
   " with Eggs, 32
   " Maitre d'Hotel, 32
   Scallops, Fried, 26
   " Poulet au Creme, 26

SHAD, 25
   Boiled, 25
   " Maitre d'Hotel, 25
   " Roe, Croquettes of, 26
   " Planked, 26

SMELTS, 27
   Terrapin, 28
   White Fish, Baked, 27
   " " Broiled, 27
   " " and Oysters, 28
   " " Planked, 28

FISH DINNER, 186

FISH HOUSE PUNCH, 300
FLAT IRONS, TO CLEAN, 314
FLOUR, BROWNED, 305

FOOD FOR INVALIDS.

BARLEY WATER, 288

BEEF—
    Essence of, 277
    Juice, 277
    Sandwich, 277

BROTHS
    Beef, 276
    Chicken, 277
    Clam, 277
    Egg, 277
    Meat, 278
    Mutton, 278
        Trotters," 278
    Veal, 278

CHICKEN, CREAMED, 290

CHOCOLATE AND
    Iceland Moss, 289

COFFEE CRUST, 288

CRACKERS
    And Cream, 291
    And Marmalade, 290
    Soaked, 291

CUSTARD
    Broth, 291
    For Invalids, 291
    Savory, 291

EGGS
    Milk of, 279
    Nog, 280
    Poached, 279
        " in Broth, 279
        " in Milk, 280
    And Port Wine, 279
    And Orange Juice, 288
    Pudding of, 281
    Tea, 281

FOOD, TO PREPARE, 276

GOOSE, 86

GRUEL
    Barley, 282
    Candle, 290
    Egg, 282
    Farina, 282
    Flour, 282
    Graham, 283
    Indian Meal, 283
    Oatmeal, 283
    Oats and Cream, 283
    Sago, 283

JELLY
    Bread, 280
    Chicken, 280
    Currant, 280
    Lemon, 280
    Restorative, 280
    Sago, 281
    Strengthening, 281
    Tapioca, 281

KOUMISS, 289

LEMONADE, 301
    Flaxseed, 288, 289

MILK PREPARATIONS, 285
    Baked, 285
    And Chocolate, 286
    Chicken, 286
    Citronized, 286
    Clabbered, 285
    Digested, 285
    Hot, 287
    Junket, 287
    Laban, 287
    Punch, 302
    Shake, 288
    Soup, 287
    Thick, 287
    Whites of Eggs, 287
    And Wine, 285

PANADA, 284

SOUPS
    Pea, 283
    Tapioca, 284
    " and Cream, 284
    " Porridge, 284

FOOD FOR INVALIDS—Cont.
  TOAST
    Cream, 289
    Dry, 289
    Oyster, 290
    Water, 290
    Wafers, Oatmeal, 290
FOOD TO KEEP WARM, 311
FONTAINEBLEAU CHEESE, 321
FRIAR'S OMELETTE, 250
FRIED CAKES, 216
  Summer Squash, 321
FRUIT, TO CLEAN, 312
FRUIT AND FARINA, 250
FRUIT PUNCH, 300
FRYING
  Batter, 184
  How to, 184
  Lard, 184
  Medium, 184
  Mixture, 183
  Suet for, 184
FURNITURE POLISH, 314

GAME
  DUCKS
    Wild, Broiled, 91
    "   Canvas Back, 92
    "   Roast, 91
    "   Roast, Virginia, 91
  GROUSE
    Broiled, 92
    Roasted, 92
    Souffle of, 92
  GUINEA FOWL, 92
  PARTRIDGE, SOUFFLE OF, 93
  PHEASANTS
    Boiled, 93
    Roast, 93

PIGEONS
  Roast, 92
  Stewed, 92
QUAIL, BROILED, 94
SNIPE ROAST, 94
TURKEY, WILD, ROAST, 94
  "   Stuffing for, 94
VENISON,
  Cold, Minced, 95
  In Chafing Dish, 190
  Rewarmed, 95
  Saddle of, 94
  Steak, 94, 95
  Roast, 94
GAME SOUP, 10
GASCONY BUTTER, 167
GARLIC WINE, 163
GELATINE, TO PREPARE, 310
GERMAN SAUCE, 143
GIBLET SAUCE, 103
GINGER BREAD, 214
  Cordial, 302
  Snaps, 215
GLASS JARS, 313
GRAPE JUICE, 265
  Mead, 301
GREEN PEPPERS AND CHICKEN, 321
GRITS, 153
GROUSE, 92
GRUELS, 283
GUMBO SOUP, 10
GUINEA FOWL, 92
HADDOCK, 30
HALIBUT PIE, 22
HAM, 70
  Butter, 168

ALPHABETICAL INDEX. xix

HAMBURG STEAK, 42, 279
HARD SAUCE, 104
HASH, 42
   Corned Beef, 41
HERMITS, 217
HICKORY NUT CAKE, 217
   Salted, 274
HERRINGS, 31
HOLLANDAISE FRITTERS, 251
   Pudding, 257
   Sauce, 104
HOMINY, 152
   Small, 153
HORSERADISH
   Butter, 104
   Sauce, 104
   Vinegar, 104
HOT MILK, 287
HOT POT, 41
ICED SAVORY, 169
ICES
   Apricot, 229
   Currant, 229
   Strawberry, 229
   Wiesbaden, 229
ICING
   Boiled, 217
   For Cake, 217
   Lemon, 218
   Soft, 218
   Royal, 225
ICE CREAM
   Apricot, 227
   Banana, 227
   Cafe Parfait, 227
   Marischino, 238
   Peach, 238
   Pineapple, 238
   Vanilla, 238
   " and Chocolate, 241
INK STAINS, 311

ITALIAN
   Cream, 251
   Cheese, 61
IRISH STEW, 51
JARDIENERE SALAD, 116
JAVELLE WATER, 322
JELLY
   Apple, 262
   Aspic, 263
   Currant, 264
   " Black, 263
   " Whipped, 264
   Crabapple, 265
   Cranberry, 264
   " Whipped, 264
   Grape, 269
   Lemon, 269, 280
   Prune, 269
   Quince, 268
   Raspberry, 270
   Wine, 269
JUNKET, 287
JUGGED CHICKEN, 322
KETTLES, TO CLEAN 310
KIDNEYS STEWED, 178
KISS PUDDING, 251
KITCHEN, PEPPER, 173
KOHLRABI, 128
KOUMISS, 289
LADY CAKE, 218
   Fingers, 218
LAMB, 51
   Braised, 50
   Breast of, 50
   Broth, 16
   Chops, 50
   Crown of, 50
   Kidneys, 51
   Pie, 54
LAYER CAKE, 218

LEBERWURST SANDWICH, 296
LEFT-OVERS, 310
LEMONADE, 301
   Calcutta, 301
   Flaxseed, 288
LEMON
   Brandy, 304
   Butter, 104
   Jelly, 269
   To keep, 307
   Pudding, 237
   Sugar, 272
   Syrup, 105
LETTUCE
   Cream of, 15
   Salad, 116
LIME WATER, 312
LITTLE CAKES, 219
LIVER AND BACON, 61
   Baked, 52
   Braised, 62
   Cake, 62
   Chafing dish, 187
   Larded, 62
LOBSTER, TO BAKE, 23
   To Boil, 22
   Bisque, 23
   Creamed, 23
   Cutlets, 23
   A la Creole, 24
   Devilled, 24
   If Fresh, 24
   Newburg, 24
   Salad, 116
   Sauce, 102
MACARONI, 188
   A la Brignoli, 150
   Italian, 150, 151
   Quenelles, 151
   And Tomatoes, 151
MAITRE D'HOTEL SAUCE, 105
MAPLE SUGAR SAUCE, 105

MARMALADE PUDDING, 252
MAYONNAISE, 106, 117
MEAT
   Care of, 206
   To Cook, 306
   To Keep, 311
MELTED BUTTER SAUCE, 105
MERINGUES, 313
METALS, To Clean, 317
MILK, 285
   Baked, 285
   Clabbered, 285
   And Chocolate, 286
   Chicken, 286
   Citronized, 286
   Digested, 286
   Shake, 288
   Thick, 287
MINCE MEAT, 237
   Pies, 237
MINESTRONE, 11
MINT SAUCE, 105
MOCK DUCK, 42
   " Hare, 43
   " Turtle Soup, 10
MONTPELIER BUTTER, 106
MOUNTAIN PUDDING, 252
MOUSSE, Etc., 229
MUSHROOMS, 128
   Powder of, 308
MUSTARD SAUCE, 116
MUTTON
   To Boil, 49
   Broth, 16
   Braised, 50
   Breast of, 49
   Brains, 49
   Chops, 51
   Chops, Thick, 51

MUTTON — Continued.
  Irish Stew, 51
  Kidneys, 51
  Leg of, Boiled, 52
  "   Roast, 53
  "   Stewed, 53
  Minced, 52
  Neck of, 52
  Pie, 53
  Roast, 53
  Saddle of, 54
  Soup, 11

NESSELRODE PUDDING, 231

NORMANDY SOUP, 11

NUT LOAF, 274

OKRA, 131

OLIVE CUSTARD, 168

ONIONS, 129
  Baked, 12
  Coloring for Soup, 107
  Juice, 107
  Sauce, 107
  Soup, 12

ORANGE
  Brandy, 304
  Pie, 238
  Salad, 117
  Sauce, 107
  Sugar, 272
  Syrup, 107

OXTAIL SOUP, 12

OYSTERS,
  Angels on Horseback, 33
  Baked, 33
  In Blankets, 33
  Broiled, 33
  Browned, 34
  Chowder, 13
  Creamed, 34, 188
  With Celery, 37, 188
  Cocktail, 35
  With Crackers, 35
  Croquettes, 35
  Curry, 35

OYSTERS
  Cutlets, 34
  Fried, 36
  "   with Tomatoes, 36
  Fricasseed, 37
  Panned, 188
  Patties, 37
  Poulettes, 37
  Pourette, 37
  Raw, 37
  Sauce, 107
  Salad, 38, 117
  Squizzled, 189
  And Sherry, 188
  Soup, 13

PAINT, TO REMOVE, 318

PANADA, 284

PANCAKES, 202, 252
  Adirondacks, 201

PARKER HOUSE ROLLS, 203

PARSLEY, 131

PARSNIPS, 132

PARTRIDGE, 93

PASTE, 317

PASTRY, 232
  A Very Good, 232
  Beef Dripping, 233
  "   Suet, 233
  Flead, 234
  Puff, 232, 233

PATTIES, 238

PEA
  Soup, 13, 283
  "   Dried, 13

PEACH
  Brandy, 304
  Canned, 267
  Ice Cream, 228
  Mousse, 230
  Pie, 239
  Preserves, 267
  Pickle, 174
  Short Cake, 239

PEAR, PICKLE, 174
PEAS, GREEN, 131
PECAN NUTS, 274
PEPPERS, 132
    Sauce, 108
PERFUME BAGS, 316
PHEASANT, 93
PIE CRUST, 234
PIES,
    Apple, 234, 235
    Cocoanut, 235
    Cherry, 235
    "   Roly Poly, 236
    Cheese, 236
    Cocoanut, 235
    Cream, 236
    Lemon, 237
    "   Cheese, 237
    Mince Meat, 237
    "   "   Little, 238
    Orange, 238
    Patties, 238
    Peach, 239
    Potato, 239
    Pumpkin, 239
    Squash, 240
    Washington, 240
PIE PLANT, 267
PICKLES
    Chili, 172
    Cucumber, 171
    "Delicious," 172
    Governors, 172
    Mixed, 173
    Mustard, to Mix, 173
    Sweet Cherry, 174
    "   Peach, 174
    "   Pear, 174
    "   Pineapple, 175
    "   Tomato, 175
    Tomato, 175
    "   Soy, 175
PIE CRUST
    For One Pie, 234
    "Afine," 234

PIGS' FEET, 69
PIGS' HEAD, 71
PIGEONS, 92
PINEAPPLE
    Ice Cream, 228
    Pickle, 175
    Pudding, 254
PIQUANTE SAUCE, 108
PLAIN CAKE, 221
PLUM CAKE, 222
    Charlotte, 254
    Preserve, 266
    Pudding, 252, 253
    "   Sauce for, 111
PLUNKETS, 224
POIVARDE SAUCE, 108
POP-OVERS, 202
    Graham, 202
    Rye, 203
PORK
    Bacon, 68
    "   Broiled, 68
    "   To Cook, 68
    "   Fried, 68
    Ham, Baked, 70
    "   Boiled, 70
    "   Broiled, 70
    "   To Cure, 70
    "   Fried, 70
    "   Steamed, 71
    Pigs' Feet, Broiled, 69
    "   "   Fried, 70
    "   Head, 71
    "   "   Pudding, 69
    Cutlets, 68
    Leg of, Roasted, 71
    "   Stewed, 71
    Meat Cakes, 72
    Poor Man's Goose, 69
    Salt for Larding, 67
    Sausage, 73
    "   Boiled, 73

PORK—Continued.
Sausage, Broiled, 73
" Fried, 73
" Rolls, 73
Scrapple, 72
Spare Ribs, 72
Sucking Pig, 67
Tenderloins, 179

POTATOES, 133
Pie, 239
Pudding, 251
Soup, 14, 82

POUND CAKE, 221

POULTRY, 74

PRESERVES—
Apples, Baked, 262
" Fried, 262
" Marmalade, 262
" Stewed, 262
Blackberries, 263
Cherries, 264
" Brandied, 265
East India, 268
Fruits, 268
Grape Juice, 265
Peaches, 267
" Canned, 267
" Marmalade, 266
Pears, 265
Plums, Brandied, 266
" Damson, 266
" Marmalade, 266
Pie Plant, 267
Quince, 268
" and Apple, 267
Raspberry, 270
Strawberry, 270
" Jam, 271
" in Sun, 271
To Sterilize, 271
Syrup for, 271
Tutti-frutti, 268
Vegetable Marrow, 271
Watermelon, 271

PRUNE JELLY, 269
Pudding, 254

PUDDING
Alberry, 241
Ambrosia, 242
Apple Dumpling, 242
" Float, 242
" Fritters, 242
" German, 242
" and Tapioca, 243
Apricot Eggs, 242
" Muscovite, 243
" Short Cake, 243
Bavarian Cream, 243
Batter, 244
Bread, 244, 245
" and Butter, 244
" Tarts, 245
Brighton, 245
Brown Betty, 245
" Bread, 245
Caramel, 246
Carrot, 246
Charlotte Russe, 246, 247
Chocolate, 248
" Custard, 248
Cocoanut, 246
Cream, 247
Cornmeal, 247
Cornstarch, 249
Custard, Baked, 247
" Boiled, 249
" Fried, 248
" Souffle, 321
Damson Dumplings, 249
Diplomatic, 249
Duchess, 322
Friar's Omelette, 250
Fig, 250
" in Cream, 250
Fruit and Farina, 250
German Ice, 251
Hollandaise, 251
Italian Cream, 251
Kiss, 251
Mountain, 252
Marmalade, 252
Pancakes, Fried, 252
Pineapple, 254
Plum, 252, 253
" Charlotte, 254

PUDDING— Continued.
  Prune, 254
  Potato, 254
  Queen of, 255
  Rice, 255
  " and Fruit, 255
  " Iced, 255
  " Plain, 256
  Roly Poly, 256
  " " Cherry, 236
  Savarin, 257
  Souffle. 256, 257
  Snow, 258
  Spanish Cream, 258
  " Puff, 258
  Sponge, 259
  Suet, 259
  " Sauce, 259
  Swedish, 259
  Toothsome, 260
  Transparent, 260
  Venetian, 260
  Venoise, 260
  Yorkshire, 261

PUFF PASTE AND BLOATER, 168
  Pastry, 232

PUMPKIN PIE, 239
  Soup, 14

QUAIL, 94

QUEEN CAKE, 222

QUEEN OF PUDDINGS, 255

QUINCE PRESERVES, 267

QUICK BROTH, 4

RASPBERRY PRESERVES, 270
  Vinegar, 174

REINE A LA SOUP, 15

REFRIGERATOR, TO CARE FOR, 311

RESTORATIVE JELLY, 280

RICE
  To Boil, 147
  Casserole, 148
  and Cheese, 148
  Croquettes, 148

RICE
  Pudding, 255
  Crumpets, 204
  Rissoto Milanese, 148
  Savory, 149
  Sweet, 149
  Socles, 149
  Timbales of, 149
  and Wine, 150

ROBERT SAUCE, 110

ROLY POLY PUDDING, 256

ROMAINE DRESSING, 110
  Salad, 118

ROMAN PUNCH, 230

ROUX, BROWN, 109
  White, 109

ROYAL ICING, 225

RUM PUNCH, 302

RYE MEAL MUFFINS, 201
  Puffs, 203

SADDLE OF MUTTON, 54
  " OF VENISON, 94

SALAD
  Artichoke, 114
  Asparagus, 114
  Calf's Brains, 114
  Cauliflower, 115
  Celery, 115
  Cheese, 114
  Chicken, 115
  Dressing for, 115
  Endive, 116
  "F. F. V.," 116
  French Dressing for, 116
  Jardiniere, 116
  Lettuce, 116
  Lobster, 116
  Mayonnaise, 117
  Orange, 117
  Oyster, 117
  Potato, 117, 118
  Romaine, 118
  Sweet Bread, 117
  Tomato, 118
  " with Caviare, 111, 118

ALPHABETICAL INDEX.

SALAD Continued.
 Vegetable, 119
 Vinegar for, 119
 Walnut and Peas, 119
 Watercress, 119
SAGE AND ONION SAUCE, 110
SALLY LUNN, 205
SALMON, 25
SALSIFY, 141
SALT FISH, 30
SALT PORK, 67
SANDWICHES
 Boiled, 292
 Caviare, 293
 Celery, 293
 Cheese, 293
  " Cream, 293
  " Hot, 294
  " Potted, 293
 Cherry, 294
 Chicken, 294
 Fish, 294, 297
 Fried, 294
 Ham, 294
 Hot, 295
 Lettuce, 295
 Mayonnaise and Olives, 296
 Leberwurst, 296
 Olives, 295
 Raisins, 295
 Roast Beef, 296
 Sardine, 292
 Sausage, 297
 Spanish, 296
 Tomato, 296
SARDINES, 32
SAUCE
 Algonquin, 96
 Anchovy, 96
 Apple, 96
 Asparagus, 97
 Bearnaise, 97
 Bechamel, 97
 Brains, 98
 Bread, 98

SAUCE
 Bread, with Onions, 98
 Brown, 99
 Caper, 99
 Cauliflower, 97
 Celery, 101
 Cider, 99
 Cherry, 101
 Clotted Cream, 100
 Cranberry, 100
 Cream, 99, 100
 Cucumber, 100
 Devonshire, 100
 Drawn Butter, 101
 Dutch, 101
  " for Fish, 102
 Egg, 102
  " Balls, 102
 Epicurean, 102
 Fairy Butter, 102
 Fish, 102, 106, 110
 Force Meat Balls, 103
 Garlic Wine, 103
 German, 103
 Giblet, 103
 Hard, 104
 Hollandaise, 104
 Horse Radish, 103
  "   "   Butter, 104
  "   "   Vinegar, 104
 Jelly, 104
 Lemon, 104
  "   Syrup, 105
 Lobster, 102
 Maitre d'hotel, 105
 Maple Sugar, 105
 Mayonnaise, 106
 Melted Butter, 105
 Mint, 105
 Montpelier Butter, 106
 Mustard, 106
 Onion Coloring, 107
  "   Juice, 107
 Orange, 107
 Oyster, 107
 Pepper, 108
 Piquante, 108
 Poivarde, 108

ALPHABETICAL INDEX.

SAUCE
  Pudding, 108, 109
  Plum Pudding, 111
  Robert, 110
  Romaine, 109
  Roux, White and Brown, 109
  Sage and Onion, 110
  Soubise, 110
  Swedish, 106
  Tartar, 111
  Thickening with Eggs, 113
  Tomato, 111
  Vanilla, 112
  White, 112
  " with Mushrooms, 113
  Wild Duck, 113
  Wine, 112

SAUSAGE, 73

SAVARIN, with Rum, 257

SAVORIES
  Anchovies, 166
  " Straws, 166
  " Toast, 166
  Bacon, 166
  Butter, 170
  Caviare Canapes, 167
  Crackers, 167
  Egg, 167
  Gascony Butter, 167
  Ham Butter, 168
  Iced, 169
  Olive Custards, 168
  Puff Paste and Bloater
  " Paste, 168
  Sardine, Butter, 168
  " Broiled, 168
  " with Cheese, 169
  Savory, 169
  Semolina, 170
  Scotch Woodcock, 170
  To Serve, 166

SCALLOPS, 26

SCORCH, on Linen, 319

SCRAPPLE, 72

SCOTCH WOODCOCK, 170

SCOTCH EGGS, 164

SHAD, 25

SHANDY GAFF, 302

SHOES, To Soften, 308

SHORT CAKE
  Apricot, 243
  Ham, 204
  Peach, 241
  Prune, 241
  Strawberry, 240

SIBERIAN PUNCH, 302

SIRLOIN OF BEEF, 67

SMELTS, 27

SNIPE, 94

SNOW PUDDING, 258

SOFT CAKES, 221

SOUBISE SAUCE, 110

SOUFFLES, 321

SOUPS—
  Artichoke, 2
  Asparagus, Cream of, 15
  Baked, 4
  Bean, 3
  " Baked, 3
  Beef, 2
  " Stock, 3
  Beets, Cream of, 15
  Bouillion, 2
  Bread, 4
  Broth, Quick, 4
  Calf's Head, 10
  Cauliflower, 7
  Celery, 5
  " Cream of, 6
  Chicken Broth, 5
  " Gumbo, 10
  Chowder, Fish, 8
  Clam, 6
  " Bisque of, 4
  Claret, 6
  Coloring for, 7
  Composition of, 1

ALPHABETICAL INDEX.   XXVII

SOUPS—Continued.
  Consomme. Royal, 6
  Corn, Cream of, 15
    "   C
  Crecy, 7
  Fish Chowder, 8
    "   S
  Flemish, 9
  Game, 10
  Glaze, 9
  Gumbo, 10
  Lettuce, Cream of, 15
  Milk, 287
  Minestrone, 11
  Mock Turtle, 10
  Mutton, 11
  Normandy, 11
  Onion, 12
    "   Baked, 12
  Oxtail, 12
  Oyster Chowder, 13
    "   Soup, 13
  Pea, 13
    "   Dried, 13
    "   and Cream, 287
  Potato, 14
  Pumpkin, 14
  Quenelles for, 14
  Quick Broth, 4
  Rice and Tomato, 14
  Reine, a la, 15
  Spinach, Cream of, 15
  Stock, Brown, 5
    "   White, 16
  Tapioca, 16
    "   Cream of, 15
  Vegetable, 16
  Veal, 16

SPICE CAKE, 221
  Plaster, 317

SPANISH BUN, 223

SPAGHETTI, 152

SPINACH, 140
  Soup, 15

SPONGE CAKE, 221
  Pudding, 258

SPONGES, To Clean, 313

SQUASH
  Summer, 143
  Winter, 143
  Fried, 321
  Griddle Cakes, 143
  Pie, 240

STERILIZE, Fruits to, 270

STOCK
  Brown, 6
  White, 16

STRAWBERRIES AND RUM, 258
  Preserves, 270
  Shortcake, 240

SUET, To Chop, 311

SUGAR, 259
  Lemon, 272
  Orange, 272

SUNSHINE CAKE, 223

SWEET BREADS, 64, 65, 66, 116, 117, 189

SWEET HERBS, 305

SWEDISH PANCAKES, 259
  Sauce, 106

SYRUP, 217

TAPIOCA SOUP, 16
  And Apple, 243
  With Cream, 284
  Cream, 284
  Porridge, 284

TARTAR SAUCE, 111

TEA CAKES, 205

TEA
  To Make, 302
  Flavors, 203
  Punch, 304

TERRAPINS, 28
  Mock, 66

THICKENING, with Eggs, 113

TOAST, 180, 289, 290

TOMATOES, 143
  Catsup, 175
  and Caviare, 118
  Salad, 118
  Sauce, 111
  Soup, 15
  Soy, 176
  Toast, 181

TONGUE, 46

TOOTHSOME PUDDING, 260

TRANSPARENT PUDDING, 260

TRIPE, 181
  Creamed, 181
  Cutlets, 181
  Digestion of, 182
  Fried, 181
  a la Mode, 182
  with Oysters, 182
  to Prepare, 181

TURKEY
  to Cook, 90
  Boiled, 88
  Broiled, 88
  Breast of, 88
  Creamed, 88
  Minced, 89
  Roasting of, 84
  Roast, 88
  Stewed, 89
  Stuffing for, 89, 90
  Wild, Roasted, 94
    " Chestnut Filling, 94

TURNIPS, 145

TURPENTINE, Uses for, 319

USEFUL HINTS:
  Black Beetles, to Kill, 308
  Blankets, to Wash, 314
  Bread Crumbs, 310
    " " for Soup, 309
    " " Fried, 310
  Breading, 309
  Burns, 312
  Cake Crumbs, 310
  Chapped Hands, 317
  Cheese, to Keep, 308
  Cleaning Mixture for Black

USEFUL HINTS
  Goods, 315
  Cleaning Mixture for Carpets, 315
  Cleaning Mixture for Clothing, 315
  Cleaning Mixture for Rugs, 315
  Cleaning Mixture for Woolens, 316
  Cornstarch, to Use, 308
  Cockroaches, to Kill, 308
  Cold Cream, 316
  Cook, Lessons for, 318
  Cracker Crumbs, 309
    " " to Make, 309
  Croutons, for Soup, 309
  Cream Cheese, 308
  Currants, to Clean, 305
  Drains, to Clean, 311
  Economy, 305
  Egg Stains, 307
  Figs, to Freshen, 308
  Flat Irons, to Clean, 311
  Flour, to Brown, 305
  Furniture Polish, 314
  Fruit, to Clean, 312
  Food, to Keep Warm, 311
  Gelatine, to Prepare, 310
  Glass Jars, to Clean, 313
  Javelle Water, 322
  Ink Spots, 314
  Kettles, to Clean, 310
  Lemons, to Keep, 307
  Left Overs, 310
  Lime Water, 312
  Meats, to Keep, 313
    " to Cook, 306
  Meat, 306
  Meringues, 313
  Metals, to Clean, 317
  Mush, 309
  Mushroom Powder, 308
  Onion Juice, 313
  Paint, to Remove Smell of, 318
  Paper Bags, to Use, 315
  Paste, 317
  Perfume Bags, for Bath, 316
  Refrigerator, to Care for, 311
  Silver, to Clean, 311
  Shoes, to Soften, 318

USEFUL HINTS—Continued.
  Spice Plaster, 317
  Sponges, to Clean, 313
  Suet, to Chop, 311
  Sweet Herbs, 305
  Scorch, on Linen, 319
  Turpentine, Uses of, 319
  Utensils, to Clean, 312
  Vegetables, Steamed, 311
  Velvet, to Restore, 315

VANILLA ICE CREAM, 228
  Sauce, 112
  Sugar, 271

VEAL
  Birds, 55
  Blanquette of, 56
  Breast of, 55
  Callops, 56
  Calf's Brains, Baked, 58
  "   "   Croquettes, 58
  "   Head, Fried, 58
  "   "   to Prepare, 58
  "   "   Boiled, 60
  "   "   Soup, 10
  "   "   Terrapin, 60
  Cream of, 56
  Cutlets, 57
  "   with Cream, 57
  "   "   Macaroni, 57
  French Pie, 60
  Fricandeau, 59
  Fritters, 59
  Italian Cheese of, 61
  Liver, with Bacon, 61
  "   Baked, 62
  "   Braised, 62
  "   Cake, 62
  "   in Chafing Dish, 187
  "   Larded, 62
  "   Stewed, 63
  "   Tarrapin, 66
  Loaf, 64
  Loin of, 63
  Minced, 64
  Pie, 54
  Sweetbreads,
    Baked, 64
    Cutlets, 64

VEAL
  Fried, 65
  Havanese, 65
  Patties, 66
  Salad, 117
  Truffled, 66
  Creamed, 180
  Sefton, 180
  Soup, 16

VEGETABLES
  Artichokes, 121
  "   Globe, 121
  Asparagus, 120
  "   Creamed, 120
  Bananas, 121
  Beans,
    Green, 122
    Lima, 122
    Boston Baked, 122
  Beets, 121
  Brussels Sprouts, 121
  Cabbage,
    Baked, 122
    Boiled, 123
    and Butter, 123
    Cold Slaw, 123
    Escalloped, 122
    Hot Slaw, 123
  Cardoons, 124
  Carrots a la Maitre d'hotel, 124
  "   Stewed, 124
  Cauliflower, Boiled, 125
    with Cheese, 126
    Salad, 115
  Celery, Salad, 115
    Stewed, 126
  Corn, Baked, 124
    Boiled, 124
    Creamed, 125
    Cake, 125
    Cakes, 125
    Escalloped, 125
    Fritters, 125
    Pudding, 125
  Cucumbers, 126
    for Fish, 127
    Fried, 127
    Dressed, 127
    to Prepare, 126

ALPHABETICAL INDEX.

VEGETABLES—Continued.
  Egg Plant, Fried, 127
    Stuffed, 127
  Kohlrabi, 128
  Mushrooms, Baked, 128
    with Butter, 128
    Stewed, 128, 129
  Onions, Baked, 130
    How to Prepare, 129
    with Cream, 129
    Custard, 129
    Fried, 129
    Fritters, 129
    in Gravy, 130
    Maitre d'hotel, 130
    Steamed, 130
    Stuffed, 130
  Okra, 131
  Parsley, Fried, 131
    to Prepare, 131
  Parsnip Balls, 131
    Boiled, 131
    Fritters, 131
    Fried, 131
  Peas, Dried, 132
    Green, 131
    Soup, 13
  Peppers, Croquettes of, 132
    for Winter Use, 132
  Potatoes, a l'Anna, 133
    Baked, 133
    Balls, 133
    to Boil, 132
    Boiled, 133
    Cadeau, 133
    and Chocolate, 134
    Cake, 137
    Cakes, 134
    Creamed, 134
    Croquettes, 134
    Crumbed, 135
    Escalloped, 135
    French Fried, 135
    Fried, 135
    " and Parsley, 136
    Hash Brown, 136
    Klosse, 136
    Loves, 137
    Lyonnaise, 137
    Maitre d'hotel, 137

  Potatoes
    Princess, 137
    Puff, 138
    Rissoles, 138
    Roast, 138
    Saratoga, 138
    Snow, 138
    Souffle, 139
    Soup, 14
    Stewed, 139
    Sweet Baked, 140
    " Boiled, 140
    " Candied, 140
    Turnovers, 140
  Salsify, Boiled, 141
    " Cakes, 141
  Sour Kraut, 142
    To Pickle, 142
  Spinach, 140, 141
  Squash, Summer, 143
    Summer, Steamed, 142
    Winter, 143
    " Griddle Cakes, 143
    Fried, 321
  Tomatoes, with Brains, 143
    Au Gratin, 144
    with Chicken, 143
    Devilled, 144
    Fried, 144
    Pilau, 145
    Stewed, 145
    Stuffed, 145
  Turnips, in Butter, 145
    and Bread Crumbs, 145
    Stewed, in Gravy, 145
    Mashed, 146
    and Peas, 146
  Vegetable Marrow, 146
    Preserves, 271
    Stuffed, 146

VENISON, 190, 93, 94
VENETIAN PUDDING, 260
VENOISE PUDDING, 260
VERMICELLI, 152
VINEGAR, for Salad, 119
VOL-AU-VENT, 241
WAFFLES, 205

ALPHABETICAL INDEX. xxxi

WALNUT AND PEA SALAD, 119

WARSHAW PUNCH, 203

WASHINGTON CAKE, 223
Pie, 240

WATERCRESS SALAD, 119
Melon Preserves, 271

WELSH RAREBIT, 159, 190

WEST POINT PUNCH, 303

WHITE FISH, 27
Grape Ice, 229

WHITE FISH
Mountain Cake, 224
Sauce, 112
Stock, 16
Puddings, 180

WIESBADEN ICE CREAM, 229

WINE
Catsup, 176
Jelly, 269
Sauce, 112

YEAST, 206

YORKSHIRE PUDDING, 261

SOUPS.

(GENERAL COMMENT.)

So much has been written on the subject of soups and of their importance or non-importance, that it is not proposed to discuss these points here. Soup is intended to *prepare* for a dinner, therefore, the rich, thick soups, which are really a meal in themselves, should be omitted when a dinner of several courses is to follow.

Light, nutritious soups and broths should, however, find a frequent place on every table.

Stock being the basis of all meat soups and sauces, it is essential that we should have a proper knowledge of the most complete and economical method of extracting from a certain quantity of meat the very best possible stock or broth.

Meat is composed of fibres, fat, gelatine, osmazome and albumen. The fibres are inseparable and constitute the remains of the meat after long cooking. Fat is dissolved by boiling; gelatine is dissolved and is the basis and most nutritious portion of the stock; when it is abundant, the stock when cold becomes a jelly. Osmazome is that part of the meat which gives flavor and perfume to the stock. When meat is roasted the osmazome appears to have a higher perfume, and so when you use the remains of roast meat in your soup you have always a finer flavor. Albumen is of the nature of the white of eggs.

Bones ought always to form a large part of the stock. They contain gelatine and a fat-like marrow, and by always breaking the bones in pieces you obtain better results.

Beef makes the best stock. Unless fowls are old and fat they give but little flavor to soup. Old pigeons make an excellent stock. The best stock is obtained from the freshest meat. When the meat boiled in the stock-pot is to be used as a meat course at dinner or for other meals it is best to have it in one piece. The stock-pot should always be kept covered, and the contents should gently simmer, the vegetables being removed when tender. The contents of the stock-pot should be carefully skimmed and strained, and above all, the stock-pot should be absolutely clean.

ARTICHOKE (JERUSALEM) SOUP.

Two slices of ham, one-half a head of celery, one turnip, one onion, two tablespoonfuls of butter, four pounds of artichokes, one pint of boiling milk or one-half cream and and one-half milk, one teaspoonful of salt, a little cayenne, two lumps of sugar, three pints of white stock. Cut the vegetables and ham into pieces and fry in the soup kettle with the butter. Cook these for fifteen minutes, stirring them well all the time. Wash and pare the artichokes, cut them in pieces and add them with one-half of the stock to the other ingredients; when the vegetables are all tender put in the rest of the stock; stir well, add the seasoning and when it has cooked ten minutes mash through a sieve; now return to the kettle and stir in the boiling milk or cream. Serve with small pieces of bread fried in butter.

BOUILLON.

Four pounds of lean beef, three carrots, three leeks, one turnip, one head of celery, one bunch of parsley, one bay leaf, one onion with four cloves stuck in it, one garlic clove. Cut the beef in pieces, put into six quarts of cold water, two tablespoonfuls of salt; put on to boil, then skim off the froth, then let it simmer slowly for an hour; skim all the fat off, then add the vegetables not cut in pieces, boil for three and one-half hours; remove the vegetables and meat, strain the soup; when cold take off all the fat and heat the soup, strain through a napkin. The fat is excellent for frying purposes.

BEEF SOUP.

Three pounds of beef, one pound of bone—the shin of beef is very good for soup, provided there is enough meat on it; have the bones all cracked. Five quarts of cold water, one teaspoonful of salt, two carrots, two onions, in which stick two cloves, six leeks, one head of celery, one urnip. Put on the fire in the soup pot the cold water and the meat and bone; when the soup boils add one-half teacup of cold water; this will accelerate the rising of the scum; skim, repeat this three times, the broth ought then to look clear, then add the vegetables; as soon after as the soup boils put it on the corner of the stove and let it simmer there for four or five hours; when the vegetables are done remove them from the soup. It may be necessary to add a little more salt when the soup is served.

BEEF STOCK.

One shin of beef cut in pieces, bones and meat; six quarts of water. Fry together one quart of onions and three carrots until they are brown, then put them into the soup pot and one bunch of parsley, one head of celery, four bay leaves, six cloves. Let the soup boil gently at least six hours, then strain; the next day remove all the fat, and when the soup is needed heat it, adding vermicelli, barley or rice to it; if vermiceli, soak it in warm water for a few minutes; if barley, it must be cooked slowly for several hours in water; rice must be cooked in boiling water; Italian paste does not need cooking; put it in the soup when served.

BAKED BEAN SOUP.

It is always good economy to make a much larger dish of baked beans than will be used at one time. Reserve a portion of them for to-morrow's salad and put the rest over the fire with a quart of water and soup vegetables and herbs; simmer an hour and press through a sieve; return to the fire, stir in a teaspoonful of flour, wet with milk to prevent settling, and dilute the soup to the proper consistency with hot milk.

BLACK BEAN SOUP.

One pint of black beans, soak them over night in three quarts of water; boil them three hours with any bones or meat you have, or with one pound of lean beef and a slice of salt pork; two onions sliced; when the beans are very soft rub the soup through a sieve, add a little spice and cloves, if liked. Cut up one lemon into thin slices and put in tureen with three hard-boiled eggs sliced and one gill of port or sherry; this addition is not necessary; strain the soup into the tureen, stirring well.

BREAD PANADA SOUP.

Three pints of water, add three tablespoonfuls of bread broken in small pieces, one saltspoonful of salt, one tablespoonful of butter. Put these on a very hot fire and stir constantly for twenty minutes.

Mix together the yolks of four eggs with one teacup of cream or milk, one tablespoonful of butter; put the boiling soup into the tureen and stir in the yolks, etc., stirring all the time, and serve at once.

BAKED SOUP.

Two pounds of any kind of meat trimmings or odd pieces, two onions, two carrots, two ounces of rice, one pint of split peas, four quarts of cold water, one teaspoonful of salt, a little pepper. Cut the meat and vegetables in pieces, add the rice and peas, season with the salt and pepper; put all into a jar, fill in with the water, cover closely and bake for four hours, then strain and serve.

This soup is very good and wholesome, and can be made in the oven when the top of the stove is occupied.

BISQUE OF CLAMS.

Take thirty clams, boil them in their own juice for five minutes, drain and chop them very fine. Put into the saucepan four ounces of butter, two ounces of flour, one-half saltspoonful of salt, one-half teaspoonful of pepper, a little cayenne, one pint of milk; stir constantly, and just before the mixture boils move from the fire, strain and heat again; the butter and flour must be quite smoothly blended before the milk and other ingredients are added.

· A QUICK BROTH.

One pound of lean beef cut in fine pieces and some chicken bones well broken up; add one quart of cold water, one carrot, one onion, a little celery and one saltspoonful of salt. Boil gently together for one hour, strain and serve with toasted bread.

BROWN SOUP STOCK.

Six pounds of beef from the shin (three pounds of meat and three pounds of bone), six quarts of cold water, one-half teaspoonful of pepper-corns, six cloves, one bay leaf, three sprigs of parsley, three of thyme, three of sweet marjoram, one carrot, one turnip, one large onion, two stalks of celery, all cut fine; one tablespoonful of salt. Wipe the meat with a clean, damp cloth—never wash meat for soup; cut the meat into small pieces, break up the bones; fry one-third of the meat with the marrow from the bones; put the rest of the meat with the bones into the soup kettle, add the water, let it stand one-half hour, then add the fried meat and cook all slowly, never boiling, only simmering, for six hours. Cover the soup tightly. One and one-half hours before finishing the soup, add the vegetables, then strain and cool quickly. The next day remove the fat before using the stock.

CHICKEN BROTH.

Take one-half of an old chicken, remove the fat and skin, break up and pound the meat and bones; then place all in a stew-pan and add one quart of cold water with one tablespoonful of cut leeks or one small onion, twenty blanched and peeled almonds, one blade of mace, and a saltspoonful of salt. Stir the broth until it boils, then skim carefully; after that remove from the hot fire to the cooler part of the stove and let the broth simmer for two hours, strain the broth and put away to cool, unless it is desired at once. Serve with slices of hot toast.

CELERY SOUP.

Take one quart of good stock either made from veal or the water in which chickens have been boiled; put on the fire one-half cupful of rice and one pint of milk and grate into this the white part and the root of two heads of celery; let the rice cook slowly, add more milk if the rice becomes too stiff; when it is tender mash it through a colander and add to the stock, with one teaspoonful of salt, a little white pepper, a pinch of cayenne and let all boil up once. Serve in hot tureen.

CLAM SOUP.

One shin of veal, cut into pieces, one bunch of herbs, three quarts of water, cook for three hours, skim carefully, strain and then put back into soup kettle, add fifty clams chopped fine one quarter of an hour before serving, with four large crackers grated.

CLARET SOUP.

One quart of boiling water; soak one cup of sago in a little cold water for a few hours; add to the boiling water, one-half cup of sugar; boil together; add one lemon sliced very thin; just before serving put one stick of cinnamon in one pint of claret, and boil for two minutes. Serve hot.

CORN SOUP.

One quart of water, six ears of corn, cut off the kernels and scrape the cob well; boil the corn in the water one and one-half hours, then mash through the colander. Take butter the size of an egg, put into the frying pan with one tablespoonful of flour, stir until smooth, but not brown, then add one pint of sweet milk; add to the corn and boil up once.

CREAM OF CELERY SOUP.

Two large heads of celery, cut very fine, put on to boil in one quart of milk and add one cup of rice, cook slowly; when the celery is tender and the rice cooked, rub them through a coarse sieve; return to the soup kettle, add a little more milk if too thick and then add one quart of good veal or chicken broth, a little salt and pepper.

CONSOMME ROYAL.

Four pounds of beef cut in pieces and one chicken which has been half roasted and cut in pieces. Put four quarts of cold water into the soup kettle, add the beef and one ounce of salt; as soon as it boils, skim, add the chicken, one carrot, one turnip, one leek, one onion with four cloves stuck in it, one bay leaf. Boil all slowly for four hours, then strain, put back into the kettle with the white of one egg beaten stiff and let it all boil up once more, then strain again. Serve with royal custard. To make this, take two yolks of eggs, and one whole egg, a little pepper and salt, one-fourth of a pint of milk, one-fourth pint of the consomme, mix well together. Butter a small cup or mold, fill with the custard, bake slowly for a few minutes or until the custard is solid; when cold, cut into small dice and serve in the soup.

CRECY SOUP.

Slice one pound of carrots, put into the stew-pan, one-half pound of butter, when hot, fry the carrots, four leeks cut fine, one onion sliced, together for five minutes, then add one quart of good chicken broth and one-fourth pound of bread crumbs; simmer until the carrots are done, then press all through a fine sieve, then return to the soup pot and add two quarts of chicken broth, stir well until it boils, then simmer for one hour, skim off all the fat and strain, serve in a tureen. Serve with fried bread, cut in small dice pieces.

PUREE OF CAULIFLOWER.

Put one small cauliflower in three pints of white stock, boil for thirty minutes. Stir two tablespoonfuls of flour well mixed with one tablespoonful of butter into this, and then boil ten minutes. Press through a sieve, add one cup of cream and let all just boil up; put into the well heated tureen one and one-half cups of whipped cream; pour over the soup; serve hot; add salt and pepper when first cream is added.

COLORING FOR SOUPS—1.

One cup of brown sugar, one-half dozen whole cloves, one cup hot water; let them all boil until the liquid is quite dark brown in color, then bottle it. Add a teaspoonful to any soup, you desire to darken in color.

COLORING FOR SOUPS—2.

Take onions and cut them in slices and put them into a moderate oven, leave until they are black chips (not burnt). These may be bottled and are by some considered far better for coloring soups and gravies than burnt sugar.

FISH CHOWDER.

Put half a pound of sliced salt pork in the bottom of a saucepan and fry brown; take it out, and put in layers of potatoes, onions and fish sliced, seasoning each layer with plenty of salt and pepper, using about three pounds of fish, and a quart each of potatoes and onions, cover with cold water, bring gradually to a boil, and cook slowly for thirty minutes; then add two pounds of sea-biscuit soaked for five minutes in warm water, and boil five minutes longer and serve.

FISH SOUP.

Put into the frying-pan one-half pound of butter, four carrots cut fine, three onions sliced, two heads of celery cut fine, two shallots cut fine or one clove of garlic, three cloves, one bay leaf, one little bunch of thyme and parsley; fry all these until they are brown; then add one pint of white wine and three quarts of boiling water, one teaspoonful of salt, and one saltspoonful of pepper; put with these six pounds of any good fish, let all simmer for two hours; when finished, strain through a cloth; serve hot.

MARYLAND CHOWDER.

There is nothing better for a chowder than a large cod or haddock. Two pounds of fish, one-half pound of water crackers, two ounces of butter, one pint of oysters or clams, one gill of cream, one gill of water, one onion sliced, one tablespoonful of salt, one-half teaspoonful of pepper, one-half teaspoonful of mace, one-third teaspoonful of cayenne. Put the water into the soup kettle, then the onion, one-half the fish, the skin side down; sprinkle in one-half the salt and pepper, etc., then one half of the oysters or clams, cover all with the butter in small lumps and one-half of the crackers; the rest of the fish, oysters, seasoning, butter and crackers; pour over the cream having first boiled it. If the oysters have much liquor, you do not need the water; if the chowder is too dry add a little more water, cover closely and cook one-half hour, serve on a platter; milk may be used instead of cream. One-half pound of bacon or salt pork gives a good flavor. To be eaten on plates with a fork, not as a soup.

FLEMISH SOUP.

One dozen sliced potatoes, two heads of celery, two onions, four pounds of shin of beef, four quarts of water, salt, pepper; boil together three hours, then add one-half pint of boiling milk or hot cream and one teaspoonful of sugar.

GLAZE.

This is one of the most valuable aids to good cooking—it will keep for years. It is not always possible to have stock in the house at all times, especially in summer—with glaze one does not need to have it.

Take six pounds of lean beef, the leg is the best; part of a knuckle of veal, with the beef to weigh six pounds; cut all into small pieces with one-half a pound of lean ham; do not let any of the outside of the ham go in the pot. Put these into the soup with five quarts of water, three onions with two cloves stuck in each, one carrot and one head of celery; let all come to the boiling point, then skim, then place on the back of the range and let it simmer for six hours—it is now an excellent foundation for clear soups or gravies by adding one teaspoonful of salt, but do not add any salt, if it is intended to reduce to glaze; just strain the stock through the colander, place in an earthern crock, put back the meat and vegetables with four quarts of boiling water and boil all four hours longer, then strain and place in another crock or bowl; next morning, take the two stocks, heat them and strain again, then unite them in one large pot and let it boil as fast as possible, be sure not to cover it; when it is reduced to three pints, then put it into a smaller pot and boil until it is thick and of a brown color; be very watchful that it does not burn, as this is the dangerous time. When you have only a little over a pint, pour it into small jars or into sausage skins which have been well cleansed, or it can be poured on to tins and dried by exposure until it is dry; if put into jars do not cover them until the glaze leaves the sides of the jar. To put the glaze into the sausage skins, tie one end very tight and pour the glaze through a funnel, into the skin, tie up the other end and hang it to dry; when the glaze is needed cut a slice off this.

CHICKEN GUMBO.

Put two slices of fat, salt pork and one tablespoonful of butter into the frying-pan. When hot put in one chicken which has been cut into pieces. Fry these brown, and then put them into the soup kettle with one pint of tomatoes, one pint of okra sliced, one onion sliced, one saltspoonful of salt and two quarts of cold water; cook together for four hours very slowly—the soup must not boil, only simmer—when desired, take out the chicken, cut all the white meat into small dice, and return to the soup; let all come to the boiling point and serve. Serve with the soup, boiled rice.

GAME SOUP.

Take the bones and trimmings of any cold game, break into small pieces and put into the soup kettle; add two quarts of stock (if you have it) or else cold water; one carrot, one onion, one small turnip, one head of celery all cut in small pieces. Let the soup boil, skim and place on the back of the stove to simmer for three hours, then strain and remove the fat. Boil two tablespoonfuls of barley until soft, take one half and mix with it the yolks of three hard-boiled eggs moistened with one tablespoonful of cream, and then stir it into the soup, slowly; put in the balance of the barley and serve.

CALF'S HEAD OR MOCK TURTLE SOUP.

Take the water in which the head was boiled, two pounds of veal, one onion, two tablespoonfuls of chopped carrots, one turnip cut fine, three stalks of celery, one blade of mace, four cloves, twenty pepper-corns, one bay leaf, a little parsley. Put all the vegetables into a pan and fry them with two tablespoonfuls of butter until they are brown; put them with the stock and veal; cook slowly for one hour, strain the soup, return to the kettle, and add two lemons cut in slices, one glass of sherry or port, some salt and pepper, two tablespoonfuls of flour mixed to a soft paste with a little water, one tablespoonful of tomato catsup, some egg and force-meat balls. Serve.

Any of the soup left is equally good re-heated the next day.

MUTTON SOUP.

Take the neck of mutton, cut it in pieces, add to it three carrots, two turnips, two onions, all sliced, a bunch of sweet herbs, one tablespoonful of parsley, one teaspoonful of salt, a little pepper and three pints of cold water; simmer slowly for four or five hours, then skim; pass the soup through the sieve and return to the soup kettle to boil just once. Serve with barley which has been boiled separately while the soup has been cooking.

MINESTRONE.
A FAVORITE ITALIAN THICK SOUP.

Three quarts of boiling water well salted, one piece of salt pork the size of an egg; one large clove of garlic; chop the garlic fine with the pork; this is absolutely essential; one handful of lima beans, one-half a carrot, one-half a small turnip, both chopped fine; add these to the water and boil for twenty minutes, then add two large tomatoes (stewed and strained), two potatoes chopped fine, one ear of corn, the kernels cut off; one-half a medium sized cabbage—use pieces of the leaves as large as your hand, but remove the thick stem, one-half a pint of rice; boil slowly, covered, one-half an hour or until the rice and cabbage are done, no longer, as the cabbage becomes watery if cooked too much.

NORMANDY SOUP.

One knuckle of veal, one quart of white button onions, four quarts of cold water, half a loaf of bread, one quart of cream, two tablespoonfuls of butter, salt and pepper to taste, two tablespoonfuls of flour. Put veal in the soup kettle with onions and water, let all simmer slowly for two hours; then add the bread cut in slices. Simmer slowly for two hours more. Remove the knuckle and press the ingredients through a sieve. Rub butter and flour together to a smooth paste, stir into the boiling soup, and stir constantly until it thickens. Add the cream, salt and pepper, and serve.

ONION SOUP.

Fry six large onions in some butter or good dripping until they are brown, then stir in with the onions one tablespoonful of flour, then add one quart of hot water; stew the onions till tender; add one teaspoonful of salt and one teaspoonful of sugar; when the onions are done, strain the soup into a hot tureen and stir quickly into it the yolks of two eggs in which put one tablespoonful of cream. Put into the soup tureen two slices of hot toast before pouring in the soup.

BAKED ONION SOUP.

Place in a dish which will stand the heat, some slices of bread with the crusts left on. Fry three onions in a pan with one tablespoonful of butter until brown, put these on the bread, and then fill up the dish with some good consomme or stock; sprinkle on the top some grated cheese, cover the dish and let the soup bake in the oven for ten minutes; the soup is really better served in the same dish. If this is not liked, be sure the tureen is hot before the soup is poured into it, and that it is served at once.

OX-TAIL SOUP.

Two ox tails, two slices of ham, one tablespoonful of butter, two carrots, three onions. one leek, one head of celery, one bunch of sweet herbs, one bay leaf, twelve pepper-corns, four cloves, one teaspoonful of salt, two tablespoonfuls of tomato catsup, one glass of port wine, three quarts of water. Cut up the tails, wash them well in cold water, put them in the soup kettle with the butter; cut the vegetables in slices, add them with the herbs and pepper-corns, add one-half pint of water; stir and cook these well together for ten minutes, then fill up the stew-pan with the water, and when boiling, skim well and add the salt; simmer gently for four hours or until the ox tails are tender, then take them out of the soup, strain it, thicken with a little flour, add the wine and catsup, put back the tails, simmer for ten minutes and serve.

A dish of boiled rice, boiled dry, is very nice to serve with the soup,

OYSTER CHOWDER.

Two slices of salt pork cut fine, one onion sliced, one pint of oysters, one pint of sliced potatoes, one quart of rich milk, one-half cup of fine cracker crumbs, a little salt and pepper.

Cook the potatoes until they are tender; fry the onion and salt pork until they begin to color, strain them into the oysters; cook the oysters in their own liquor until they are plump, add the potatoes, cracker crumbs, and last of all the milk. Keep it hot, and stand for one-half hour where it will not cook, to ripen—this chowder depends on two things—the richness of the milk, and the ripening process.

OYSTER SOUP.

One quart of oysters, one quart of milk, one-half pint of cream, two tablespoonfuls of butter, one dessertspoonful of flour.

Put into the stew-pan the oysters in their own liquor, do not let them boil; stir together in another stew-pan the butter and flour. When mixed, add the milk, let them boil and then add the oysters drained from the liquor, add the cream, a little salt, pepper and two blades of mace.

PEA SOUP.

One pint of fresh or canned peas, boil them until they are perfectly soft in one pint of water, then mash them through a sieve. Add to the pulp and liquor one pint of cream or one pint of milk, one teaspoonful of sugar, a little salt and pepper and one tablespoonful of butter. Let these all come to boiling point. Serve hot, with toasted crackers.

DRIED PEA SOUP.

Soak one pint of yellow split peas over night. Next morning place them in the soup pot with two quarts of water, with just a little bit of soda, add one carrot cut fine, one turnip cut in pieces, one onion sliced, one head of celery cut fine; when the vegetables are tender add one teaspoonful of salt, one-fourth teaspoonful of pepper, one teaspoonful of sugar. Strain the soup through a colander, rubbing the vegetables well, then return to the soup pot, and keep hot. Fry some little cakes of bread until brown in butter and serve with the soup.

POTATO SOUP.

Boil the potatoes, rub them through the colander into two quarts of rich hot milk, one tablespoonful of chopped parsley, one onion, a little salt and pepper; cook one-half hour, then stir in one tablespoonful of butter—beat two eggs with one-half teacup of cream, stir in qnickly, and serve with fried bread cut in small cubes.

PUMPKIN SOUP.

Two pounds of yellow pumpkin, take off the rind and remove the seeds, cut into small pieces; put into the stew-pan with one tablespoonful of sugar, a little salt and one pint of boiling water; simmer together until the pumpkin is tender, then drain and mash through a colander; put back into the stew-pan, add one quart of boiling hot milk, boil for a minute longer and then pour into the soup tureen over a slice of bread.

QUENELLES FOR WHITE AND CLEAR SOUPS.

One tablespoonful of butter, when melted add one dessertspoonful of flour and one tablespoonful of cream so as to make a thick cream, add one tablespoonful of grated cheese, a little salt, pepper and nutmeg; beat the mixture until it is smooth and firm, and leaves the sides of the saucepan. Mold into quenelles with a teaspoon dipped in hot water; when needed, poach them in hot stock or water and serve in the tureen.

RICE AND TOMATO SOUP.

Five cups of brown soup stock; cook in this, one-half cup of rice until it is tender. Cook together one bay leaf, two cups of strained and stewed tomatoes, two slices of onion, ten peppercorns, two stalks of celery cut fine; cook for one-half hour, then strain into the stock, add one tablespoonful of Worcestershire sauce; rub together one-half tablespoonful of butter and one and one-half tablespoonfuls of cornstarch; stir this into the soup and cook for fifteen minutes, add one teaspoonful of salt, a little pepper, and serve hot.

SOUP A LA REINE.

One chicken, one ounce of sweet almonds, one cup of bread crumbs, one-half pint of cream, one lump of sugar, two quarts of good veal stock. Boil the chicken until it is tender, then remove from the soup kettle, pull off the meat from the bones, pound it with the almonds in the mortar; when smooth, return to the soup kettle with the bread crumbs and let all simmer for one hour, then rub through the sieve, add the sugar, a little salt, and the cream; take the crust of the loaf and place in the tureen; pour over the soup.

CREAM OF SPINACH.

Wash and pick the spinach and put it on to boil; boil until soft and tender, then press enough through a sieve to make a generous pint of the pulp, add to this one quart of rich chicken or any good, white stock; when it becomes very hot, take one tablespoonful of butter and two tablespoonfuls of cornstarch and rub together until smooth, stir this into the soup and continue to stir until very smooth. Season with salt and white pepper; return to the soup pot and add a cup of cream, beat all the time after the cream is added with an egg-whip—this you will find makes it very light. Serve immediately; it should be very hot.

Cream of Asparagus, Cream of Celery, Cream of Beets, Cream of Corn, Cream of Lettuce, and Cream of Green Peas are all made in the same manner.

TOMATO SOUP.

Boil one can of tomatoes or four large raw ones in one quart of boiling water for twenty minutes, then add one pint of sweet milk, a pinch of soda, one teaspoonful of salt, a little pepper, and two tablespoonfuls of butter; let the mixture come to boiling point, then strain and add eight small crackers, rolled fine.

TOMATO-CREAM SOUP.

One quart of canned or three quarts of ripe tomatoes; boil slowly for one hour, then strain, add a little chicken broth if convenient, one saltspoonful of salt, one-half saltspoonful of pepper, a small pinch of soda; boil five minutes and add one pint of whipped cream. Stir together and serve at once.

TAPIOCA SOUP.

Boil three pints of broth with two tablespoonfuls of tapioca, when well mixed cover the stew-pan and let the soup simmer for a half hour, then skim and serve.

VEGETABLE SOUP.

One quart of good stock, two carrots cut fine, two onions cut fine, one potato cut fine, one turnip cut fine, one bunch of parsley, one teaspoonful of salt, a little pepper. Cook the vegetables in the stock until tender, and then serve all together. The stock can be omitted and water substituted. Vegetable soups, clear and thick, are extremely palatable; the former being agreeable and wholesome, especially in warm weather, when fresh vegetables are abundant and full of juice and fragrance, and the latter, or thick soup may be very nutritious also. Nutritious and palatable soup may be made from fish of the cheaper sorts, using fish in place of meat for the stock.

VEAL OR MUTTON BROTH.

To each pound of meat and bones add one pint of cold water, skim and add one teaspoonful of salt, six peppercorns, one blade of mace, one bunch of sweet herbs, two carrots cut in pieces, two onions cut fine, one potato, one turnip cut fine, one teaspoonful of sugar, one-half cup of rice; boil slowly together for four hours, strain and let it cool, then skim off the fat, and re-heat.

WHITE STOCK.

One knuckle of veal, any cold poultry, four slices of ham, three carrots, two onions, one head of celery, twelve pepper-corns, one teaspoonful of salt, one blade of mace, one bunch of sweet herbs, four quarts of water, one tablespoonful of butter. Cut the veal, put it and the trimmings of poultry and the ham into the soup kettle with the butter, moisten with one-half pint of water and simmer until the gravy flows, then add the four quarts of water and the remainder of the ingredients; simmer slowly for five hours, skim, and then strain through a fine sieve, and it is ready for use.

FISH.

Fish is better fried than boiled; water extracts the juices and flavor; always use a deep vessel with plenty of fat for frying.

Roasted or baked fish are always good, and Sir Henry Thompson advises that fish be so prepared. He says: "Even a coarse kind of fish if baked with a few slices of bacon will yield a good nutritious meal, which will cost only one-third of an average meat meal."

To bake, place the fish in a tin vessel only slightly deeper than its own thickness, with a lid to prevent the escape of the flavor; the dish to be well buttered, placed in a closed oven and the fish served in the original dish if possible.

FISH BOILED IN COURT BOUILLON.

Put on the bottom of your fish kettle a bed made of sliced carrots, onions, one lemon, some parsley, thyme, bay leaf and one tablespoonful of whole pepper grains. On this bed place the fish and cover with half white wine and half cold water, or water with three wine glasses of good vinegar. Have a moderate fire and as soon as the liquid boils, take off the kettle and remove the fish. Serve with a white sauce. The bouillon can be strained and kept for several days and used several times, but be sure to re-boil it every three days.

BOILING FISH.

In boiling delicate fish, such as salmon cod or halibut, the plunging into boiling water tends to break the fish; it should be put first into water that is on the point of boiling, kept at this temperature for a few minutes and then allowed to fall several degrees and cooked at about 180 degrees F. The fish will be delicate and have preserved its form.

FISH CREAMED.

Boil a white fish, about three pounds for fifteen minutes, then take from the water and let it cool; when cool, mince it very fine after having carefully removed all the bones; butter a baking dish. Boil one pint of milk; stir together three tablespoonfuls of flour, and two tablespoonfuls of butter; when smooth stir into the hot milk with three sprigs of parsley, two onions minced fine, and the yolk of one egg beaten light. Place a layer of the fish in the dish, then a layer of the sauce and so on until the dish is full. Spread a thin layer of bread crumbs, which have been lightly buttered, over the top, and bake for one-half hour.

FRIED SMALL FISH.

Do not split the fish; clean them, dip them in beaten egg and bread crumbs, or in flour seasoned with salt and pepper; have some fat hot in the pan, put in the fish, cook them for ten minutes, turn and brown on the other side, and serve. For the fat take some slices of salt pork and fry in the pan; when all the fat is out remove the pork and fry the fish in the fat remaining. Serve on hot dish.

FRIED PERCH, SMELT, PORGY OR ANY SMALL FISH.

After each fish is cleaned, put into it a thin slice of fat salt pork, three slices of onion and a little green pepper, or red pepper, with the seeds removed; add a sprig of mint if obtainable; tie up the fish or skewer it, bread it and dip in beaten egg and fry. The heat drives the flavoring into the fish. This is a Cuban recipe.

FISH CHOPS.

These can be made with salmon or any other fish.

Take one-half pound of cooked fish, carefully remove all the bones and particles of skin, shred very fine; add to the fish two teaspoonfuls of salt, one-half teaspoonful of pepper, one-half teaspoonful of cayenne and one teaspoonful of onion juice. Boil one cup of milk; when boiling, stir into it three tablespoonfuls of flour, well mixed, with one tablespoonful of butter; when thick remove from the fire and add the yolks of three eggs; stir them well into the milk, add the fish, place on the fire again for two minutes, then add one teaspoonful of chopped parsley and one teaspoonful of lemon juice. Spread the mixture on a platter and let it rest on the ice for several hours to become stiff; when required take one tablespoonful of the mixture, form into a chop, and make all of the mixture into chops; roll each one in beaten egg, then into fine crumbs and fry in deep hot fat for two minutes; serve with a Tomato or Hollandaise sauce.

FISH PIE.

Four pounds of haddock or bass, boil with plenty of salt in the water; take off the skin and bones, then flake the fish. Boil one quart of cream or milk, add one tablespoonful of flour stirred into cream until perfectly smooth, add one tablespoonful of parsley and one-half an onion chopped fine, also one-fourth pound of butter; after all is boiled add a little cayenne; grease a pan, put in it layers of fish, then sauce; let the last layer be of the sauce; strew on the top a thin layer of bread crumbs; bake one-half hour.

FISH PUDDING.

Cold boiled fish makes an excellent pudding; salmon is particularly good. To one pint of fish add two well beaten eggs, three tablespoonfuls of cream, two tablespoonfuls of chopped parsley, a little salt and paprika. Mix them well together, breaking the fish into medium-sized pieces. Turn the mixture into a bowl that has been well buttered and sprinkled with crumbs. Place the bowl in a pan of hot water and put into a hot oven. Bake twenty minutes and turn out on a heated dish, and have a cream sauce to pour around it.

TIMBALES OF FISH.

To every half pound of fresh fish add one cup of bread crumbs, and one-half cupful of sweet milk; boil the crumbs and milk together, pound the fish to a smooth paste, gradually adding the crumbs and milk, then add one-half teaspoonful of salt, a little cayenne, three drops of onion juice; when all the mixture is smooth fold in quickly the beaten whites of five eggs. Have the timbale tins greased, pour in the mixture, cover them with white paper and steam for twenty minutes; serve with a white sauce.

CLAMS RAW.

Serve on powdered ice, same as oysters.

QUOHOGS CLAM CAKES.

One pint of quohogs chopped fine, two eggs, one teaspoonful of sugar, one teaspoonful of baking powder, a little salt, just enough flour to stick them together, which is very little. Do not use the liquor that comes with the quohogs. Fry on griddle or drop in hot fat ; season with butter and pepper.

STUFFED CLAMS.

Chop your clams very fine, add as much bread crumbs soaked in milk as you have clams ; season with salt, pepper and parsley ; mix well and add the yolk of one egg. Put one tablespoonful of butter into the saucepan, when hot add the clam mixture, fry and add one tablespoonful of tomato sauce ; fill the clam shells. keep warm until served.

Crabs can be served in the same manner.

CLAM FRITTERS.

An excellent breakfast dish is clam fritters. Chop fine two dozen clams, make a batter with one pint of flour, in which has been sifted a level teaspoonful of baking powder ; add a cup of sweet milk and nearly as much of the clam liquor, and two eggs beaten light ; beat hard until it is a smooth batter, then stir in the chopped clams ; put plenty of lard in the frying pan and let it become boiling hot ; put in the batter by the spoonful and cook slowly, wnen one side is browned turn the fritters and brown the other side. The batter may be cooked on a griddle like pancakes if preferred.

CREAM OF CRAB.

Put one large tablespoonful of butter in a sauce-pan, let it brown, then stir in one tablespoonful of flour, when thick put in one pint of milk, a little cayenne, one saltspoonful of salt and one blade of mace ; add two cups of crab meat and let all boil together for fifteen minutes ; add lastly one-half teacupful of cream and one teaspoonful of chopped parsley, and serve.

DEVILED CRABS.

Crabs are in season in May, June, July and August. Crabs must be boiled alive, like lobsters. Boil twelve crabs, when cold take out the meat.

Put four tablespoonfuls of cream in the double boiler, when hot add two tablespoonfuls of butter as soon as this sauce thickens, add the crab meat, one tablespoonful of finely chopped parsley, one teaspoonful of salt, one-half saltspoonful of cayenne, one-half teaspoonful of lemon juice and the finely mashed yolks of four hard-boiled eggs; fill the shells, which should be washed clean and dried, with the mixture, closely to the edge of the shells; take the beaten yolk of an egg and baste the crabs well with it, and then sprinkle with bread crumbs; fry for two minutes in deep boiling fat; only put two shells at a time in the fat. If the fat is not convenient omit the egg and pour over each shell a little melted butter and bake in the oven for five minutes.

SOFT SHELL CRABS FRIED.

Remove the spongy part and the sand bags from the sides; wash, wipe, dry and drop them into deep, hot fat; cook for five minutes, take them from the fat, with a skimmer, sprinkle over them a little salt and serve very hot. Only fry two crabs at one time in the fat.

SOFT SHELL CRABS BROILED.

Wash, dry, remove the spongy parts and sand bags, brush the crabs over with melted butter or with cream; lay them on a hot broiler and cook for five minutes; serve on hot toast.

CREAMED BAKED COD.

Three pounds of fresh cod, one pint of cream, two tablespoonfuls of butter, one even tablespoonful of flour, yolk of one egg, one saltspoonful of salt and pepper. Boil the fish twenty minutes and then pick it fine with a silver fork. Heat the cream in a double boiler; mix the butter and flour together and add to the cream when boiling hot; when thick, take it off the stove, stirring constantly and add the yolk beaten with one tablespoonful of water, then add the fish; mix together and put into a dish, cover the top with cracker crumbs and pour melted butter over the top; bake until brown.

HOT HALIBUT, OR COD PIE.

Two pounds of fresh halibut or cod; remove all bones and chop the fish fine; butter a china baking dish, sprinkle on the bottom two tablespoonfuls of chopped parsley and shallots, then place a layer of the fish, a little salt, pepper and nutmeg, some bits of butter and slices of hard boiled eggs (two eggs will be enough for the pie), then add another layer of fish, seasoning, butter and eggs; fill the dish and then pour in enough good white sauce, one tablespoonful of white vinegar or white wine; cover the dish with a good paste, puff or plain. Make a a hole in the center of the cover; bake slowly for an hour and a half in moderate oven.

FROGS' LEGS FRIED.

Place the frogs' legs in boiling water with one teaspoonful of salt and one tablespoonful of lemon juice; let them remain for five minutes, then drain, wipe dry, dip in fritter batter and fry in deep boiling fat.

FROGS' LEGS STEWED.

Scald the legs, then put into the stew pan with hot water enough to cover them; add a little salt, pepper, a few sprigs of parsley, one tablespoonful of lemon juice, one-half an onion, one bay leaf and one carrot; stew until tender, then take from the pan. Strain the liquor and add one-half cup of cream; let this boil, then pour it over the frogs.

TO BOIL A LOBSTER.

Put one-fourth of a pound of salt to each gallon of water. Be sure that the lobster is alive; select a heavy one and one that keeps in motion. As soon as the water boils, drop in the lobster and boil for twenty-five minutes; skim the water, remove the lobster from the pot and cool.

LOBSTER—TO BROIL.

Cut down the back with a sharp knife (you will find a line on the shell), remove the stomach and intestine; place on the broiler—shell side down—and broil for twenty-five minutes; put a little melted butter on the lobster to keep it from drying. When cooked serve with butter, salt and pepper, or with a sauce.

LOBSTER—TO BAKE.

Cut the lobster in the same manner as for broiling, remove the stomach and intestine, place in a baking pan, with a little butter spread over; when about half cooked sprinkle a few bread crumbs over and some melted butter; bake thirty minutes and serve hot.

LOBSTER BISQUE.

One lobster, chop the meat very fine; put one pint of cream in the stew pan, when hot add the lobster meat, one-half tablespoonful of butter, three crackers rolled fine, one-half saltspoonful of pepper, one saltspoonful of salt; let all come to the boiling point, then remove from the fire and add one tablespoonful of Madeira or Sherry wine. Serve at once.

CREAMED LOBSTER.

Take the meat from a boiled lobster, cut it into small pieces, mix two tablespoonfuls of butter, one tablespoonful of flour; when hot stir into the mixture, the lobster, a little grated nutmeg, a teaspoonful of salt. one teacup of cream and one teaspoonful of sherry; stir well together and let cook for ten minutes, then serve either in the shell of the lobster, which must be carefully washed and dry, or in a silver covered dish.

LOBSTER CUTLETS.

Cut the meat from the lobster into small pieces, place in stew pan on the fire one tablespoonful of butter, one tablespoonful of flour; mix; when smooth and thick, add the yolks of two eggs and one teacupful of cream, a little cayenne and salt and the lobster, stir well and let cook for five minutes, then spread the mixture on a platter, when cold and firm form into cutlets. Dip first into bread crumbs made very fine, then into an egg beaten, then into crumbs. Place in ice box two hours; when needed fry in deep hot fat. Serve with tartar sauce. A small piece of claw should be stuck into the end of each cutlet to resemble a bone.

LOBSTER A LA CREOLE.

One pint of highly seasoned stock, add one cup of tomatoes, one garlic clove; let these cook together for ten minutes, strain and return to the fire. Take one tablespoonful of butter and one tablespoonful of flour well mixed together and stir into the stock, add some sliced mushrooms and some fresh, green peppers chopped fine and the seeds removed—the sauce must be of the consistency of thick cream. Have the meat of the lobster cut into pieces, cook it in the sauce long enough to become very hot, or a better plan is to warm it in a little of the stock before it is thickened, then add the balance of the stock.

DEVILED LOBSTER.

One lobster, take out the meat and cut into fine pieces; put into stew pan one tablespoonful of butter, one tablespoonful of flour, stir until they are smooth and then add one tablespoonful of mustard, one saltspoonful of cayenne and one pint of milk; when the mixture is hot, stir in the lobster meat, let these cook together for five minutes, then fill small individual dishes and sprinkle fine bread crumbs over the tops with bits of butter and cook in the oven for five minutes before serving.

A lobster tail is curled under if fresh, or if alive when boiled.

LOBSTER NEWBURG.

The meat from two lobsters cut into one-inch pieces; put the lobster into the sauce pan with one ounce of butter, a little salt, one-half saltspoon of cayenne and two truffles chopped fine; cook together for five minutes, then add one wine glass of sherry. Beat the yolks of three eggs in a bowl with one-half pint of cream, add to the lobster, stir all together for two minutes longer; serve very hot.

BROILED FRESH MACKEREL.

Split the fish down the back, broil on a well-greased gridiron until the inside flesh is white and the outside skin brown; place on a hot platter, the skin side uppermost; put over the fish some Maitre d'hotel sauce.

BOILED SALMON.

To cook salmon in perfection a slice should be plunged into boiling water enough to well cover it and allowed to boil eight minutes. Serve with drawn butter sauce.

BROILED SALMON.

Take a slice of salmon weighing two or three pounds, have the gridiron hot and greased, place the salmon on it, turn often to prevent burning. Cook ten minutes, butter on both sides, then place on hot platter, add a little salt and pepper.

DEVILED SALMON.

Two pounds of cooked salmon, two tablespoonfuls of butter, one tablespoonful of flour, one tablespoonful of mustard, one-half teaspoonful of cayenne, one pint of milk. Put the butter into the sauce pan, when it bubbles add the flour, mix well together, then add the milk; when the mixture is smooth and creamy, add the mustard which must be made into a soft paste before adding, and the cayenne. Put the salmon into a pudding dish, pour over the mixture, and on top of this spread a thin layer of bread crumbs and a few bits of butter. Bake ten minutes in a hot oven.

SOUCED SALMON.

Boil the salmon; to one pint of liquor in which it is boiled add one pint of vinegar with all kinds of whole spices, a little cayenne pepper; pour this mixture over the salmon for twenty-four hours.

BROILED SHAD.

Split the shad on the back, remove the roe and the spine; have the gridiron hot and greased, broil the shad for thirty minutes, then put on a platter and put into the oven for five minutes. Spread over the shad some butter and serve very hot with slices of lemon about the platter.

BROILED SHAD WITH MAITRE D'HOTEL BUTTER.

Split the shad in two, broil until done; then place on a hot platter, pour over it a maitre d'hotel sauce.

CROQUETTES OF SHAD-ROES.

Two shad-roes, put them into a sauce pan with boiling water slightly salted, let them cook slowly for fifteen minutes, then take from the fire, pull off the fine skin and mash them. Put one tablespoonful of butter into the sauce pan, add two tablespoonfuls of flour; when hot, add one-half pint of cream, stir until perfectly smooth and thick; remove from the fire and stir in at once the yolks of two eggs, add to this mixture one tablespoonful of chopped parsley, one saltspoonful of salt, a little pepper, one-half a grated nutmeg, one-half teaspoonful of cayenne and the shad-roes. Mix well together, spread on a platter to cool. When cold flour your hands and make the mixture into croquettes. Have one egg beaten, dip the croquettes into the egg first, then roll in fine bread crumbs, then in the egg again. Let them stand in the ice-box for fully an hour before frying, then have your fat very hot (see general directions for frying), when they are a golden brown color, drain them on folded brown paper. Serve with slices of lemon and a Tartar Sauce.

PLANKED SHAD.

The famous Planked Shad of the Delaware River are usually split down the back; when the fish is split, proceed as for planked White Fish.

FRIED SCALLOPS

Wash the scallops, drain them well, then dip them into fine cracker crumbs seasoned with salt and pepper, then into an egg beaten and again into the crumbs; fry in smoking hot fat. A Mayonaise dressing is delicious with fried scallops.

SCALLOPS POULET AU CREME.

Two tablespoonfuls of milk flavored with a little onion water or juice. Into this put one quart of scallops, chopped fine and the breast of one small boiled chicken, cut fine. Add a pint of cream, a lump of butter rubbed with a tablespoonful of flour, pepper and salt. Let this boil two or three minutes until of the consistency of cream and serve.

FRIED SMELTS.

Draw the smelts at the gills, wipe them dry, dip them in beaten eggs, then in bread crumbs; fry in hot, deep fat. Serve them crisp and dry with Tartar Sauce.

CREAM SALMON OR TROUT.

Have the head and tail cut off, put the fish into boiling water which has been slightly salted and simmer for five minutes, then remove from the fire and drain. Put the fish into a stew pan with a little mace, nutmeg, cayenne, all mixed together; then cover the fish with cream, adding bits of butter. Keep the pan covered and let the fish stew for ten minutes, then dish the fish; keep it hot while you make the sauce. Take one dessert-spoonful of flour mixed smooth with milk; stir this into the cream, add the juice of one lemon, let this just boil, then strain, and pour over the fish.

TO FRY BROOK TROUT OR ANY OTHER SMALL FISH.

Clean the fish and let them lie for a few minutes on a clean towel; season some cornmeal with salt and pepper, roll the fish in this and fry them in two-thirds butter and one-third lard; drain on a sieve or on coarse brown paper and serve quickly.

BAKED WHITE FISH.

Bone the fish and cut into small squares or rounds, place them in a deep plate and put bits of butter over, some green peppers chopped fine and a little salt; pour over some white wine, cover the dish closely and bake the fish for one-half hour; serve with the following sauce:

Cook one tablespoonful of butter until it is a delicate brown, put in one teaspoonful of capers, and one teaspoonful of flour; either add a little more wine or drain the sauce from the fish into the butter, then pour it over the fish and serve hot.

BROILED WHITE FISH.

Split the fish down the back, remove the backbone; have the gridiron hot and greased, the fire clear; broil for five minutes, turn, cook five minutes, then again for five minutes; serve on hot platter, with melted butter over and some chopped parsley, a little salt and pepper; garnish with slices of lemon.

WHITE FISH BAKED WITH OYSTERS.

One white fish, weighing about five pounds; do not split, wipe dry on the inside and outside and rub well with a mixture of salt, pepper and flour, prepare the oysters for stuffing the fish. Take one full pint of oysters, drain them and roll each oyster in well seasoned bread crumbs, fill the fish, put slices of salt pork over the fish and bake for twenty minutes or until the fish is well browned; baste frequently with the water which comes from the fish; serve with a tomato sauce.

PLANKED WHITE FISH.

Cut the fish on the underside, bone it, wash and wipe dry; remove the line of opaque-looking fat on each edge. One hour before cooking rub the fish with a little olive oil and sprinkle over with one teaspoonful of brown sugar to which has been added a little cayenne and one saltspoonful of salt.

The plank should be made of some hard wood and always heated before the fish is placed upon it: while the fish is cooking it should be well basted with melted butter; cook for a half hour; when cooked serve with a garnish of slices of lemon and cucumber.

STEWED TERRAPIN.

(Washington).

Put the terrapin into boiling water and then simmer them until the feet are tender to the touch. Remove from the water, clean and pick them from the shells, cut into pieces ready for the dressing. To prepare the dressing take one pound of butter to three terrapins, melt the butter; when hot add the terrapins with one saltspoon of pepper, but no salt. Take for each terrapin the yolks of three hard boiled eggs, mash the yolks perfectly smooth and add one wine glass of Madeira wine, a little at a time, until the yolks are reduced to a thin paste ; it may be necessary to add more wine, add one-half a nutmeg grated ; place the paste over the terrapins (it should just cover them) and make very hot. The greatest care should be taken not to break the gall bladder, as the whole dish will be spoiled if even a drop of the gall should touch it.

TO FRESHEN COD FISH.

Cover the piece with cold water and let it heat gradually; when it boils the fish will part easily from the bones, remove from the stove; when cool pick it fine.

COD FISH BALLS.

Cut the fish in pieces and soak an hour in luke warm water, then you can remove the skin and bones easily; then put on the stove in cold water and when it begins to boil change the water and repeat twice; this removes the salt sufficiently; then let it cook slowly until very tender. As soon as the fish is ready, the potatoes (which must be cooked at the same time), must be well mashed and added to the fish while hot, with a piece of butter the size of an egg, and one egg. You must have twice as much potatoes as fish, one cup of fish, two of potatoes. Mix well together, moisten with milk until of the consistency, that will hold together, then mold into balls and fry in boiling lard, or if you prefer you can fry out slices of salt pork and cook the fish balls in it—either is good.

COD FISH CAKES.

Wash and boil one quart of potatoes, putting them on the fire in cold water enough to cover them, and a tablespoonful of salt. Put one and a half pounds of salt cod fish on the fire in plenty of cold water and bring it slowly to a boil; as soon as it boils throw off that water and put it again on the fire with fresh cold water; if the fish is very salt change the water a third time. Free the fish from skin and bones; peel the potatoes, mash them through a colander with a potato masher, season them with a quarter of a saltspoonful of pepper and an ounce of butter; add the yolks of two eggs and the fish; mix well and make into cakes, using a little flour to prevent sticking to the hands. Fry them golden brown in enough smoking hot fat to nearly cover them; observe that in frying any article of food it will not soak fat if the latter be hot enough to carbonize the outside at once, and smoking hot fat will do that.

CREAMED COD FISH.

Soak the cod fish for fifteen hours in a large quantity of cold water, skin the fish, pick it all from the bones, cut it in small dice pieces. Take a large skillet, put the fish one inch deep in this, pour over cold water to cover the fish, let it simmer, but not boil, for two hours. About twenty minutes before serving pour off the water and cover the fish with milk; add one-half pound of butter to one quart of fish, add a little pepper, a very little salt; let the fish boil, then take one tablepsoonful of flour mixed smooth with a little water, stir it into the fish while it is boiling; then just when ready to serve the fish add two eggs well beaten; do not let the eggs boil. The fish can be prepared at any time, but must be kept covered with cold water; do not let it stand after draining.

COD FISH ON TOAST.
(Cuban).

One teacup of freshened cod fish shredded fine; fry one onion and one tablespoonful of butter until brown, then put in the cod fish with enough cold water to cover it, add one-half can of tomatoes or six fresh tomatoes; cook all slowly for one hour, add a little salt and pepper. Have ready slices of hot toast and pour on them the cod fish.

SALT FISH.

Soak the fish in cold water for two days, changing the water several times; when required, dry it well; fry in the pan with one tablespoonful of butter two onions sliced; fry until yellow, remove the bones from the fish, season with pepper, one teaspoonful of mustard and one tablespoonful of vinegar; mix with the onions and cook for ten minutes and serve very hot. Fish should always be split open for broiling.

TO FRESHEN SALT FISH.

Lay the fish in cold water with the skin side up, otherwise the salt sinks into the skin and the fish will not freshen.

CROUTES OF HADDOCK.

Take a finnan haddock about a pound in weight, free it from skin and bones, and put it into a stew-pan with two ounces of butter, four tablespoonfuls of milk, a well-beaten yolk of egg, a little pepper and a teaspoonful of lemon juice. Whisk these ingredients over the fire for five minutes, by which time the fish will be smooth. Pile this on some small rounds of hot buttered toast. Sprinkle the tops lightly with some finely minced parsley and red pepper, and serve.

FINNAN HADDIE.

One pound of finnan haddie, put into a pan and cover with boiling water, let it boil for five minutes, drain off the water from the pan, add one-half tablespoonful of butter stir the fish in this, so as to season both sides. Serve hot.

HERRINGS ON TOAST.

Cut three good bloaters down the backs, bone them, put them in spiced vinegar for ten minutes, then dust pepper and salt on the white side; dip each one into heated fat and broil them over a clear fire; when ready serve on toast and add one tablespoonful of lemon juice and one tablespoonful of chopped parsley. Be sure to serve the fish very hot.

PICKLED HERRINGS.

Take twenty-four best fresh roe herrings, have them well cleaned; place them in a large stone crock, putting first a layer of herrings, then cover them with salt, a few cloves, a little allspice, mace and whole pepper corns; then another layer of herrings; repeat this until the crock is full; cover the whole with vinegar. Place on the range, and let all simmer, but not boil, for twelve hours, then the preparation is ready to use; but it will keep for weeks if kept covered with vinegar, and the crock tightly closed.

SALT MACKEREL—TO BOIL.

Soak the fish, skin side upward, for twenty-four hours; drain, cook in boiling water for five minutes; pour off the water and cover fish with sweet milk; cook for fifteen minutes; remove the fish, thicken the milk with one tablespoonful of flour and one-half tablespoonful of butter rubbed together; saltspoon of pepper; pour this sauce over the fish and serve hot.

SALT MACKEREL BROILED.

The fish from Norway are the finest. Soak the mackerel for two days in cold water, change the water two or three times, wipe dry. Broil over a clear fire, place on hot dish, pour one pint of boiling water on the fish, let it stand for a minute, then pour it off; put on the fish a little butter, lemon juice and minced parsley, and serve.

The boiling water poured on and off removes all taste of oil from the fish. Do not drink any liquids while the fish is being eaten; if this rule is observed the fish will not be apt to disagree with any one, or prove indigestible—and salt fish is really a valuable food.

DEVILED SARDINES.

Take six sardines and spread over them on both sides some made mustard and a dash of cayenne, broil them and serve on hot buttered toast; garnish with slices of lemon.

SARDINES MAITRE D'HOTEL.

Take six sardines, a dessert-spoonful of chopped parsley, one thin slice of onion pounded fine, one tablespoonful of Chili vinegar, half a pint of melted butter, and a round of toast; scrape the sardines, arrange them neatly on the toast, and put the above sauce over them, adding a squeeze of lemon juice and cayenne to it.

SARDINES WITH EGGS.

Fry some bread in boiling lard or butter; cut it into fingers; scale and wipe some sardines, make them hot in the oven, and place one on each finger of bread; then pour over them the following sauce: The yolks of four eggs well whipped, half an ounce of butter, one teaspoonful of tarragon vinegar, one teaspoonful of common vinegar, a mustard spoonful of made mustard and a little salt. These must be well stirred over the fire till the sauce thickens, but does not boil.

KIPPERED SALMON.

Rub the salmon with an equal mixture of salt and sugar; let this fish stand twelve hours, then smoke it for twelve hours. Put the fire far away from the fish, so that the smoke will blow over the fish steadily.

OYSTERS.

ANGELS ON HORSEBACK.

Take very thin slices of fat bacon, cut all the rind off. Then take an oyster (or two if very small), pour on it two drops of essence of anchovy, four of lemon, and a grain of cayenne and roll it in the slice of bacon. Tie them together. When there are sufficient of these rolls, put them on a small skewer and fry them; when cooked take each one separately and place on a small piece of toast. This is a dish which must be served very hot.

BROILED OYSTERS—1.

Dry large oysters on a napkin; roll them in fine cracker crumbs, then into melted butter and again into the crumbs, add a very little salt and pepper with the crumbs; broil them on a wire gridiron well greased; they are done as soon as they are a light brown. Serve with slices of lemon.

BROILED OYSTERS—2.

Select large oysters, drain them, lay them on a well-greased broiler, place it over a clear fire and turn it as the oysters cook; when done, serve at once; pour over them some melted butter, seasoned with salt and pepper and some finely chopped parsley.

OYSTERS IN BLANKETS.

Take large oysters, season with cayenne, wrap up each one in a thin piece of bacon, fasten with a little wood tooth pick; fry them for a few minutes, serve very hot.

BAKED OYSTERS WITH SHERRY.

Fifty oysters; put one-third in a deep dish; add a tablespoonful of melted butter and cover with bread crumbs, seasoned with salt and pepper; then put one-half of the remaining oysters in and proceed as above, then the balance;

pour in sherry enough to cover the oysters, add a layer of bread crumbs and one tablespoonful of melted butter. Bake until colored brown, serve hot.

BROWNED OYSTERS ON TOAST.

Mix yolks of two eggs with a little flour. Season twenty-four oysters and dip in the batter. Brown the oysters in hot butter. Then add the oyster liquor to the flour and eggs, stir into the butter, simmer three minutes, add oysters again, and serve on toast.

CREAMED OYSTERS.

Blanch twenty-five oysters and drain them; take one tablespoonful of butter, one tablespoonful of flour; stir together in the saucepan until smooth, then add one cup of cream, a little salt and pepper and one-half teaspoonful of nutmeg; when the mixture boils, add the oysters, cook for five minutes.

OYSTER CUTLETS—1.

Mix about half a pound of veal with the same weight of large stewing oysters; chop all very finely, then pound them together in a mortar, adding two ounces of finely-chopped veal suet and three tablespoonfuls of bread crumbs which have been soaked in the liquor from the oysters; season with a little salt, white pepper and a teaspoonful of lemon juice and one tablespoonful of cream. Now add the beaten yolks of two eggs and mix thoroughly, pounding all a little more, and make up into the shape of small cutlets. Fry them in butter after dipping them in egg and bread crumbs. Drain them well and send to table very hot. Garnish with sprigs of parsley and slices of lemon.

OYSTER CUTLETS—2.

Two dozen oysters, two ounces of butter, one ounce of flour, one-fourth pint of cream, three eggs, pepper, salt and bread crumbs. Melt the butter, add the flour, the yolks of three eggs, pepper and salt. Cut the oysters in half, and cook about five minutes in the sauce, but do not let them boil; turn on to a dish to cool, when cold, form into cutlets. Cover with the whites of the eggs, and fry in boiling hot fat; serve very hot.

OYSTERS ON CRACKERS.

An appetizing dish that is easily prepared is oysters baked in crackers. Take little butter crackers or any small round crackers that will split readily; split them; dip the pieces in hot water and then spread each half thickly with soft butter. Lay half the pieces upon a biscuit tin and place an oyster upon each piece; put a few drops of lemon juice upon each oyster and sprinkle them with salt and pepper and a dash of mace. Cover the oysters with the remaining buttered halves of crackers, brush the tops with melted butter, place them in a hot oven and bake them from five to ten minutes and serve as soon as they are taken from the oven.

CURRY OF OYSTERS.

Three pints of oysters, including the juice; one tablespoonful of grated cocoanut, one apple cut fine, one small onion cut fine, one tablespoonful of butter, one-half a cup of cream, one tablespoonful of curry powder, two tablespoonfuls of flour, one-half a tablespoonful of lemon juice. Fry the cocoanut, apple and onion in the butter until they are soft, then add the oysters and let all come to the boiling point, then add slowly the cream with the curry and flour rubbed together into the cream; let all boil, and take from the fire in a minute, then add the lemon juice. Serve at once as the oysters harden by long cooking. Serve with boiled rice. Lobsters, Crabs and Shrimps can be cooked in the same way.

OYSTER COCKTAIL.

(To Serve Before a Dinner.)

The juice of two lemons, half cup of tomato catsup, four drops of tobasco sauce, one teaspoonful of Worcestshire sauce, one-half teaspoonful of salt: mix together. Fill small punch glasses with oysters, pour over the sauce. Serve hot toasted crackers with the oysters.

OYSTER CROQUETTES.

One quart of oysters, stew them for three minutes in their own liquor, then drain them; when they are cool slice them; this is a better way than to chop them. Prepare a sauce with one tablespoonful of butter and one tablespoonful of flour, a few drops of lemon juice or one tablespoonful of chopped shallots; let these boil for five minutes; if too thick thin with a little of the oyster liquor, then add the yolks of three eggs well beaten, a little cayenne, one saltspoonful of salt, one teaspoonful of chopped parsley and the juice of one lemon; put in the oysters and let all boil three minutes, then spread the mixture on a platter; when cool make into balls, flattened at each end and about one inch thick; roll them in fine cracker crumbs. then in beaten egg, then in cracker crumbs. Have the fat deep and very hot, place the croquettes in the frying basket and fry for only two minutes. Serve the croquettes hot and with slices of lemon.

FRIED OYSTERS.

Fifty large oysters; always use large oysters for frying; wipe them dry in a clean towel. Beat one egg lightly, add to it one teaspoonful of warm water. Roll some cracker crumbs very fine. season the crumbs with salt, pepper and a very little nutmeg. Dip the oysters into the egg, then roll them in the crumbs, place them on a platter so that they will not touch each other; place in the ice box for two hours, Put fat into the frying kettle; when it is very hot put in the oysters; the fat must be deep so as to cover the oysters, when brown drain them. Keep hot until served. Garnish the dish with slices of lemon and parsley.

FRIED OYSTERS WITH TOMATO SAUCE.

Select large oysters, drain them and wipe them dry with a clean coarse towel, then dip them into the following batter: Cook one cup of tomatoes, when hot put in one tablespoonful of flour, a little salt and cayenne, a very little nutmeg and three drops of onion juice (if liked), the batter should be very thick; strain through the sieve and let it cool, then dip each oyster into this instead of into beaten egg, then into fine bread crumbs. Place them on the ice for two or three hours before frying; when needed—fry them in deep, boiling fat and serve hot.

FRICASSEED OYSTERS.

One hundred oysters, one-fourth pound of butter. Brown the butter, then put in the oysters and let simmer for ten minutes; rub one tablespoonful of flour and butter together, one tablespoonful of chopped parsley, a little salt and pepper, and add just before serving three yolks of eggs well beaten.

OYSTER PATTIES.

Fill the shells of puff paste with oysters. Cook the oysters first in rich cream, slightly thickened, seasoned with salt and powdered mace.

OYSTERS A LA POULETTE.

One pint of oysters, put them into a stew-pan and let them come to the boiling point, but not let them boil. Place in another stew-pan one tablespoonful of butter, when melted add one tablespoonful of flour; stir until these boil. Mix with one-half a cup of cream the yolks of two eggs, a little cayenne and salt; pour this mixture into the stew-pan with the butter and flour, slowly and stir constantly until it boils, then remove from the fire and strain it over the oysters, and serve hot.

OYSTER POURETTE.

Boil fifty oysters in their own juice, drain them and add a dressing of rolled crackers, two yolks of eggs, one large tablespoonful of butter, one wine glass of wine, one tablespoonful of chopped parsley. Serve hot.

OYSTERS WITH CELERY.

Twenty-five oysters; take one tablespoonful of butter, when hot, add one tablespoonful of flour; when these bubble add the oysters and one-half cup of chopped celery, a little salt and pepper. Cook for five minutes.

OYSTERS TO SERVE RAW.

Have the oysters opened carefully; see that no bit of shell is left on them; serve on their own shell; arrange five on each plate; place the oyster shells on a small bed of pounded ice; put one-quarter of a lemon with each portion.

OYSTER SALAD.

Boil one hundred oysters in a little of their own liquor, or in half liquor and half milk—the milk makes the oysters whiter than the liquor alone; let the oysters boil for five minutes, remove from the fire, drain them carefully, pour over them a French salad dressing and place them on the ice. When required drain them from the salad dressing and pour over a mayonnaise dressing.

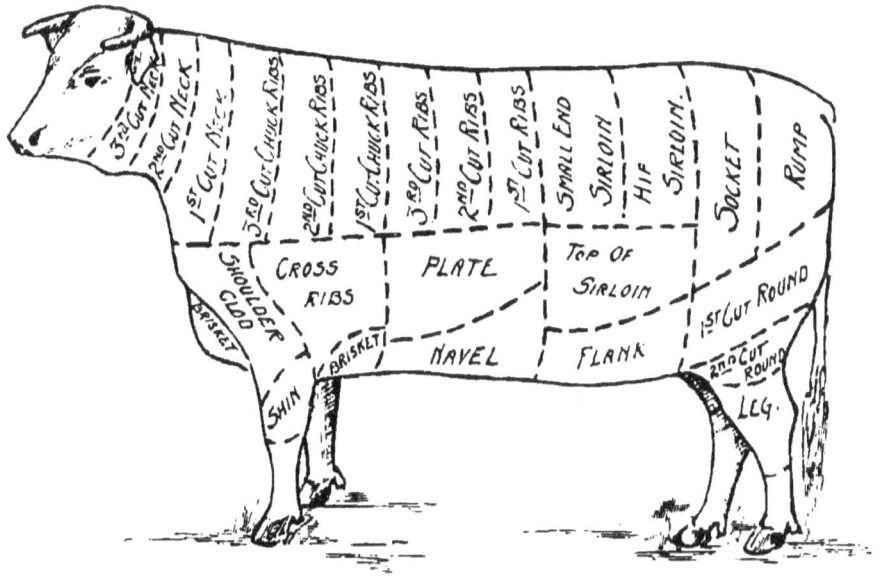

BEEF.

TO BOIL BEEF.

Always simmer the meat, in this way meat which otherwise would be tough, is rendered tender and savory and inexpensive pieces are made palatable, juicy and nourishing.

BOULETTES.

A palatable way of using cold meats, roasted meat only; mince the meat very fine, add a little fat bacon or salt pork; chop an onion a teaspoonful of herbs one teaspoonful of parsley together, add one teaspoonful of salt, one-half teaspoonful Worcestershire sauce, juice of one-half lemon, two eggs. Mix all well together, make into flat balls about one-half inch thick, fry in lard or butter until a light brown.

BRAISED BEEF.

Lay a piece of beef of about five pounds in a broad pot; place sliced onions on the top, a little salt and one cupful of stock or gravy, and one cupful of boiling water; cover the pot tightly, add more stock or water if the gravy sinks too low; when done—one hour will cook the meat—dredge the beef with flour, take it from the pot, put into a pan and place in a hot oven; as the flour browns, baste the beef with butter-water. Ten minutes will be time enough to brown the beef; strain the gravy, take off the fat, take one tablespoonful of flour, one teaspoonful of tomato catsup, boil until the gravy is thickened; pour one-half over the meat, the other serve in the gravy-boat.

BEEF A LA MODE.

Fourteen pounds round of beef with bone; make in this four incisions half way through; take one tablespoonful of black pepper, one tablespoonful of salt, rub these into the cuts, then mix together one pound of beef chopped fine and one pound of suet chopped coarsely, mix, season and add one tablespoonful of cloves, two tablespoonfuls of allspice, one clove of garlic, fill the cuts, bind a cloth around the beef, cook like roast beef—do not baste. Make a rich gravy.

CORNED BEEF.

The best piece is from the round, though both the rump and brisket pieces are very good. Put the beef into a kettle, cover with cold water, bring it to the boiling point, skim carefully and put back on the range to simmer—do not let it boil at all; allow twenty-five minutes to each pound. Keep the water in which the beef was boiled; return the beef which was left from dinner into this, cover and put away to cool; this renders the beef very tender. Do not cook cabbage with the beef, cook separately, if both are desired. The water in which the beef was boiled, if not too salt, is a good foundation for either split pea, potato or bean soup.

CORNED BEEF HASH.

The corned beef should be quite salt, cured with some salt-petre; simmer, not boil, until very tender; when done spread a napkin wrung out in cold water over it to prevent it turning black. Potatoes that boil mealy are not good; boil them with the skins on rather underdone and do not use until cold. Chop the beef very fine, the potatoes coarser, twice as much potato as meat. Put milk or cream (cream is better), butter and pepper into a large old-fashioned spider; when hot add the hash, not more than one and one-half inches deep; do not stir it. Keep drawing away from the sides of the pan with a spoon, but not to mash it. Cook for an hour or more, quickly at first, then set back on the range to simmer.

Prepare the beef and potatoes the night before using, pack all into a bowl and cover closely : it is ready then for breakfast—do not spare the butter, if you use cream not so much butter is necessary.

CORNED BEEF WITH CREAM.

Two cups of cooked corned beef grated, one-half a cup of cream, one tablespoonful of butter, a saltspoonful of pepper. Mix together, heat thoroughly, and serve on toast.

BEEF DRIPPING, TO PREPARE.

Cut the beef suet into small pieces, place in saucepan with a very little water; be careful the suet does not burn, as it melts pour into a bowl; when cold all the impurities will be on the bottom of the cake and can be scraped off.

BROILED FILLET OF BEEF.

Take one pound of fillet of beef, broil it nicely, but not too much; have in readiness some maitre d' hotel butter made thus : Three ounces of butter, one dessert-spoonful of minced parsley, one teaspoonful of lemon juice, and a little pepper and salt; work all these ingredients into a cake and let it grow cold. After broiling the fillet, place a piece of maitre d'hotel butter as big as a walnut on the top.

HOT POT.

Cut small pieces of beef from the shank or round, cut potatoes in thin slices; put layer of beef, a little salt and pepper, add little bits of butter and a few drops of onion juice, if onion flavoring is liked, continue the beef and potatoes, having potatoes the last layer, until the dish is nearly full, then add a cupful of good stock or hot water. Cover the dish tightly and bake for two or three hours; it is well to serve it in the dish in which it is baked.

HASH.

Hash, made as the recipe for corned beef hash, of either corned beef or roast meat, is very nice baked in gem pans, instead of cooking it in the skillet; when baked turn from the pans and serve on slices of hot toast.

HAMBURG STEAK.

Use for the steak the ends of the beefsteak, or meat from the round of beef; chop very fine two pounds of meat, with a little of the suet, remove as much of the meat fiber as possible; add one saltspoonful of pepper one teaspoonful of salt, one tablespoonful of minced onion (this is not necessary), press the meat together and make into small flat cakes, or in one large one; broil for five minutes over a clear fire, or cook in the skillet, which must be very hot and slightly greased before the meat is put in; five minutes will cook the meat; put melted butter over the cakes, and serve very hot.

MOCK HARE.

Three pounds of round steak, one-half pound of salt pork, all chopped fine; one onion scraped or grated, two eggs well beaten, six crackers rolled fine, one tablespoonful of pepper, one-half tablespoonful of salt, two tablespoonfuls of milk or stock, and make into two loaves, like bread, scatter cracker crumbs over the tops and bits of butter, and baste often. Bake one hour. Thicken the gravy with one tablespoonful of butter and flour, then add one can of mushrooms. Serve one loaf hot with the mushrooms or a tomato sauce; the other loaf serve cold, sliced thin.

MEAT FIBRIN.

For enriching sauces and soups. Take four pounds of liver; cut it into long, slender strips; roll it in a mixture of the following. One-half ounce each of allspice, mace, nutmeg, celery salt, black pepper and cloves, all well pounded, after which roll it thickly in flour. It will take longer to dry in the oven than any other meat. When quite dry grind it and mix it with one-quarter pound of heated salt. Bottle and cork. Use it in the proportion of one dessertspoonful to one pint of good stock.

MOCK DUCK.

Two pounds of beefsteak from the round, one cup of bread crumbs seasoned with salt and pepper, one-half tablespoonful of melted butter, a little cayenne, one-half teaspoonful of chopped onion ; mix well together and spread on one side of the steak, roll it and fasten with a little skewer; roast for one hour, then remove from the pan ; place it on a hot dish. Thicken the gravy with one tablespoonful of flour and strain over the steak.

BEEF OLIVES.

Have thin slices cut from the round of beef, slightly beat them to make them level ; brush them over with a beaten egg, sprinkle with some sifted sweet herbs ; season with a little salt and pepper ; roll up the slices and fasten with a little wooden toothpick. Put into the stewpan one pint of stock or one pint of hot water, then lay the olives side by side, closely ; put over them some thin slices of bacon, stew them *very* slowly for two hours ; take them from the pan, remove the skewers ; thicken the gravy with one-half tablespoonful of flour and one-half tablespoonful of butter rubbed together ; pour this over the olives. A few drops of Worcestershire sauce or tomato catsup can be added if liked.

OX HEART.

This is a very economical dish ; it is really very nice. Soak the heart in vinegar and water three hours, then cut off the lobes and gristle ; stuff the heart with salt fat pork chopped fine, the same amount of fine bread crumbs, a little parsley chopped, a little thyme, pepper and salt ; tie up the heart in a cloth and let it slowly simmer for two hours, the large end up, then remove from the fire take off the cloth, flour the heart and roast it until it is browned ; lay some pieces of fat pork in the pan and some over the heart, make a gravy by stirring in the pan a tablespoonful of flour and a teacupful of hot water.

VIRGINIA PICKLE FOR BEEF.

To one gallon of water, add salt enough to float an egg ; one tablespoonful of saltpetre, cover closely and let it stand for three days. Rub the beef to be corned well with salt and let it remain in the dry salt for three days, then wash carefully; rub again with salt, adding one tablespoonful of saltpetre to the salt; let the beef remain in the dry salt for ten days, then place in the pickle, and cover closely for one month. Beef prepared in this manner can keep perfectly for a year, but it is absolutely necessary that all the blood be extracted from the beef.

BEEFSTEAK PIE.

One and one-half pounds of fine, juicy beefsteak, cut into pieces about an inch square, season them well with salt and pepper and dredge flour over them. Make a suet crust, butter a quart bowl well and line it with the crust, press the crust gently on to the bowl; fill the bowl with the meat and one small cupful of cold water; leave enough crust over the edge to form a cover—be sure there are no holes in the crust for the gravy to escape, pinch the edges together, tie a floured cloth over the bowl—be careful to tie it well and firmly down, bring up the four ends of the cloth over the top and tie them, plunge the bowl into boiling water, and boil gently for two hours.

BEEFSTEAK PUDDING.

Make a paste of one pound of flour, one-half pound of finely chopped beef suet, one-half teaspoonful of salt, and one-half pint of cold water. Roll out the paste until one-half an inch in thickness; line the pudding bowl, leaving enough of the pastry to fold over the top. Take one pound of beefsteak, dredge with flour, cut into small pieces, with one teaspoonful of salt, one-half teaspoonful of pepper, one tablespoonful of water; fill the pudding dish, fold over the crust, and cover the bowl with a clean cloth floured—tie it over tightly, put the pudding into boiling water and boil three hours, remove the cloth, turn the pudding out; cut a small hole in it to let out the steam, and serve.

POT ROAST—1.

Eight pounds of the "round" of beef; tie around round the beef a broad tape to keep it in round form—add two quarts of hot water, a little salt and pepper, simmer slowly for two hours; remove the beef, place it in a pan, and brown in a hot oven for ten minutes. Use the water in which the beef was boiled for the gravy.

POT ROAST—2.

Place the roast in an iron pot without any water, but with a few slices of fat pork on the bottom; let the roast brown on one side, then turn it on the other; when both sides are browned add one pint of hot water, one tablespoonful of chopped parsley or an onion sliced. The roast requires nearly three hours to cook; when done, remove the meat, strain the gravy and put back into the pot; add one tablespoonful of flour, one saltspoonful of salt and a little pepper. Serve hot.

BEEF ROLLS.

One pound of lean beef, one-third of a pound of sausage meat, one-third of a pound of bread crumbs; mix the sausage and crumbs together with one saltspoonful of salt and one-fourth saltspoonful of pepper. Cut the beef into slices one-half an inch thick, spread the sausage and crumb mixture over the beef and tie firmly; dredge with flour, put into the stew pan with one onion, cut in pieces, two tablespoonfuls of tomato catsup or tomatoes, one-half a teaspoonful of Worcestershire sauce, two slices of salt pork, one-half pint of water; cover closely and cook for two hours.

ROLLED BEEF.

Cut the bones from the ribs of beef, or take any part of the beef that can be made into a long roll—chop very fine together one garlic clove, one onion, one-fourth pound of fat salt pork, add one saltspoonful of salt, one-fourth saltspoonful of pepper, one-fourth teaspoonful of ground cloves (if liked); mix these well together and spread over the beef, roll the beef, bind with a string and skewers. Put one-half tablespoonful of butter in the stew pan; when it is hot put in the roll of beef, brown, add one glass of wine or vinegar, one glass of water or stock, one bay leaf, a little pepper and two cloves; let the beef cook slowly for two hours, then remove from the pan, skim off the fat from the gravy—put into the gravy a slice of toasted bread—in five minutes strain the gravy through a coarse sieve and serve; garnish the beef with slices of lemon.

SPANISH OLLA PODRIDA.

One pound of beef, one pound of mutton, one pound of lean pork, one-half pound of bacon, one handful of green peas. Place all these in a stew pan with enough water to cover and simmer slowly; as soon as the meats are half cooked add one-half head of cabbage, two pieces of pumpkin, one handful of kidney beans, a few potatoes and two sausage; boil together for one hour, season with salt, pepper, cayenne, one garlic clove and a little cloves and allspice, add one tomato cut in pieces and one onion, boil together one-half hour longer and serve.

BEEF STEAK.

A beef steak should be at least one and one-half inches thick; trim the steak slightly, beat it in order to flatten it, have the broiler very hot—the coals bright, turn the steak very often and broil for ten minutes—do not stick a fork into the steak while it is broiling. When cooked, place on a hot platter and put over it a good lump of butter or a maitre d'hotel sauce.

RUMP STEAK STUFFED AND ROLLED.

Two pounds of rump steak, two ounces of suet, three ounces of bread crumbs, six olives, one dessert spoonful of chopped parsley, pepper, salt and two eggs. Peel and chop the olives small, chop the suet, put into a basin with the crumbs, parsley, olives, suet, pepper and salt; mix well with the eggs. Spread the mixture on the steak, roll and tie securely; place in a greased paper and roast about three-quarters of an hour.

STEWED TONGUE, FRESH OR SMOKED.

Put the tongue into water, enough to well cover it, add a small handful of salt, parboil the tongue, then peel it and rub it well with mace, pepper, ginger, cloves and allspice. Strain the first water, put the tongue back into it, boil three hours, throw in two large handfuls of raisins, one tablespoonful of brown sugar, one-half cup of vinegar. One-half hour before it is done add one lemon cut fine, strain the gravy and serve. It should cook in all, four hours.

FRESH TONGUE.
(A Good Entree).

Boil a fresh tongue until tender, slice it in thin slices on a dish, and keep hot, pour over and around the tongue a sauce made as follows: Take one cup of raisins, one cup of currants, half a cup of citron, one cup of port wine, one cup currant jelly, half a cup of butter and a half a cup of vinegar—melt all together and pour very hot over the tongue.

ROAST BEEF.

In roasting meat the oven should always be hot so that the meat will brown at once—the gravy which exudes, congeals on the outside and forms a glaze; this glaze seals the pores of the meat. Never put water in the pan, and do not flour the meat, and never put the salt or pepper on the joint before it is cooked or while it is cooking; when the meat is done pour off the fat from the pan, remove the meat, pour a little boiling water into the pan, carefully scrape off every bit of the glaze on the bottom of the pan, add a little salt and pepper, but no flour—the gravy will be thick enough without any.

SIRLOIN OF BEEF.

The sirloin of beef, about ten pounds, makes three good meals; the thin end can be corned; the fillet is considered the "epicure's piece." The roast is a good one and looks well on the table. It is important to remember that the smaller the cut to be roasted the hotter should be the fire, for an intensely hot fire coagulates the exterior and prevents the drying up of the meat juices. Do not apply this to large pieces of meat, for meat is a poor conductor of heat, and a large piece of meat exposed to intense heat would burned and changed to charcoal before the heat had penetrated to the interior.

A GOOD STEW.

Take an earthenware jar, put in the bottom a few slices of bacon, on this a layer of potatoes, then a layer of onions, some chopped parsley, a little sprinkle of sweet herbs, pepper and salt, and a little grated nutmeg, then a layer of good beef or mutton, then repeat the vegetables, etc., until the jar is filled, finishing with a few slices of bacon; cover tightly and place in a deep pan half filled with boiling water and bake for three hours.

BEEF TRIFLES.

Take a pound of cold roast beef, mince it very finely, then put into a basin and mix with it a seasoning of salt and pepper, three ounces of melted butter, two tablespoonfuls of finely grated horse radish, six tablespoonfuls of fine bread crumbs, and a tablespoonful of minced onion. Mix these ingredients thoroughly, then moisten well with two beaten eggs. Put the mixture into small well buttered cups or molds, bake in a moderate oven for twenty minutes, then turn out and garnish with sprigs of fresh parsley and serve with or without horse radish sauce.

BONNAR STEW.

Cut small pieces of meat from the leg, about three pounds; roll all in flour until very white, place in stew pan with salt and pepper. Cover with cold water; simmer slowly for five hours. This stew will be found very good and most nourishing.

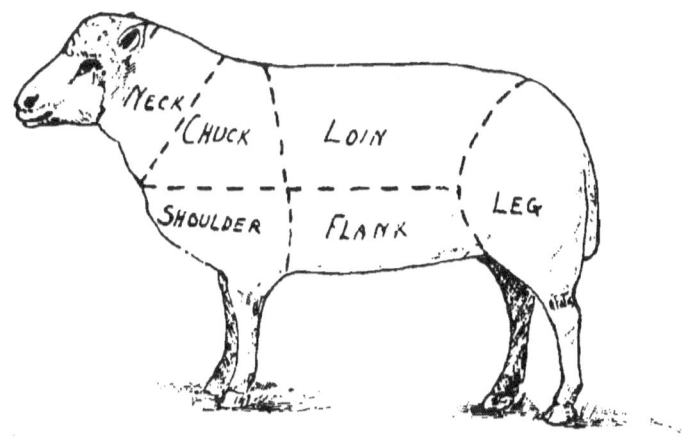

MUTTON AND LAMB.

MUTTON.

A leg of mutton for boiling should be fresh and not hang as long a time as for a roast.

BREAST OF MUTTON BOILED.

Place the breast of mutton in the kettle with just enough hot water to cover it; let it come to the boiling point and then place on the back of the stove and let it simmer for three hours; then remove from the fire and pull out the bones. Make a force-meat of one cup of bread crumbs, one tablespoonful of chopped parsley, one teaspoonful of thyme, one teaspoonful of salt, a little pepper, one-half teacupful of chopped suet; spread this over the breast of mutton, roll it up and fasten with a skewer, dip the roll into beaten egg and then into fine bread crumbs, place in the oven and brown, basting often with butter-water, for twenty minutes or until well browned. Serve hot, with stewed onions.

SHEEP'S BRAIN WITH BROWN SAUCE.

Take four sheep's brains—be careful not to break them, put into a basin, cover with warm water, remove the skin and let them remain for two hours, then put them into a saucepan, cover with boiling water, add one tablespoonful of vinegar, one teaspoonful of salt; cook until they are firm, then put them into cold water for five minutes; when needed, put the brains into one pint of stock, one onion stuck with two cloves, one sprig of parsley, one slice of salt pork or bacon, and cook for twenty-five minutes. Put on a hot dish. Serve with a brown sauce.

BREAST OF LAMB BROILED.

Put the breast of lamb into cold water with one onion, some parsley or celery, salt and pepper, two cloves and a little lemon peel; simmer until nearly cooked, then take out the meat and let it cool; when cold remove bones, divide it into narrow slices, dip each slice into melted butter, then into bread crumbs and broil them five minutes and serve.

BRAISED MUTTON.

Prepare and cook the same as Braised Beef.

COLD MUTTON.

Cut the mutton into chops, dip each piece in beaten egg in which put one tablespoonful of milk, then into fine bread crumbs and fry in deep hot fat.

LAMB CHOPS BROILED.

Proceed as for Mutton Chops.

CROWN OF LAMB.

The crown is the side of the lamb with all the ribs turned around in a circle to form a crown. The center is filled with the trimmings from the bones, when they are "Frenched," and a string is tied around the outside to keep the crown in shape, and then you proceed as follows: Season the lamb with salt and pepper, place it in a roasting pan, put one whole onion in center of the crown. Baste the meat all over with melted butter, place the pan in a hot oven, roast until the meat begins to brown, then add one cup of boiling water or meat stock. Roast, basting very frequently till done, which will take about an hour and a half. When done, lay the meat on a hot dish, garnish with green peas, carrot balls and potato balls. Remove all fat from the gravy, mix one tablespoonful of corn starch with a little cold water, add it to the gravy, cook and stir five minutes, add sufficient meat stock or water to make one pint of sauce, cook five minutes, strain and serve with the lamb.

BROILED CHOPS.

Remove the fat, beat them with the steak beater, dip in melted butter, sprinkle over a little pepper and roll them in pounded cracker crumbs, then place over a clear fire and broil eight minutes, four for each side; turn them often, serve very hot. A thick chop will take twelve minutes to cook; a thin one nine minutes. Always have the gridiron hot before putting on the chop.

BROILED MUTTON CHOPS.

Remove the fat from the bone, beat the chops slightly to level them. Have the gridiron hot and greased, the fire bright and clear; broil the chops eight minutes, place them on a hot platter, arrange them neatly; put a small piece of butter on each chop and a little pepper and salt. Serve the chops very hot. Mutton chops should be broiled over a clear but not fierce fire; pour a little salad oil over the chops and sprinkle them with a little pepper and salt an hour before broiling them.

IRISH STEW.

Take two pounds of pieces of mutton (the trimmings of chops and the neck make a good stew), two pounds of potatoes cut in pieces, one teaspoonful of salt, one-half teaspoonful of pepper, two onions may be added if liked, and one carrot, all cut in pieces; add one pint of water; let the stew simmer for two hours; add one tablespoonful of butter, then serve hot.

MUTTON AND LAMB KIDNEYS.

Fry in butter some slices of bread trimmed free from crusts; split six fresh kindeys, after they are washed, freed from fat and skin. Season them well with salt and cayenne, lay them in the pan and fry in a little butter; when they have cooked for ten minutes remove from the pan, place on the slices of fried bread; thicken the gravy with one tablespoonful of flour, and one teaspoonful of tomato catsup or one teaspoonful of Worcestershire sauce and one teaspoonful of sherry or port wine. Serve the kidneys very hot.

BOILED LEG OF MUTTON.

Have the water boiling; put in the leg and let it simmer, not boil, until cooked—all meats are more tender if not allowed to boil hard. Allow twenty minutes to each pound; put one onion and one bay leaf into the water, and a little salt and pepper. Serve with caper sauce.

MUTTON PIE.

Use two pounds from the neck or loin of mutton and two kidneys; take out the bones, put them into one pint of water and cook for one-half hour; cut the meat into small pieces, cut up the kidneys, mix with the meat, sprinkle over one tablespoonful of flour, one teaspoonful of salt, a little pepper, one tablespoonful of minced onion. Put these into a deep pie dish with the gravy; cover with a good pastry, puff paste or suet; bake for one and one-half hours and serve hot.

MINCED MUTTON ON TOAST.

Mince very fine the remains of cold mutton left from the roast or boiled mutton, add to the mince one teacupful of milk, one tablespoonful of butter, one-half teaspoonful of salt, a little pepper, three drops of onion juice (if liked); let all become hot, then serve on hot toast. A poached egg may be placed on each portion, and will be an addition.

NECK OF MUTTON BOILED.

Place the neck of mutton in boiling water, to which add one tablespoonful of salt; let it simmer slowly for two hours; then remove from the stew pan and serve with caper sauce, or with parsley or butter sauce. The liquor in which the neck was boiled should be strained, and the next day it will serve as the foundation for a good broth or soup.

ROAST MUTTON.

Four days before using, bone and season with the following mixture: One teaspoonful ground ginger, one teaspoonful of ground cinnamon, one-fourth teaspoonful ground black pepper, one-fourth teaspoonful ground cloves, one-fourth teaspoonful ground mace; mix together in one-half pint hot vinegar in which has been steeped two bay leaves and a small bunch of thyme and sweet marjoram and a clove of garlic; rub the mutton thoroughly with this mixture—put in a cool dry place for one and one-half days. Fill the cavity left by the bone with a stuffing made of celery chopped very fine and cooked until tender, mixed with a pint of white sauce (the bone will make the necessary stock). When the meat is needed, cover with mushrooms chopped fine and one-half pound of almonds chopped; then roast in hot oven, baste constantly while cooking, with mixture of strained tomatoes and rich stock, one pint of each. A glass of claret may be added if liked.

ROAST LEG OF MUTTON.

Select a good sized leg of mutton of ten pounds; in winter let it hang for three weeks, unless it has been hung for a long time at the butcher's. Before roasting, beat the leg well, all over, with the rolling-pin; this adds greatly to the tenderness and delicacy of the meat. Put a clove of garlic or a few slices of shallots into the hock end of the leg, dredge with flour, spread a little butter over and roast for one hour and thirty minutes; baste the mutton frequently with a little boiling water at first, then from the juice in the pan. When the mutton is cooked, place on hot platter, strain the gravy, skim off the fat. Serve currant jelly with roast mutton.

LEG OF MUTTON STEWED.

Beat the leg well and rub over a little salt; grease a tin baking pan with butter; put on the bottom two sliced onions, two bay leaves, one carrot sliced, one tablespoonful of vinegar, one-half a pint of water, one saltspoonful of salt, one-fourth saltspoonful of pepper. Lay the mutton in the pan and bake in a hot oven until it is brown, basting often with the gravy in the pan; when brown, put the mutton in a stew pan with all the sauce and vegetables and slowly simmer closely covered for two hours; if the gravy dries away add a little water; remove the mutton, skim the gravy and strain it over the meat. One cucumber stewed in the gravy is an addition.

ROAST SADDLE OF MUTTON.

Trim off all unnecessary fat. Wrap the saddle up well in greased paper, tie the paper over, roast in the oven, baste it frequently—allow fifteen minutes to each pound. Within one-half hour of the time for serving, remove the paper, brown the mutton. Serve with a clear gravy, very hot.

VEAL OR LAMB PIE.

Have your dish well buttered Place first a layer of cold veal or lamb cut in small dice, then a layer of cold boiled potatoes cut in small dice, then a layer of sliced hard boiled eggs, pepper, salt and a little chopped onion and parsley, till the dish is within an inch of the top; add enough stock well seasoned to fill the dish; cover with a pie crust, and bake ten minutes or long enough to brown the crust.

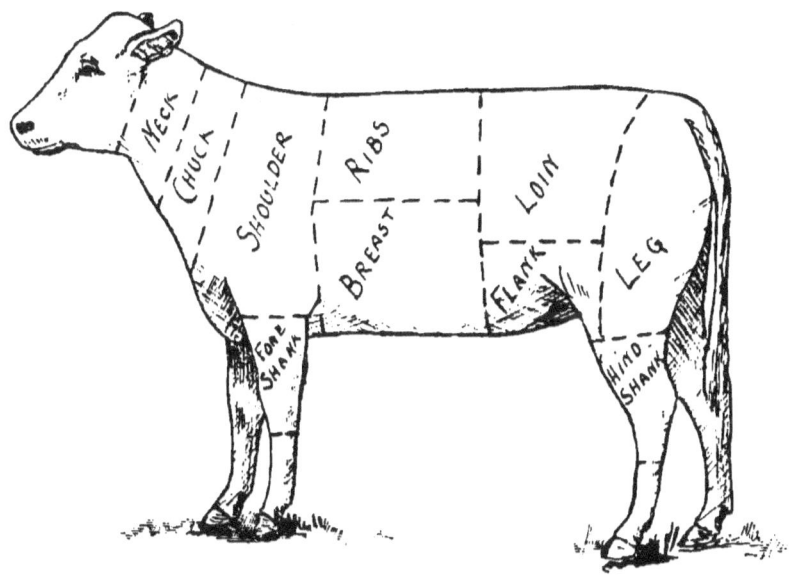

VEAL.

BREAST OF VEAL FRICASSEED.

Lay the breast of veal in warm water to whiten for a few minutes, then cut the meat into small pieces. Put in the stew-pan one-half a tablespoonful of butter, one onion, one carrot, a sprig of thyme and a thin slice of lemon peal, a little salt and pepper; dredge the meat with flour, put it in the stew-pan with one pint of water; simmer for two hours—the meat must not brown; when ready to serve, take out the meat, skim the fat from the gravy and add the yolks of two eggs well beaten, and the juice of one lemon, one cup of white bread crumbs, a little salt and nutmeg; stir these well into the sauce and serve with the veal.

VEAL BIRDS.

Veal birds are made in Austria from slices of uncooked veal, covered with thin slices of bacon and a sage leaf, then tied up and roasted. There is, however, no reason why they should not be stewed in this way. A foundation gravy is made of a mixture of white stock and cream, flavored with lemon peel, parsley, cayenne, and a dash each of salt and nutmeg. The "birds" must stew in this for about two hours; they are nicest when made small enough to serve one to a person. This same gravy is good to serve with cooked veal minced.

BLANQUETTE OF VEAL.

Use the breast of veal. Take three pounds of veal, cut into pieces about two inches square; put these into the stew-pan and cover with water; add one saltspoonful of salt and one-half saltspoonful of pepper; boil, and then add two onions, two cloves, a bunch of sweet herbs; simmer gently together for one hour, then drain the veal from the broth. Stir one tablespoonful of flour and one tablespoonful of butter together in a stew-pan until smooth, add the broth, which must have been strained, stir together; add the beaten yolks of two eggs, strain over the veal and let it all just come to a boil, add one tablespoonful of chopped parsley and serve hot. Blanquette of veal can be made from the remains of cold roast veal; avoid boiling the veal again, only let it become hot.

VEAL SCALLOPS.

Take thin slices of veal, cut them into pieces about an inch square, season with a little salt and pepper and some sweet herbs, dip each piece in the yolk of egg, then into bread crumbs; fry some pieces of salt pork, remove these from the pan and put in the scallops, fry them brown and then add one cup of stock, one-half cup of cream or milk, one cup of oysters or mushrooms and one tablespoonful of lemon juice.

CREAM OF VEAL—1.

Take a pound of fillet of veal, pound it in a mortar with an equal part of milk panada. Mix and stir in the beaten yolk of one egg and the whipped whites of two, and sufficient cream to make into a paste; add a little pepper and salt. Place this in well-buttered molds; steam for an hour; be sure and do not let it boil. Turn out and serve with either tomato sauce or a puree of spinach.

CREAM OF VEAL—2.

Two pounds of veal cutlet, pound it until soft and thin, then cut into finger lengths and about one inch wide, dip each piece into beaten egg, then into fine bread crumbs, seasoned with salt and pepper and a little nutmeg. Put one tablespoonful of butter into the pan; when it is hot put in the veal, brown the slices on both sides, then place them on a hot dish. Pour into the pan two tablespoonfuls of cream, let it boil once, then strain this gravy over the veal. Serve with slices of lemon.

VEAL CUTLETS.

Have the cutlets free from bone if possible; trim them into a proper shape and beat them well with the pastry roller until the fibre of the meat is broken; this process improves veal, but it is injurious to many other meats. Dip each cutlet in flour or in beaten egg and bread crumbs and fry for fifteen minutes in good fat, either of dripping or lard, not a deep fat. Then remove the cutlets from the fat and pour out the fat. Put into the pan one tablespoonful of flour and one tablespoonful of butter; cook these together for a minute, then add one cup of broth or boiling water, one spoonful of lemon juice, a saltspoonful of salt, one-half a saltspoonful of pepper; strain the gravy over the cutlets and serve hot.

FRIED VEAL CUTLETS WITH CREAM GRAVY.

Take two pounds of veal from the leg, cut into small round pieces; dip each piece into flour with one teaspoonful of salt and a little pepper. Put two tablespoonfuls of butter in the frying pan, when hot put in the cutlets and fry slowly until they are brown and tender, then remove; pour into the pan one teacup of cream, let it just boil, then strain over the meat. Serve hot.

VEAL CUTLETS WITH MACARONI.

Use three pounds of veal cutlets from the neck, one-fourth pound of macaroni broken into four-inch pieces; put into one pint of boiling water; when boiling put on the back of range to simmer for thirty minutes, then pour in one teacupful of cold water; this is the correct way to prevent the macaroni from pulping; add one saltspoonful of salt. Make a gravy from some fine stock, thicken with one tablespoonful of flour, add one tablespoonful of some good catsup, drain the macaroni and put it into the gravy. Cook the cutlets; first put them in the beaten yolk of egg, then into bread crumbs, fry them in fat until they are brown, add a sprinkle of thyme over them and a few drops of lemon juice. Place the macaroni and cutlets on a hot dish and sprinkle with paprika. Serve the gravy in small dish.

TO PREPARE CALVES' BRAINS FOR COOKING.

Wash the brains in cold water, drain them, cover again with cold water, in which put a tablespoonful of good vinegar or lemon juice and one saltspoonful of salt; let the brains soak in this mixture for twenty minutes. Put in the saucepan some boiling salted water, drain the brains and put them into the saucepan with one onion, one bay leaf, six peppercorns and six cloves; let them cook for thirty minutes, then drain them and put them again into cold water; when cold pinch off all the fibers you can without breaking the brains.

CALF'S BRAINS.

Soak the brains in cold water for one hour, remove all the skinny parts, be careful not to bruise the brains; when they are clean and white put them into a stew-pan with one quart of water, one teaspoonful of salt, one tablespoonful of vinegar, and boil gently for twenty minutes, then remove from the pan and let them become cold; cut them in pieces, dip each piece in beaten egg, then into bread crumbs; fry in deep hot fat. Serve with a tomato sauce.

BAKED OR FRIED CALF'S BRAINS.

Wash the brains, then cook them in salt water for twenty minutes, place on a plate and put a plate over them and a weight; when cold, slice the brains, dip in beaten egg, then in cracker dust, then in egg, and fry them in a little butter, or bake them in the oven.

CROQUETTES OF CALF'S BRAINS.

Wash the brains thoroughly till they become white, remove the skin and fibers, then pound them till smooth in a mortar. Season with pepper, salt and a pinch of white sugar. Add two ounces of milk panada, a beaten egg and a teaspoonful of flour; leave the mixture to get quite cold before rolling into balls, then dip in beaten egg and bread crumbs and fry a pale color. Oyster sauce or sauce piquante should be served with this dish.

FRICANDEAU OF VEAL—1.

Use three pounds of the fillet of veal, take out the bone, trim the piece nicely and lard the top with thin strips of salt pork; put into the stew-pan the bone and trimmings of veal, with one carrot, one onion cut fine, a little salt and pepper; lay on the top of these the veal, add one-half pint of broth, boil until the broth is thick, then add one pint more of broth, and simmer all for one and one-half hours; baste the fricandeau every few minutes, when it is browned take from the pan. Skim off the fat and strain the gravy and serve over the meat; place the fricandeau on a bed of cooked spinach.

FRICANDEAU OF VEAL—2.

Use four pounds of veal (the fat side of the leg), one pint of broth, four ounces of lean ham, one faggot of sweet herbs, one carrot, one onion, two bay leaves, one blade of mace, one-fourth pound of fat bacon for larding, eight artichoke bottoms, six truffles, four mushrooms. Beat your fricandeau with a rolling-pin, take off the skin and trim off the rough edges, lard the top and sides, cover it with fat bacon, lay it in a stew-pan with some trimmings of raw veal underneath it, also the onion and carrot cut up small, the herbs, mace, the lean ham, pepper, add salt and a pint of broth. Cover the pan close and let it stew slowly three hours, then take up the meat, remove all fat from the gravy, boil quickly to a glaze, then glaze the fricandeau. Make a rich gravy, add the mushrooms, truffles and artichoke bottoms, and serve round the meat.

CALF'S FEET FRITTERS.

Boil two calf's feet as for jelly, but do not let them stew till they fall to pieces, but while they are still firm take them out of the stock, split them open, remove the bones (which you return to the stock for sweet jelly), and lay the coverings of them flat in a dish to get cold. Then cut them into small, cutlet-like pieces, dip each into batter and fry a light color. Drain them well from the fat, pile high on a dish and pour either tomato sauce around or a sauce composed of a half pint of stock, two tablespoonfuls of tarragon vinegar, one of chutnee, a little salt, a lump of sugar, thicken with corn-starch and boil the sauce well before serving.

CALF'S HEAD BOILED.

Have the head thoroughly cleaned, scraped and split open; see that the ears are clean; then put the head in cold water for an hour. Remove the brains; be careful not to break them and put them into a basin and cover with cold water. Put the head into a large enough kettle that the water will entirely cover it, bring the water quickly to the boiling point, skim and then put the kettle on the cooler part of the stove and simmer the head for three hours; add one teaspoonful of salt and one-fourth teaspoonful of pepper, remove from the fire; remove the large bones and pour over the head either Brown, Parsley, Tomato or Bechamel sauce. The water in which the head was cooked may be used for mock turtle soup, or a white soup.

CALF'S HEAD TERRAPIN.

One pint of cold calf's head cut into small pieces, one cup of the water in which the head was cooked, one-half a teacupful of cream, one-half teaspoonful of salt, a little cayenne, two tablespoonfuls of sherry, the yolks of two eggs, one tablespoonful of butter and one tablespoonful of flour.

Put the stock into the stew pan or chafing dish; beat the flour and the butter well together and stir into the boiling stock, stir constantly until thick and smooth; add the meat, salt and pepper and cook for five minutes, then remove from the fire or put out the lamp of the chafing dish and add the sherry.

Cold chicken, turkey, game and veal are all very good treated in this manner.

FRENCH PIE.

One and one-half pounds of calf's liver, one-half pound of unsmoked fat bacon, one-fourth pound of cold roast veal, rabbit or chicken, one-half teaspoonful of white pepper, one and one-half ounces of gelatine, one onion, one pint of stock, cayenne, nutmeg, mace and salt to taste. Boil the calf's liver till tender; when cold put twice through the mincing machine with the onion, pound in a mortar and season highly with pepper, salt, cayenne, mace and nutmeg. Soak the gelatine and melt it with the stock; line a china mold with the bacon cut into very thin slices, then put a layer of the cooked meat or poultry, next a layer of the pounded liver, and so on, till the mold is full; pour in some of the stock in which the gelatine has been melted, cover the top with bacon, and bake in a moderate oven. Do not turn it out of the mold till next day.

ITALIAN CHEESE.

One pound and a half of calf's liver, cover it with boiling water for five minutes, then dry with a soft cloth and chop it very fine; chop one pound of veal and one-half pound of ham fine and mix with the liver, add one onion chopped fine, two tablespoonfuls of chopped parsley, one teaspoonful of salt, one-fourth teaspoonful of pepper, a little cayenne and a pinch of powered sage. Mix all well together and put into a buttered mold, cover tightly and steam or boil for three hours, then remove the cover, pour off any liquid from the top, pour this into a saucepan and while hot, add to it one-fourth of a box of gelatine which has been previously soaked in a teacup of cold water, stir until the gelatine is dissolved, add a little salt and pepper, pour this into the mold over the cheese; it will fill up all the places which have shrunk in the cooking; shake the mold so as to have the liquid settle around the sides; leave it to cool, when cold turn on a platter and garnish with slices of lemon and sprays of parsley.

LIVER AND BACON.

Cook in a frying pan as many slices of bacon as may be required; place them on a heated dish and put them where they will keep hot. Lay the liver in the frying pan where the bacon has been cooked, sprinkle it generously with salt and pepper and cook rare. Place the liver on a hot plate and with a sharp knife cut the meat into thin strips, removing all the stringy and gristly parts. Return the liver to the frying pan, add a generous piece of butter and more salt and pepper, and stir it around with a fork, letting the meat become thoroughly heated. Turn it into the center of a hot platter, place the bacon around it and serve.

BRAISED LIVER.

Two and one-half pounds of calf's liver, three small onions, one can of mushrooms, one bunch of parsley, one-eighth pound of butter, one-half pound of salt pork, one lemon. Lard the liver with the pork, melt the butter in the pot (a small iron one, with a tight cover, is the best for this preparation), then put in the onions, mushrooms, parsley and lemon; put in the liver, cover tightly that no steam escapes. Cook for two hours; remove from the pot, strain the gravy and pour over the liver.

BAKED CALF'S LIVER.

Take one liver, pour over it boiling water and skin it; wash it in several waters, lard with bacon or salt pork. Put in a pan a little bit of sliced onion, a carrot sliced and a little water, put in the liver, which you cover well with onions sliced; sprinkle all with flour, and baste often in a hot oven. Bake one and one-half hours.

CALF'S LIVER CAKE.

Pound in the mortar the best part of the calf's liver; it must be perfectly fresh; add an equal quantity of boiled salt pork, pound this in a mortar with some parsley, a little salt and pepper. Slice two onions very fine and fry them with a little suet dripping. Cut into fine dice enough ham to make one-half a cupful, add this to the liver and pork, add three eggs beaten separately, beat these well into the meat; grease a plain mold and fill with the mixture and steam for three hours. Turn out the cake on a platter and garnish with thin slices of broiled bacon.

CALF'S LIVER LARDED.

The operation of larding is done by passing strips of larding pork, which is firm, white, fat pork, cut two inches long, and quarter of an inch square, in rows along the surface of the liver, placing the strips of pork in the split end of a larding needle, and with it taking a stitch about a quarter of an inch deep and one inch long in the surface of the liver, and leaving the ends of the pork projecting equally; the rows must be inserted regularly—the ends of the second coming between the ends of the first, and so on, until the surface is covered. The liver is then laid in a dripping pan on one ounce of carrot, one ounce of onions and one ounce of salt pork sliced, half a teaspoonful of salt, quarter of a saltspoonful of pepper, three sprigs of parsley, one of thyme, three bay leaves, and six cloves; a gill of of Spanish sauce or brown gravy is poured over it and it is cooked in a moderate oven about an hour until it is thoroughly done.

STEWED CALF'S LIVER.

Two pounds of fresh liver, lard it with strips of fat, salt pork, season with salt and pepper, and put into a stewpan with two tablespoonfuls of butter and fry well on both sides; then take out the liver and mix one tablespoonful of flour to the butter, and add one pint of water, one glass of wine, one onion with two cloves stuck in it, one teaspoonful of salt, one-half teaspoonful of pepper, a little bunch of sweet herbs; stir until boiling. put back the liver with two carrots cut fine, two onions; simmer slowly for two hours; put the liver on a dish, skim the gravy, take out the vegetables, garnish the liver with the carrots and onions, strain the gravy and pour over the liver, and serve.

BRAISED LOIN OF VEAL.

Four pounds of loin of veal, take out the bone and tie the veal round with a string; put it into the stew-pan with one-half tablespoonful of butter; brown it on both sides, and then add one quart of good stock, one carrot cut fine, one onion in which stick two cloves, one little bunch of sweet herbs, one teaspoonful of salt, one-half teaspoonful of pepper. Simmer on a slow fire for two hours; keep the stew pan half covered. Take out the meat, put it on the platter and keep it warm while you strain the gravy; skim off all the fat, let the gravy boil hard for a few minutes to reduce it, then pour it over the meat. Serve spinach with veal.

VEAL LOAF—1.

Three pounds of minced, raw, lean veal; one-half pound of salt pork chopped fine, one teaspoonful of pepper, one teaspoonful of salt, one-half teaspoonful of sage, three Boston crackers, rolled fine; one egg, two tablespoonfuls of cream. Mix all together, shape into a loaf, put a few bits of butter on the top and bake one hour slowly; when cold slice in thin slices.

VEAL LOAF—2.

Four pounds of veal, one chicken, one-half pound of salt pork, one-half teaspoonful of cayenne, one teaspoonful of salt, two eggs well beaten. Chop the meat all very fine; mix together and add one onion finely chopped, four powdered crackers, a little salt, pepper and truffles, if you like. Mix, make into a loaf and bake three hours, basting well with butter water; when done pour over a meat jelly made of veal.

MINCED VEAL WITH POACHED EGGS.

Take one pound of cold veal, mince it fine and place in the stew-pan, add one cup of milk, one tablespoonful of butter, one saltspoonful of salt, one-half saltspoonful of pepper, a little nutmeg. Mix well together and let the mixture boil once, then have slices of hot toast ready; put the mince on the toast and poached eggs on top.

BAKED SWEETBREADS.

Parboil the sweetbreads, then put them into cold water for a few minutes, remove the skin and any gristle, lard the sweet breads with narrow slices of salt pork and place them in a baking pan. Put into a stew-pan the water in which the sweetbreads were cooked, add one tablespoonful of browned flour and one tablespoonful of butter mixed together; a little salt and pepper, one bay leaf, one small onion in which stick two cloves; let all boil for five minutes, then strain this over the sweetbreads and bake them in the oven for twenty minutes.

SWEETBREAD CUTLETS.

Soak one pair of sweetbreads in salt and water for an hour, then drain; remove any strings and blood and put them in the saucepan with one half pint of good stock; boil for a half hour, drain them and let them get cold; cut off all the fat and gristle; chop them fine with one tablespoonful of boiled ham, one-half pint of canned mushrooms, or fresh ones; one saltspoonful of salt, one-fourth teaspoonful of pepper, a little cayenne and a very little grated nutmeg, three drops of onion juice. Take one tablespoonful of butter in the saucepan with one tablespoonful of flour, stir them over the fire; when they are smooth add two tablespoonfuls of cream and one tablespoonful of stiff jellied stock, stir together until smooth, then add the sweetbread mixture—it should be a soft mass, not at all stiff; pour it on to a plate; when cold form into cutlets, dip each one in beaten egg then into fine cracker crumbs—put them on the ice for an hour or more. When needed, fry them in very hot fat for two minutes.

FRIED SWEETBREADS—1.

Trim and wash thoroughly two sweetbreads; have the skillet hot, put in one-half tablespoonful of butter, when hot add the sweetbreads, fry them brown on each side, then set them on the cooler part of the stove to cook slowly.

FRIED SWEETBREADS—2.

Parboil the sweetbreads, when cold remove the skin and any gristle, rub the sweetbreads with lemon juice, cut them in slices and dip each slice in beaten egg and then into fine breadcrumbs seasoned with salt and pepper, then fry in deep hot fat for three minutes.

Make a cream sauce of one tablespoonful of flour, one tablespoonful of butter well cooked together and two tablespoonfuls of cream with a little nutmeg and two drops of onion juice; serve hot with spinach.

SWEETBREADS—HAVANESE.

Fry the sweetbreads without blanching, in butter; when they are evenly browned, serve with a tomato sauce, to which add five or six fresh, red peppers chopped fine. Serve with the sweetbreads, green peppers stuffed with mushrooms, truffles and bread crumbs mixed together, cook the peppers in the sauce—the skins are easily taken off the peppers by placing them in the oven for a few minutes, then pull off the skins before stuffing the peppers.

SWEETBREAD PATTIES.

Sweetbreads boiled, cooked and cut in pieces when cold, the white meat from a cooked turkey, all make good fillings for patties, or they can be filled with cold game, prepared the same as chicken patties.

TRUFFLED SWEETBREADS.

One pair of sweetbreads, three truffles, one-half pint of stock, one tablespoonful of flour, a little pepper and salt. Soak the sweetbreads in water for two hours, then boil them from ten to fifteen minutes, throw them again into cold water for half an hour, then drain them. Chop up the truffles and make a thick layer of them and place on one of the sweetbreads, put the other bread on the top of it. Bind them together and stew gently in the stock for half or three-quarters of an hour, season with pepper and salt; thicken and brown the sauce and serve with fried pieces of bread round the dish.

MOCK TERRAPIN.

Cut the calf's liver into small pieces; you must first wash the liver and let it cook in a hot oven for one-half hour. Shake over the liver one teaspoonful of flour, one teaspoonful of mustard, a little cayenne, one teaspoonful of salt, a quarter of a teaspoonful of ground cloves. Stir these together and add the gravy which came from the liver while in the oven and add one small cup of boiling water. Keep all the mixtures hot but not boiling. Just before serving add two hard boiled eggs chopped, one tablespoonful of butter, one wine glass of wine and one teaspoonful of lemon juice.

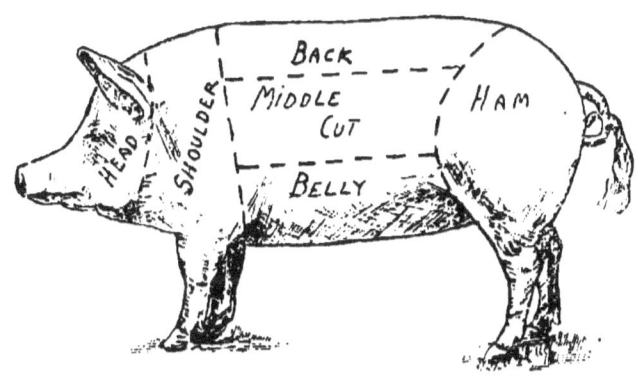

PORK.

ROAST SUCKING PIG.

After the little pig is scalded and prepared for cooking wipe it dry and stuff the body with bread crumbs mixed with one teaspoonful of sage, one teaspoonful of salt, a little cayenne, a little melted butter, all well mixed together. Sew up so that the stuffing will not fall out; cut off the feet and place the pig in a pan with an apple in his mouth; score the skin, baste the pig constantly with the gravy that comes from the pig, roast four hours; when ready to serve split open the body and remove the stuffing, cut off the head, split it open and take out the brains; mix the stuffing and the brains well together, add one glass of sherry and the gravy which has come from the pig, a little nutmeg, one tablespoonful of lemon juice and a little cayenne. Serve this sauce in the gravy-boat or Piquante sauce. Serve apple sauce with the pig also. The pig must be well basted at first with hot water, in which put a pinch of salt, then pour off the water from the pan and baste with olive oil.

SALT PORK FOR LARDING.

Salt pork used for larding should be cut in very narrow strips and thrown into ice-water for a few minutes before using. The ice-water hardens the pork.

BACON.

Bacon can be boiled the same as ham, three hours' time required for a piece of four pounds; when cooked remove the skin, sprinkle the top with fine bread crumbs and a little brown sugar and brown in the oven. Boiled bacon is especially nice, served with boiled chicken.

BROILED BACON.

Slice the bacon in very thin slices, cut off the hard lean and the rind; put on the fine wire broiler, cook over a clear fire, five minutes. Keep the bacon in a cool, dry place; if the slices are placed in the ice-box for a few hours before needed, it will be found an improvement.

CLEAR BACON FRIED.

Cut off the hard, lean strip from the bacon, then cut the slices one-eighth of an inch thick; have the frying-pan very hot, lay in the slices of bacon, turn as soon as they are clear, cook a moment on the other side and remove from the fire.

TO COOK BACON.

Cut the slices very thin, let them stand in the refrigerator for some hours before cooking.

PORK CUTLETS.

Three pounds of the loin of pork, three ounces of butter, lemon juice, three tomatoes, one carrot, one turnip, one parsnip, one apple, one ounce of glaze, chopped parsley, one pound of chestnuts, pepper and salt. Take a very young and tender piece of loin of pork, cut it into delicate cutlets, fry the cutlets in two ounces of butter quickly; boil your carrot, turnip, apple, parsnip, and cut them into thin strips; keep the vegetables warm. Boil your chestnuts very soft and take the shell and skin off. Pound with pepper, salt, and an ounce of butter, and rub through a sieve; arrange as a wall on which to dish your cutlets. Bake your tomatoes and use them to garnish the dish. Fill the center of the chestnut wall with the cut-up vegetables; pour the melted glaze round the cutlets; squeeze the lemon juice over all.

"POOR MAN'S GOOSE."

Take the liver, heart and sweetbreads of the pig, wash them thoroughly. Slice four onions fine, put into the baking pan, with one teaspoonful of dried sage; cut the liver into small pieces, lay them with the onions, then cut up the heart and then the sweetbreads, pepper all well, and cover with thin slices of bacon or salt pork; set the tin in a good oven, bake for one hour, then add one cup of boiling water. Send this to the table in the pan in which it was cooked. Serve with it, plain boiled potatoes.

The bacon mentioned in Foreign Cook Books, is equivalent to our salt, pickled, or mess pork; not the smoked sides and shoulders we call bacon.

Children as a rule do not like meat fats; but use bacon fat for frying potatoes and they will like it.

VIRGINIA LIVER PUDDING.

Soak the pigs' livers over one day and night in salt and water, changing the water frequently. Soak the pigs' heads in salt and water for the same time, allow two livers to every head. After soaking the livers and heads, wash them carefully and boil them until soft, remove the bones from the heads, put livers and heads through the meat chopper, season the meat highly with salt and pepper, mix together, heat thoroughly and pour into shallow pans. Keep in a cool dry place; when required, slice in thin slices, and fry in a hot pan and serve.

PIG'S FEET BROILED.

Have the feet well washed and cleansed, then place in a large stew-pan, cover with boiling water, with one tablespoonful of salt for twelve feet; let the water boil once, skim, then place the stew-pan on the back of the stove and let the feet simmer for six hours. At the end of this time, take from the fire, and let the contents become cold. When cold place in a stone crock and if desired pour over two cups of vinegar and two teaspoonfuls of whole spice boiled together. When desired dip the feet in flour which has been well seasoned with salt and pepper and broil over hot coals for eight minutes.

PIG'S FEET FRIED.

Prepare as for broiling, dip them in beaten egg then into fine crumbs and fry in hot fat for six minutes.

HAM BROILED.

Slice the ham in thin slices; have the gridiron hot, put on the ham and cook quickly.

HAM FRIED WITH EGGS.

Slice the ham in thin slices, fry them in the frying pan; when cooked, remove to a dish and keep hot; break the eggs into the hot fat, cook them until the white of the egg is set, then put them on the ham and serve.

Many persons prefer cold, boiled ham for broiling or frying.

HAM BOILED.

Soak the ham over night, next morning wash it thoroughly, place in kettle with hot water to cover it; put one pint of cider vinegar and two onions into the water; let the ham simmer five hours—turn it once. Then take from the kettle, remove the skin, sprinkle fine bread crumbs over the ham, in which mix one tablespoonful of sugar and one tablespoonful of pepper; bake the ham for one hour, or, in place of putting into the oven, the ham can be put back into a smaller kettle, and one pint of white wine poured over it and the kettle tightly closed and the ham cooked in this for one hour.

LIVINGSTON HAMS.

For every three hundred weight of hams; seven quarts of fine salt, two pounds of brown sugar, one quart of molasses, one pound of saltpetre. Rub the hams with this mixture once a week until the mixture is exhausted. Then change about the hams, putting bottom ones on top, etc. Keep in a cool place for two weeks, and then smoke.

HAM (BAKED).

One ham, twelve pounds, seven pounds of flour. Make the flour into a paste with water, completely cover the ham with it; put into the oven and bake four hours. Take the crust off as soon it comes out of the oven; when cold, glaze.

STEAMED HAM.

Put the ham in cold water for twelve hours, wash it thoroughly, rubbing with a stiff brush to dislodge any salt on the outside, put into the steamer, cover closely and put over fast boiling water, allowing thirty minutes to each pound; keep the water on the steady boil, skin and sprinkle fine crumbs over the ham, and serve.

PIG'S HEAD.

Boil the head including the tongue in a good sized sauce-pan with sufficient water to cover the head, add a little salt; when sufficiently cooked the flesh will leave the bones. Chop it very fine while hot, add pepper and salt to taste and a little chopped sage, if sage is liked; put into a bowl, press it firmly into the bowl and place a weight on top. Return the bones to the stock which, when carefully skimmed, will serve for a good soup of peas, oatmeal, etc.; the fat to be used for frying. Oatmeal is very good in the soup, dredge in the meal, carefully stirring all the while.

LEG OF PORK ROASTED.

Take a leg of pork of about seven pounds, roast it, allowing twenty minutes to each pound, baste it frequently with the gravy which runs out from the leg; when done place on a platter, pour off the fat in the pan, add a little hot water, scrape the pan well; if the gravy is liked thickened, add one tablespoonful of flour, one saltspoonful of salt and a little pepper.

STEWED LEG OF PORK—1.

Take a leg of young pork, rub it well with salt and let it lie in the salt for a week. When ready to cook it, place it in an iron pot with just enough water to cover it and let it simmer for four hours, skimming off the fat. Then remove the leg of pork, strain the water, put into the pot one pint of good vinegar, one-half pound of brown sugar, one pint of the water in which the pork was boiled. Put in the pork, cover well and place the pot in the oven and let it cook for two hours or longer. The pork should be well browned. Serve with the gravy in the pot, and apple sauce.

STEWED LEG OF PORK—2.

Put into the kettle one leg of young pork, one carrot cut fine, two onions sliced, a bunch of sweet herbs, one tablespoonful of butter and water to half cover the leg; cover the kettle tightly, and cook the pork for two hours. Turn the leg once. When cooked, remove the pork, add a little boiling water to the gravy, thicken with one tablespoonful of flour, add a little salt and pepper, and pour this sauce over the pork and serve.

PORK MEAT-CAKE.

Chop some cold pork very fine; grate two potatoes and one onion; mix with the pork; add two eggs well beaten, a little salt and pepper, and two tablespoonfuls of milk; make into a cake and fry in a little fat. Serve hot.

BONED SPARE-RIBS OF PORK STUFFED.

Six pounds from the piece of spare-ribs of pork, it consists of the flat bones cut from the loin; slip out the bones, flatten the meat with chopper, dust it with pepper and then spread on it this stuffing: Two well-cooked onions, one tablespoonful of dried sage, one pound of chopped apples, a little pepper and salt; mix well together. Roll the meat up tightly, fasten at each end with string, place in the oven and baste often, it will be cooked in one and one-half hours; dish it very hot—serve with roasted potatoes and a dish of good apple sauce.

SCRAPPLE—1.

Four pounds of pork, the lower part of belly with skin on, one pound of beef liver; after cleaning pork, boil both together with plenty of salt and pepper, cook until tender, then chop fine, each separately. Sift into the liquor two teacups of cornmeal, let boil until well cooked, add salt, pepper and sage to taste, then add pork and liver and one cup of buckwheat flour—don't make it thick, pour into pans.

SCRAPPLE—2.

Boil together six pig's feet and a jowl, until they are so tender you can pull out all the bones; then chop the meat fine. Put into the liquor when boiling, enough cornmeal to thicken the mixture, cook all well together, season with salt and pepper, then add the meat. Put into shallow dishes, slice when needed and fry.

SAUSAGE.

For forty pounds of meat, thirteen ounces of salt, four ounces of pepper, one ounce of sage. Spread the meat out on a table, and sprinkle the salt, pepper and sage over it, stir well; then grind the meat very fine, by seasoning before grinding every bit is well done. It is wise to make the meat up into balls and fry, then pack away. If the meat is to be kept, cover well with lard.

Sausage can be kept for several months, perfectly sweet, if after it is prepared, it is made into small balls (enough for one person) and fried a little on each side; then pack the balls into a stone crock and pour over the top some melted lard. Keep the sausage meat in a cool, dry place. When needed, fry the balls in a very little lard.

BOILED SAUSAGE.

Put the sausage into boiling water and cook for ten minutes; serve with a turkey or chicken.

BROILED SAUSAGE.

Have the broiler hot and greased; broil the sausage for five minutes; serve on hot toast.

FRIED SAUSAGE.

Have the pan very hot; put in the sausage, fry for ten minutes, turn them once, and serve hot.

SAUSAGE ROLLS—1.

Make a light biscuit dough with milk, let it rise over night; in the morning roll it out very thin, cut into biscuits, place a sausage in the center of each, fold over the dough; let it rise again, then bake in hot oven.

SAUSAGE ROLLS—2.

Roll out some good pastry, a puff paste is best; roll out to one-eighth of an inch in thickness, then cut the paste in five-inch squares; wet the edges with a little beaten egg; mince up any cold meat with a little ham, season with salt and pepper or use sausage meat. On each square spread two ounces of the meat, fold, press the ends together, brush over the rolls slightly with the egg, and bake in a quick oven for fifteen minutes. Send them to the table on a napkin.

POULTRY.

HOW TO CHOOSE AND PREPARE POULTRY.

An old test in choosing poultry is the condition of the breast bone. Touch the end of it and if it bends easily from side to side the bird is under a year old, and tender. If not it will serve best in fricassees and stews. The skin of the chicken should be firm, smooth and white; the feet short and soft, the legs long, smooth and yellow, the spurs small and comb red and fresh, while the eyes are bright and full. Pin feathers denote a young chicken, while on fowls there are long hairs. The drawing should be done as soon as the bird reaches the kitchen. The first step consists in removing the pin feathers and hair. This is usually done by holding the bird by the head and feet and turning it continually over a flaming newspaper. As there is danger of smoking the flesh by this process it is really better to use a small quantity of ignited wood alcohol.

Cut off the head, cut the skin down the back of the neck and fold it over, while you carefully remove the crop and wind pipe, then cut the neck off close, leaving the skin to fold back over the opening.

Next cut a small opening under the rump, run the finger around so as to loosen the entrails. Do the same at the neck. Carefully draw them out in one solid mass without any part being broken; cut around the vent to free the large intestines. If by accident the gall sack or the intestines should be broken the inside of the chicken must be washed quickly and wiped immediately, otherwise the outside treatment here will suffice. Cut the oil sack away from the rump; cut the gall sack from the liver.

Cut open the outer coat of the gizzard and draw it away from the inner sack, leaving this last unbroken. Open the heart and wash free from blood. These inner organs and the giblets are to be saved for the gravy.

Nothing improves a bird more than the drawing of the sinews from the legs. This, if done, is accomplished before the entrails are drawn. Bend the leg back slightly and carefully cut the skin at the joint just enough to expose the sinews; run a skewer in each of them in turn and carefully draw them out. After a little practice has given skill you can get out as many as eight. The one on the back of the leg is the one you should be particularly persistent about, since it is so large and strong. In turkeys especially these sinews are so tough that in cooking they become almost as hard as bones, but if removed the drumstick is as tender as any other part.

If frozen the fowl should be put into a warm room to thaw several hours before needed. Do not soak it to thaw it.

BREADED SPRING CHICKEN.

Cut the chicken before cooking, season with salt and pepper. Take two eggs beaten lightly, put them into one-half cup of milk, and stir into this mixture two tablespoonfuls of flour; dip each piece of chicken into this and afterwards into bread crumbs.

Bake the chicken in an oven on a pan; make a gravy of one cup of cream, one tablespoonful of chopped parsley, one tablespoonful of butter, boiled together.

BOUDIN OF CHICKEN AND TRUFFLES.

Put half a pint of water into a stew-pan with a pinch of salt and an ounce of butter; when it boils stir into it enough flour to make a thick paste; put it by to get cold. Take the flesh from a fowl and pound in the mortar, add half its bulk of the above paste, and half that quantity again of butter, then salt, pepper, a small piece of shallot and a little nutmeg. Mix the whole in the mortar and work into this mixture one whole egg and the yolks of three. Pass the whole through a sieve and work in a gill of cream. Take a mold, butter it well (or use several small ones); cut truffles in slices, stamp them in any shape and arrange them against the molds in pretty devices. Half fill the mold or molds; tie a piece of paper on the top; place in a stew-pan half full of water and steam for fifteen to twenty minutes. Turn out carefully and serve with truffle or tomato sauce.

BROILED SPRING CHICKEN.

Split the young chicken down the back, remove all the entrails, wipe dry, flatten with the rolling pin; place in the oven for five minutes to heat it, then dip the chicken into some melted butter, place on the hot gridiron with the inside down; broil for fifteen minutes, turning it once; when cooked, place on a hot platter and spread some butter over it with salt and pepper or some maitre d'hotel butter.

TO PREPARE SPRING CHICKENS.

Young spring chickens are often dry; dip them in melted butter or olive oil before broiling them. It is a very good plan to place the chickens in a hot oven for ten minutes before you put them on to broil.

CHICKEN AU CASSEROLE—1.

Put about one and one-half ounces of butter into a fireproof casserole with two ounces or so of fat bacon cut up into dice, a pinch of salt, a sliced onion, or two or three shallots and a sliced carrot; let all this brown gently, and when quite hot lay in the fowl dressed as for roasting; let it color till of a pale golden color on both sides, then pour into the pan half a pint or so of good stock; cover down very closely and let it stew gently in the oven till done, and either serve neatly dished on a hot dish, or better in the pan in which it was cooked. This is the simple form of "poulet au casserole," but needless to say, it can be made richer in a variety of ways, adding a tablespoonful of sherry or a sherry glassful of chablis to the stock; or rich, strong gravy, put in with the fowls, truffles, mushrooms, tiny silver or pickling onions, some small slices of ham, or some of the small French sausages,—these can all cook with the fowl as before.

Almost any meat can be cooked in this way. Beefsteak cut up and stewed thus, with half stock, half red wine and silver onions is particularly good.

CHICKEN AU CASSEROLE—2.

Put a small spring chicken into the casserole with a little water, one tablespoonful of butter and some potatoes cut into round balls with the vegetable cutter.

Place in the oven and cook thirty minutes, then add one can of mushrooms, a flat tablespoonful of chopped onion, one-half a wine glass of extract of beef or one-half cup of rich stock, one-half a wine glass of sherry, a little salt and pepper, and thicken the gravy with one tablespoonful of flour; to do this, push the chicken on one side, return to the oven and cook for five minutes and serve at once. If the chicken is old, parboil or steam it for one hour, then put in the casserole and cook as for spring chicken.

CHICKEN CROQUETTES—1.

Boil one chicken and two sweet breads; when cold chop them fine. Take one tablespoonful of butter, one tablespoonful of flour; fry together; then add one-half pint of cream, a few drops of onion juice, add the chicken and sweet bread; stir well together, add salt, mace and cayenne. Spread the mixture thinly on a platter; when cold shape into croquettes, dip each into beaten egg, then into bread crumbs or cracker crumbs; have the fat boiling hot and deep; before frying put the croquettes on the ice for two hours.

CHICKEN CROQUETTES—2.

(Washington.)

Take two chickens, boil them in a little water until tender. Two sets of brains, prepared as "brains, to cook." When the chickens are cold remove the meat and chop it very fine; one teacupful of suet chopped fine, two sprigs of parsley minced as fine as possible, the juice and rind of one lemon, one nutmeg, one tablespoonful of finely chopped onion, one teaspoonful of salt, one saltspoonful of pepper. Mix these all well together and add enough cream to make the mixture very moist; have it as soft as possible and be able to mold it. Make the mixture into croquettes, either with a mold or with the hands; dip them into beaten egg, then into fine cracker crumbs; fry them in deep, hot fat or lard. This quantity should make twenty-four croquettes.

Cold veal or lamb can be used in the same manner.

CURRY OF CHICKEN.

One good-sized, young chicken, two tablespoonfuls of butter, two onions sliced, one small, even tablespoonful of grated cocoanut, one-half an apple cut fine, one pint of stock, one tablespoonful of curry powder, one tablespoonful of flour, four tablespoonfuls of cream, one tablespoonful of lemon juice; cut the chicken into pieces, fry the onions, cocoanut and apple in the butter; when fried add the stock and stew gently for fifteen minutes, then add the curry powder and flour rubbed together with a little stock; stew for fifteen minutes, then add the cream, which should be hot, and lastly the lemon juice.

DEVILED CHICKEN.

Take any cold, cooked chicken and cut into small pieces; dip them into a little melted butter, then into a paste made of one teaspoonful of French mustard, one-half teaspoonful of English mustard, one teaspoonful of Worcestershire sauce, one-half saltspoonful of cayenne, one saltspoonful of salt. Then place the pieces of chicken in a dish, cover them with fine bread crumbs and a few bits of butter, and bake for fifteen minutes. Turn the chicken on to a hot plate, garnish with some watercress seasoned with salt and pepper and a little oil and vinegar.

Any cold game or poultry can be deviled in the same way.

ESCALLOPED CHICKEN.

Boil two chickens until they are tender; when cool pick the meat from the bones and cut into small pieces. Butter a pudding dish, put in one layer of chicken, then a layer of sauce made of one cup of cream, one tablespoonful of butter, one tablespoonful of flour cooked together. Put the butter that has been heated into a saucepan; stir in the flour; when smooth add the cream, a little salt, pepper and powdered mace; fill the dish with alternate layers of chicken and sauce; on top put some very fine bread crumbs in which one tablespoonful of butter has been rubbed. Bake one-half hour. Serve in the dish it was baked in.

BONES FOR SOUP.

Return the bones to the water in which the chickens were boiled; boil together one hour and strain, and when cold take off the fat. This will make a good broth, or a good foundation for a white soup.

FRICASSEE OF CHICKEN.

Take one chicken weighing about three pounds, cut it into pieces neatly; let these stand in cold water for a half hour, then drain and put them into the stew-pan with one quart of water, one onion with two cloves stuck in it, one teaspoonful of salt, one-half teaspoonful of pepper, one-half pound of salt pork cut in small pieces; boil, skim and then place the saucepan on the back of the stove for two hours, then remove the chicken; take out the onion; stir together one tablespoonful of flour and one tablespoonful of butter and one tablespoonful of cream; stir this into the broth; when the broth thickens pour it over the chicken and serve.

VIRGINIA FRIED CHICKEN.

Cut the chicken into pieces, dip each piece into flour which has been well seasoned with pepper.

Take slices of salt pork, put them on the frying pan and cook until the fat is all extracted; remove the pork and fry the chicken in the fat; fry slowly for twenty minutes if the chickens are quite young—rather longer if they are old, Then remove the chickens, arrange neatly on a platter and keep warm while you make the gravy; stir into the fat one cup of milk (of course, cream is better) in which you have mixed a tablespoonful of flour; as soon as it thickens, pour over the chickens.

HUNGARIAN CHICKEN OR PAPRIKA HULM.

Take one large tablespoonful of butter, put into the stew-pan; add two onions sliced fine; when they are of a light brown color add one-half teaspoonful of paprika; let the onions brown a few minutes longer, then add the chicken cut into pieces and one-half teaspoonful of salt; brown the chicken; when this is done add one pint of good stock or boiling water; stew very gently with the pan closely covered until the chicken is cooked; remove from the pan, put on a hot dish; add to the gravy one teacup of rich sour cream; let this scald only in the gravy and then strain the gravy over the chicken.

CHICKEN HASH.

Mince cold roasted or boiled chicken, not too fine. To each cupful of meat add two tablespoonfuls of butter, one-half a cup of milk, one minced onion, one teaspoonful of salt, a little pepper. Mix well together, cook, and stir frequently. Serve on toast with a garnish of parsley.

CHICKEN HASH WITH EGGS.

Prepare as above, but just before serving poach as many eggs as required and place on the hash.

CHICKEN HASH ON RICE TOAST.

The night before, prepare some boiled rice and set away in a dish, with a weight on top. The next morning cut it in slices one-half an inch thick; brush over with melted butter, lay between a double broiler and toast a delicate brown; put bits of butter on each, season with salt and pepper, squeeze over a few drops of orange or lemon juice; hash the chicken, heat in brown or cream sauce and place it on the rice.

CHICKEN JELLY.

Cut up one-half an old chicken, one calf's foot and one-half pound of veal; put in soup-kettle with three pints of cold water, one-half teaspoonful of salt; boil and then skim carefully; add one tablespoonful of chopped carrots, one tablespoonful of onions chopped fine, one-half tablespoonful of blanched almonds. Simmer the broth until all the meat is tender; skim again, and then strain the broth through a fine sieve or napkin; if desired very clear, after straining, add the white of an egg beaten very light; stir this into the broth and let it boil up, then remove and strain again. Put into small molds or cups and place on the ice.

JELLIED CHICKEN—1.

Boil one chicken; when cold cut the meat into small pieces; place in the mold a layer of the chicken seasoned with salt and pepper, then a layer of a few capers or truffles, then the chicken; press all down to make it solid. When the mold is full, pour over the water in which the chicken was boiled, in which you have put one tablespoonful of butter. Cover and place in the ice-chest for a few hours.

JELLIED CHICKEN—2.

Cut up a good-sized chicken, leave the breast whole; put all into a stew-pan including the liver, gizzard and heart, put over it one quart of cold water and let it come to the boiling point slowly, skim and add one bay leaf, four cloves, one sprig of thyme, three sprigs of parsley, three slices of lemon; simmer for one hour; do not let it boil, or the meat will be tough; cut off the meat in small pieces, excepting the breast, cut this in four long strips; put back the bones into the pan with one-half an ounce of gelatine which must be previously soaked in a little cold water. Let the bones stew a little longer, then strain through a napkin; take the jelly mold, pour into it a little of the gravy; let it harden; cut one hard-boiled egg into slices, place these in the jelly; slice the liver and put them over the eggs and the breast; pour over some of the jelly, then when it is hard put in the meat and pour over the balance of the jelly.

Remains of cold turkey or game can be made into a jellied dish; their bones stewed down for the gravy, and if liked, some lean ham can be chopped fine and added.

JELLIED CHICKEN—3.

Jellied chicken is a delicious cold dish to serve with cresses or lettuce. Cut a fowl into four parts and cover them with boiling water; add a stalk of celery, one slice each of carrot and onion, a bay leaf, a couple of cloves and half a dozen of peppercorns. Cover the kettle and let the liquid slowly simmer over the fire until the fowl is tender. Remove the chicken and let the liquid become cold; then take off all the fat and reheat the liquid. Season it with salt and a little cayenne pepper, and then add half an ounce of gelatine that has been soaked in a little cold water an hour or more, and stir until it is entirely dissolved; then strain the liquid into an earthern bowl. Free the chicken from skin and bone and cut it into moderate sized pieces. Wet a plain mold with cold water and lay upon the bottom and sides some slices of hard-boiled eggs; then put in the prepared fowl and some shreds of cold boiled ham or tongue scattered among the chicken; very thin slices of cucumber pickles are also frequently added. Pour over the whole the liquid jelly and place the mold in a cool place to harden. Turn it out upon a platter and garnish with cresses or salad leaves.

CHICKEN LIVER WITH BACON.

Take the livers, roll them in melted butter, then in fine bread crumbs; season with salt, pepper and a little cayenne. Broil them for five minutes, first flattening them a little. When cooked, serve in a hot dish with a maitre d'hotel butter, and garnish with crisp slices of bacon.

Broiled squabs, quail, grouse and woodcock are properly served with garnish of bacon.

CHICKEN A LA MARENGO.

Prepare the chicken as for fricassee; put the pieces into a stew-pan with one tablespoonful of olive oil, two shallots, one teaspoonful of salt, one bay leaf, one-half teaspoonful of pepper, one garlic clove, one bunch of parsley, one sprig of thyme, fry these together for twenty-five minutes, or until the chicken is tender, then take from the pan and keep hot. Take one tablespoonful of flour, mix it with a little cold water, stir it into the broth, cook for ten minutes, then drain over the chicken and serve; do not skim the broth.

CHICKEN PATTIES.

Cut in very small pieces the breast of a cooked chicken. Put in the stew-pan one tablespoonful of butter, one tablespoonful of flour; stir together; when smooth add one tablespoonful of cream, a little nutmeg, one-half teaspoonful of salt, a little cayenne, then add the chicken. Do not let the mixture brown; fill the patty-cases and bake.

CHICKEN PIE—1.

Cut in pieces a good-sized chicken, pull off all the skin you can; cook the chicken in the stew pan with a pint of water, one slice of lean ham, one onion, four peppercorns, one-fourth pound of salt pork cut in pieces, until tender; then remove the chicken and the pork, place the pieces in a deep pudding dish. Rub together one tablespoonful of flour, and one tablespoonful of butter, stir this into the liquor in which the chicken was cooked, add one-half cupful of cream or milk or more; when the gravy is thickened and smooth, strain into the dish with the chicken. Cover the dish with pastry and bake until the pastry is done—one-half an hour is generally the time required. Make the pastry either with suet or butter.

Veal pie can be made in the same manner, only substituting veal for chicken, and leaving out the salt pork.

CHICKEN PIE—2.

Cut into pieces two chickens, put them into a kettle and cover with water; add one saltspoonful of salt and one-fourth saltspoonful of pepper. Simmer the chickens until they are tender, then remove from the fire, take from the kettle, leaving the gravy in the kettle, and put the pieces into a deep dish which has been buttered. Make a batter with one pint of sweet milk and two eggs well beaten and enough flour to make the batter the consistency of thick cream; add one pinch of salt, season the chicken with a little salt and pepper and add one tablespoonful of butter; pour over the batter and bake one-half hour. Thicken the gravy with one tablespoonful of flour, rubbed smooth with a little milk, and boil for five minutes. Serve it in a gravy boat with the pie.

CHICKEN POT-PIE.

Cut a chicken into pieces, put it into the stew-pan with water enough to cover the pieces, one-half pound of salt pork cut in pieces, one saltspoonful of salt, a little pepper; let the chicken simmer slowly; when it is nearly done, put in the dumplings, made the same as soda biscuits, cover the pan and let them cook for one-half hour. Put the pieces of chicken in the center of the platter, the dumplings around them. Thicken the gravy with one tablespoonful of flour mixed with one tablespoonful of butter, add two tablespoonfuls of cream or milk; strain the gravy over the chicken and serve.

CHICKEN WITH POACHED EGGS.

A nest made of bits of cooked chicken for serving poached eggs in, is a tempting way to use up the ragged pieces. Chop the meat very fine, and for two cups of meat add one tablespoonful of melted butter, the same quantity of cream, one tablespoonful of chopped parsley, a little salt and cayenne pepper, and two beaten eggs. Put the ingredients in a saucepan and let them thoroughly heat so as to set the eggs. Turn the mixture on a hot platter and form it in a flat mold with a ridge around the edge. Meanwhile poach the eggs required and place them carefully on the meat. Garnish the dish with parsley and slices of hard-boiled eggs around the mold.

ROASTING TURKEY OR CHICKEN.

Before roasting either a turkey or chicken, after it is stuffed, pound it well all over with the rolling-pin; the pounding renders the fowl tender and plump; then spread the fowl all over with butter and flour mixed to a smooth paste; this mixture is the greatest possible improvement. Another way is to blanket the fowl all over with thin slices of salt pork; use the dry salt pork always for larding or for blanketing. It is far better than pickled pork for this purpose. If the chicken is very fat, bind over the breast the chicken fat.

ROAST CHICKEN.

A chicken a year old is generally used for roasting; if an older fowl is used, steam it for one hour before roasting. Have the chicken nicely prepared; it can be stuffed or not; draw the drum sticks together, tie them; blanket the chicken with thin slices of salt pork; baste frequently in the oven; allow fifteen minutes for each pound; just before the chicken is ready, rub some butter over the breast and legs with some salt and pepper. Serve with a gravy made of the giblets.

SWEDISH CHICKEN.

Young spring chickens are the nicest for this preparation, though chickens a year old can be used. Have the chickens left whole; clean them. Take one-fourth pound of butter and one large bunch of parsley—take the leaves only—chop them fine and mix with the butter and a little salt; fill the chickens with this mixture. Put into the braising-pot (an iron pot with a closely-fitting iron lid), two tablespoonfuls of butter; brown the chickens in this; then put the pot on the back of the stove; add one pint of cream to the chickens; cover the pot and let the chickens simmer, not boil, for one and one-half hours if young ones are used; two hours if older. Cook the giblets with the chickens. When ready to serve remove the chickens and thicken the gravy with one tablespoonful of flour; strain this gravy and serve with the fowls.

CHICKEN STEWED.

For one chicken weighing three pounds, take one tablespoonful of butter, three tablespoonfuls of flour, one large onion cut fine, three slices of carrot, three slices of turnip, three pints of boiling water, one saltspoonful of salt, one-half saltspoonful of pepper. Wash the chicken, put it into a large stew-pan and let it boil gently, put the carrot, turnip, and onion with the butter in a saucepan and cook slowly for one half hour, stirring them often; skim off two tablespoonfuls of the fat from the chicken, remove the vegetables from the saucepan, put in the fat, add the flour and stir until a dark brown; mash the vegetables through a sieve into the stew-pan with the chicken, stir in the brown sauce, and let all simmer together until the chicken is cooked. A year-old chicken will require two hours. Twelve minutes before serving let all boil once. Serve with boiled bacon, ham or sausage.

CHICKEN SANDWICHES.

Cook the chicken until the meat will fall from the bones, season as it is being cooked with salt, pepper and a small onion and a little mace. Remove the meat, strain the gravy, then put the chicken back on the fire; add cream, about one pint, and a good piece of butter, unless the chicken is very fat. Boil the gravy, then set away to cool; when the meat is cold cut it very fine, add the gizzard and liver cut very fine. Cut the bread thin, spread it with layer of meat, then layer of gravy; roll the bread, and fasten with little wooden toothpicks.

CHICKEN SOUFFLES.

Take the breast of a chicken, pound it well in the mortar, press it through a sieve; to two tablespoonfuls of the meat, after it is pounded, add the yolks of two eggs, two truffles cut fine, a saltspoonful of salt, a little cayenne and a little nutmeg; mix these well together and add to the mixture one-fourth pint of whipped cream, and the well-beaten whites of three eggs.

Fill little paper cases, which can be purchased at the

confectioners, two-thirds full with the mixture and bake in a moderate oven for fifteen minutes; then serve on a napkin on a dish. Tomato or cream sauce can be served with the souffle if wished.

TIMBALES OF CHICKEN.

To every pound of the breast of an uncooked chicken pounded to a smooth paste, add one cup of bread crumbs and one-half cup of milk; cooked together, and add this gradually to the chicken meat; add one teaspoonful of salt, a little cayenne and a little nutmeg, then add the well-beaten whites of five eggs—put them in very gently. Grease the timbale molds or tins, sprinkle on the bottom of each a little finely chopped truffle; steam the timbales. Be careful not to let any water boil into the tins, by covering them with white paper. Steam for twenty minutes and serve with white sauce.

ROAST GOOSE—1.

Prepare the goose for roasting, then stuff it with the following preparation : Peel, wash and dry a platefull of potatoes; cut them into small dice. Put into the stew-pan one and one-half tablespoonfuls of butter; when hot put in the potatoes, one onion minced fine, one garlic clove minced; cover the pan; shake the potatoes to prevent burning, steam them until they are half cooked, then take from the fire and stir with them the liver of the goose, cut very fine; one saltspoonful of salt, one-fourth saltspoonful of pepper, one-fourth teaspoonful of powdered sage, one grate of nutmeg; stuff; or in place of this stuffing use apples cut into small pieces and make a rich gravy with the giblets. Prunes half stewed, make a very good stuffing; almonds chopped fine and mixed with apples and bread crumbs can be used also.

ROAST GOOSE—2.

Take a young, fat goose, chop two onions fine and fry them for five minutes in a little butter; mix the onions with one pint of mashed potato, one-half teaspoonful of sage, one teaspoonful of salt and a little pepper; stuff the goose with this. Roast the goose for two hours, basting frequently with butter-water.

Cut six large apples into halves, fill a baking-pan with them, put over them little bits of butter and some powdered sugar; bake until they are soft, then place them around the goose and serve.

Make a gravy by boiling the giblets in one-half pint of water. When they are done, chop the gizzard fine, rub the liver with one tablespoonful of flour and one-half spoonful of butter; stir this into the water in which the giblets were boiled until it thickens, Or stuff your goose with apples and add two ounces sultana raisins.

TO RENDER DOWN GOOSE FAT.

Take all the fat that was removed from the inside of the bird when drawing it, or any other superfluous pieces. Put all into cold water and leave one day. Change the water once or twice. Then drain off the water and cut the fat into small pieces, put into a clean stew pan, and slowly melt it till nothing but skinny pieces remain and liquid fat. Strain it into a jar through a piece of unbleached calico or muslin; when cold cover tightly and keep in a cool place.

ROAST TAME DUCK.

The ducks may be stuffed with mashed potatoes and onions, with a little sage added or with apples chopped fine and seasoned with salt and pepper. Baste the ducks very often while roasting. If large, one hour and a half is necessary to properly roast them; ordinary sized ducks, about one hour. Serve with a gravy made from the giblets.

STEAMED DUCK.

Rub the duck with warm butter; put into the oven to acquire a slightly yellow color; then put into the stew-pan with one carrot sliced, one celery root or three stalks, one onion, three cloves, one bay leaf, two sage leaves, one pint of water; lay the duck on these, the breast upward, let it steam, closely covered until the vegetables are cooked; add one saltspoonful of salt, and more water if it is needed. When the duck is cooked remove from the pan, skim the gravy, strain through a sieve, then return it to the pan and thicken with one tablespoonful of flour; boil once and serve with the duck.

CREAMED TURKEY OR CHICKEN.

Chop fine one quart of cold boiled turkey or chicken; take one pint of fresh white bread crumbs, without crusts; add one-half pint of rich milk and cook together until soft. Be sure to stir the mixture constantly that it may not burn. When cooked add the turkey or chicken meat, seasoned with salt and pepper and a little celery salt. Beat the yolks of four eggs until light, add to the preparation, then stir in the whites, beaten a little, not too frothy, just broken. Butter a mold, put in the mixture and place the mold in a pan half full of hot water and bake twenty minutes. Turn the mixture from the mold and serve either hot or cold; if hot, serve a white sauce with mushrooms added. Serve green peas with the dish.

BROILED TURKEY.

For broiling, only a young, half grown turkey is used. Split in half, broil over a clear fire for twenty minutes; serve with melted butter, salt and pepper.

BOILED TURKEY.

Clean, rub with salt, pepper and lemon juice, and stuff with oyster or bread stuffing. Really the turkey is better without the stuffing, and an oyster sauce is nicer. Crush the wings and legs close to the body, pin the fowl in a clean cloth, put a little salt in the water, cook slowly, allowing twenty minutes for each pound. A turkey is nicer steamed than boiled, serve with oyster or celery sauce.

A boiled turkey can be stuffed with celery seasoned with salt and pepper or with macaroni, which has been partially cooked before using in the fowl.

BREAST OF TURKEY BROILED.

Cut each breast off cleanly in one piece, dip into melted butter, broil fifteen minutes. Every five minutes dip again in melted butter seasoned with salt and pepper; serve with some of the butter poured over each piece. This way of cooking a turkey will make it very delicious.

ROAST TURKEY.

Stuff the turkey with bread crumbs seasoned with salt and pepper, one tablespoonful of powered thyme and one-half cup of melted butter; mix well together. Rub the turkey well with butter and dredge with flour and a little salt; put in hot oven; as soon as it is brown reduce the heat of the oven, put one pint of hot water and one tablespoonful of butter into the pan, and baste with this every few minutes, dredging with flour often.

If chestnut stuffing is desired take one quart of large chestnuts, pour over them boiling water to soften the shells, remove the shells and the brown skin, boil in salted water until tender, mash them (keep a portion for the gravy), add to the chestnuts one cup of rolled cracker crumbs, one teaspoonful of salt, one-half teaspoonful of pepper, one teaspoonful of chopped parsley, one-half cup of melted butter. For the gravy remove all the fat from the baking pan, add one pint of boiling water, stir in one tablespoonful of flour which has been rubbed into one tablespoonful of butter, add a little salt and pepper and the remainder of the chestnuts.

STEWED TURKEY.

Cut the turkey into nice pieces, put on to cook with one quart of water, a few pieces of salt pork, one onion, one teaspoonful of salt and a little pepper; stew gently for one and one half hours. Remove the pieces of turkey, thicken the gravy with two tablespoonfuls of flour, mixed with one tablespoonful of butter.

MINCED TURKEY.

Chop very fine the remains of cold turkey. To each cupful of meat, add one tablespoonful of butter, one tablespoonful of milk or cream, one teaspoonful of flour dissolved in the milk, a saltspoonful of salt, a little pepper; let the preparation boil once; put it upon toasted bread and place poached eggs on the top if desired.

STUFFING FOR TURKEY OR CHICKEN.

Bread crumbs grated fine put into the roasting pan; add salt and pepper and a good large lump of butter; brown on the top of the stove, stirring all the time, then stuff the fowl; the stuffing will be found to be very light and digestible. Place the fowl in the same pan without washing the pan.

STUFFING FOR ROAST TURKEY.

Substitute pork sausage meat for the suet, add one-fourth pound of chopped Sultana raisins.

TO COOK A TURKEY.

Three hours will cook a ten pound turkey; it is well to have the oven hot at first, then a slower one; baste frequently with butter-water.

BREAD CUPS.

To fill with creamed sweetbreads, chicken, veal, beef, etc.

Cut slices of bread six inches thick; cut with a deep cutter. A half-pound baking tin is nice for this purpose. Fry these cups in hot lard until brown then remove the centers It is well to make a round mark on the tops of the cups before frying. Fll the cups with any of the above preparations. Serve at once.

GAME.

BROILED CANVAS BACK DUCK.

Clean as for roasting; split the duck on the back, season with salt and pepper and spread over it some olive oil; put on the hot gridiron; cook over a very hot fire for fifteen minutes, then put on a hot dish; pour over the duck melted butter, one tablespoonful of lemon juice, salt and pepper.

BROILED WILD DUCKS.

Pick, singe and draw the ducks, slit them down the back, crack the bones, flatten the ducks with a cleaver, season with a little salt and pepper. Have the gridiron hot and greased with a little fat; have the fire clear—a charcoal fire is the best for broiling. Broil for ten minutes. Serve very hot with a little butter over them.

ROAST WILD DUCK (AN OLD VIRGINIA RECIPE).

Mince the livers of a pair of wild ducks with a tablespoonful of scraped bacon; mix with an ounce of butter a slice of onion chopped fine, a little salt and cayenne; fill the bodies of the ducks with the mixture; lay them in a baking pan, cover with thin slices of fat bacon, wrap in letter paper and set in a hot oven. When the ducks are brown take them out, garnish with slices of orange and pour over them a sauce made by adding the juice of an orange, two minced onions, with a teaspoonful of butter, a pinch of cayenne, add a little salt to the gravy in the pan. Twenty minutes will cook the ducks.

ROAST DUCK.

Do not stuff the duck; have oven very hot and roast just twenty minutes, to be in perfection; the blood should follow the knife in carving. Be sure to serve very hot, and baste often with melted butter while roasting.

GUINEA FOWL.

One guinea fowl; truss and lard it, roast exactly like a pheasant. Put a buttered paper over the breast to prevent it getting dry. Cook one hour. Serve with bread sauce.

GROUSE ROASTED.

When cleaned put a small piece of butter in each grouse, cover them well with slices of salt pork, place in your dripping-pan some slices of toast and place each bird on a piece; baste the grouse well with butter-water (melted butter and water, a tablespoonful of each). Roast for thirty minutes. Serve on hot platter with the toast.

BROILED GROUSE ON TOAST.

Pick, singe and draw two grouse; slit them down the back, pound them a little to flatten them, season with a little salt and pepper. Have the gridiron hot and greased with fat; broil the birds for fifteen minutes. Have pieces of hot toast; serve the grouse on these; pour over them Maitre d'Hotel sauce, and serve hot.

SOUFFLE OF GROUSE.

Mince, pound and rub through a sieve the breasts of two grouse; mix with this one-half pint of stiff whipped cream, a little salt and pepper. Put the mixture into a buttered mold, steam for twenty minutes. Serve with either sauce supreme, truffled sauce or mushroom puree.

ROAST PIGEONS.

Dry the pigeons, put the heart, liver and gizzard inside each bird; spread some butter over them and dredge them with flour; season with salt and pepper; place in the stew-pan a few slices of salt pork and put in the pigeons, frequently basting them; cover and cook for half an hour, then remove the pigeons and thicken the gravy with a little flour.

STEWED PIGEONS.

Take two pigeons, cut off their heads, draw them; put the liver inside the birds. Take one-half pound of salt pork, cut it into small square pieces, fry it in the stew-pan until light brown, then remove from the pan; put the pigeons into the same pan and fry them until they are brown, then put them on a plate with the bacon. Mix one tablespoonful of flour and one-half tablespoonful of butter in the stew-pan; add one pint of broth, season with a little salt and pepper, stir on the fire until boiling, then strain; return to the stew-pan the pigeons, the bacon, the broth and two onions; simmer for thirty minutes, then remove the pigeons, skim the gravy and strain over the pigeons; put the bacon around them and serve. A pound of fresh mushrooms stewed in the broth is an improvement.

BOILED PHEASANT.

One pheasant, one pound of chestnuts, one teaspoonful of anchovy sauce, one-half pound of sausage meat, one teaspoonful of white pepper, one teaspoonful of salt. Have ready a pheasant trussed for boiling; stuff the bird at the neck end with sausage meat and seasoning. It should not have been shot more than two or three days. Place the bird breast downward in well salted water, and see that the water covers it; bring it to a boil and then simmer three-quarters of an hour; skim well. Serve with a thick white sauce, poured over the bird. Garnish the dish with small cooked chestnuts, tomatoes, tufts of fried parsley, and cut lemon.

ROAST PHEASANT.

Roast the pheasant in a hot oven; keep it well basted, flour it fifteen minutes before serving; serve with a rich brown sauce, or a bread sauce.

PARTRIDGE SOUFFLE.

Roast two partridges, remove all the meat from the bones, and put it into a mortar and pound well with two ounces of cooked rice, one ounce of butter, a little pepper and salt and one gill and a half of stock. Pass all through a sieve, and add the yolks of four eggs, and then the whites of two eggs, whipped to a stiff froth; put into a mold and bake in a quick oven. Serve with a good gravy made from the bones and trimmings, and thickened with butter and corn starch. A puree of spinach may be served round it.

BROILED QUAIL.

Split each bird down the back; put on the broiler over a clear fire; turn them often; in fifteen minutes remove and pour melted butter with salt and pepper over them. Serve hot.

ROAST QUAIL.

Place in each bird a bit of butter, cover the breasts with slices of salt pork or bacon; put into the dripping-pan, each bird on a piece of toast; cook twenty minutes, basting often with butter water. In place of the butter, an oyster can be put into each bird.

SNIPE.

Cook the liver and heart until they are tender, then pound them in the mortar, adding a truffle; cook the birds in a hot oven for ten minutes, and remove from pan; dip slices of hot toast into the gravy from the birds, spread the pounded mixture on the toast, and serve the birds on the toast.

WILD TURKEY ROASTED.

Fill the turkey with chestnut filling and roast the same as tame turkey, or roast without any filling.

CHESTNUT FILLING FOR WILD TURKEY.

One and one-half pounds of chestnuts, large; one-fourth pound of sausage meat; a small amount of beaten soaked bread; boil the chestnuts in milk after thoroughly cleansing them, mash fine and mix all together; season with salt, pepper and a pinch of sugar.

SADDLE OF VENISON ROASTED.

Wipe the meat carefully, and spread over it a layer of butter. Venison is apt to be dry. Roast in the same manner as a leg. A saddle weighing nine pounds will take one hour; baste the meat frequently with the gravy in the pan. Serve very hot with currant jelly. If desired, add one wine glass of sherry to the gravy in the pan.

VENISON STEAK—1.

Cut the venison either in small pieces or in portions. Put in the chafing dish or stew-pan two tablespoonfuls of butter, one teaspoonful of salt, one-fourth teaspoonful of pepper, a little cayenne and one tablespoonful of currant jelly; when these are melted together add the steaks and cook for five minutes. One wine glass of sherry or port can be added if desired.

VENISON STEAKS—2.

Cut the steaks an inch thick, dip them in melted butter, have the gridiron hot and greased; broil over a hot fire for six minutes. Serve at once on a hot platter; season the steaks with butter, salt and pepper.

COLD VENISON MINCED.

Mince the venison fine. Put one tablespoonful of butter into the stew-pan with one onion cut fine; let these brown; then add one tablespoonful of flour and stir until smooth; then add one cupful of stock or the gravy left from the day before; season with salt and pepper; then strain this and add the minced venison; let this cook together for five minutes, and serve on slices of hot toast.

COLD VENISON WARMED OVER.

Cold venison can be warmed over either in the chafing dish or in the sauce-pan. Take any gravy left from the day before, add to it one-half tablespoonful of butter; when hot put in the venison and let it become thoroughly hot, then serve.

SAUCES AND GARNISHES.

ALGONQUIN SAUCE FOR CHOPS OR STEAK.

Two onions chopped fine, three green peppers chopped fine; cook these in one-fourth of a pound of butter; when they are tender, add one pound of fresh mushrooms chopped, or one teaspoonful of mushroom catsup; cook ten minutes longer; then add one claret glassful of sherry and one large spoonful of glaze or strong stock, and cook five minutes; when ready to serve, sprinkle in one tablespoonful of parsley chopped fine.

ANCHOVY SAUCE—1.

Prepare some melted butter (see "Melted Butter"), add a little cayenne, and add when the sauce is over the fire, a teaspoonful of essence of anchovies.

ANCHOVY SAUCE—2.

One tablespoonful of butter, one-half tablespoonful of flour; mix them well together and add two tablespoonfuls of cold water; put into the saucepan and stir constantly on the fire until the sauce thickens and boils; then take from the stove and add one and one-half teaspoonfuls of Anchovy essence, stir this well and add six drops of Chili vinegar.

APPLE SAUCE—1.

Apple sauce should be made in a porcelain lined kettle or one of graniteware. To prepare the apples, peel them and cut into pieces, dust a little salt over them; put into the kettle with a little water so that the apples will not burn. Cover them up tightly. It will not be necessary to stir them if the fire is not too strong. When the apples are done for making one quart of the sauce; put one-half of the sauce into the dish in which it is to be served, add two tablespoonfuls of sugar, unless the apples are very sour, then the rest of the apples and then one tablespoonful of sugar, one saltspoonful of salt; cover until served. A small piece of butter about the size of a walnut, is liked by many.

APPLE SAUCE—2.

Take half a dozen good-sized apples and throw them into cold water, after paring and coreing them. Then put them into a saucepan with sufficient water to moisten them, and boil till soft enough to pulp. Beat them up, adding a little sugar and a small piece of butter and one saltspoonful of salt.

SAUCE FOR ASPARAGUS OR CAULIFLOWER.

Two tablespoonfuls of flour, a tablespoonful of butter, one tablespoonful of sour cream. Mix all well together, then add one tablespoonful of cold water, put over a slow fire and let all come to a boil; then add a little water from the asparagus or cauliflower to thin if necessary. Just before serving add yolk of one egg well beaten.

BECHAMEL SAUCE—1.

Four onions, slice them and boil with one small slice of ham, either raw or cooked; some peppercorns and two tablespoonfuls of butter. Cover all closely and steam until soft; be careful the sauce does not burn or color. When the onions are tender add one tablespoonful of flour, one tablespoonful of cream, one cup of white sauce or good white stock. Cook five minutes; strain; add one saltspoonful of salt and a little pepper and serve hot.

BEARNAISE SAUCE—1.

Take the yolks of five eggs, one tablespoonful of butter, one saltspoonful of salt, a pinch of pepper; put into the saucepan and stir until the yolks begin to set, then take off from the fire, and add another tablespoonful of butter; then stir again over the fire; then add another tablespoonful of butter and one teaspoonful of tarragon vinegar.

BEARNAISE SAUCE—2.

The yolks of four eggs, four tablespoonfuls of olive oil, four tablespoonfuls of hot water, one tablespoonful of tarragon vinegar. Beat the eggs lightly, add the olive oil gradually, then the hot water a little at a time. Put in the double boiler, stir constantly until the sauce begins to thicken; it is best to remove from the fire a few times and stir, as eggs always cook better at a low temperature. When the mixture is quite thick, let it cool; when cool add one tablespoonful of tarragon vinegar, a little cayenne and a teaspoonful of salt.

BREAD SAUCE—1.

One pint milk, one-third cup bread crumbs, two tablespoonfuls chopped onion, one tablespoonful butter, one-half teaspoonful salt, one-half teaspoonful pepper, two-thirds cup of coarse bread crumbs. Boil the fine crumbs and onions in the milk for twenty minutes, then add butter, salt and pepper. Fry the coarse crumbs in one tablespoonful of butter; pour the sauce around the birds, or boiled chicken, and put the brown crumbs over them.

BREAD SAUCE—2.

One-half pint of bread crumbs, one-half pint of milk; pour the milk boiling hot on to the crumbs and cover closely for thirty minutes, then put into the saucepan with one saltspoonful of salt, one-half teaspoonful of nutmeg, or powdered mace, one-half tablespoonful of butter, and a little cayenne; stir for five minutes, then add one tablespoonful of cream, boil all together for a minute, then serve. The bread crumbs should be from stale bread and made very fine, so that the sauce will be smooth when ready for use.

BREAD SAUCE WITH ONION.

One-half a pint of bread crumbs and one onion cut in pieces; boil with one-half pint of milk, stir frequently and cook until the onion is tender, then press through a sieve, put back into the stew-pan and boil rapidly for a few minutes, then add a little salt and pepper, one tablespoonful of butter, a little nutmeg, two tablespoonfuls of cream; stir together and serve.

BRAINS FORCE-MEAT BALLS.

Soak the brains in cold water for an hour, then remove the skin, rinse the brains and tie them in a piece of cheesecloth, and place in the stew-pan with boiling water enough to cover them, add to the water one onion, one bay leaf, a few peppercorns and a little salt; boil for twenty minutes, remove the brains and let them cool; when cold, mash them perfectly smooth, and add one-fourth of a teaspoonful of thyme, one teaspoonful of chopped parsley, one teaspoonful of lemon juice, one egg, beaten; one-half a cup of cracker crumbs, two tablespoonfuls of melted butter. Mix all these together and let them stand for one-half hour, then form into small balls, roll them in beaten egg and then in fine bread crumbs, fry them in deep, hot fat for one minute. The balls are a nice garnish for any dish of calf's head, or served with tomato sauce, make a nice entree.

BOILED CIDER APPLE SAUCE FOR APPLE TARTS.

One peck of greening apples, quartered; pour over them one quart of boiled cider and cook together until the apples are soft, then mash through the colander and add one pint of melted butter, eight cups of brown sugar, six tablespoonfuls of cinnamon. While the apples are cooking stir often to prevent burning.

BROWN SAUCE.

One slice of lean ham and one-half pound of veal or beef cut into pieces, one pint of stock, one bay leaf, one bunch of sweet herbs, two onions, one blade of mace; stew these all together one hour, then take off every particle of fat, strain and return to the saucepan and add one wine glass of sherry, and a little cayenne with one tablespoonful of flour and one tablespoonful of butter rubbed together. When the sauce thickens it is ready to serve.

CAPER SAUCE.

Add to a white sauce two tablespoonfuls of French capers. Serve with boiled mutton. Caper sauce is equally good with roast mutton.

CREAM SAUCE—1.

One tablespoonful of flour, two tablespoonfuls of butter; take one tablespoonful of the butter, put in saucepan, when melted add the flour, stir until smooth; then add one teacup of cream or milk, some salt and pepper. When the sauce is thick remove from the fire and add the remaining butter; stir together until it is melted. Keep hot over a kettle of boiling water; keep it well stirred, or a crust will form over it.

CREAM SAUCE—2.

Three eggs, yolks only, a piece of butter the size of an egg, one tablespoonful of flour, one-half pint of cream, a little nutmeg and salt; stir constantly over the fire until the sauce thickens; then remove at once, for if it boils the eggs will curdle.

CUCUMBER SAUCE.

Slice two good-sized cucumbers, drain off the liquor and put them with four onions into a saucepan with one tablespoonful of butter; when quite soft, mash through a sieve, add one teacup of cream, one teaspoonful of flour, a little cayenne; boil for fifteen minutes, then add one saltspoonful of salt.

DEVONSHIRE OR CLOTTED CREAM.

Strain new milk into a shallow, wide pan; let it stand for twenty-four hours in summer, thirty-six hours in winter —place it then on the stove to warm slowly—bring the milk to the scalding point, but it must not boil or even simmer; as soon as it is ready, little bubbles of air will appear on the surface and small rings, then take the milk from the fire and put in a cold place to stand for twelve hours; the cream will be thick and clotted; it can be quickly made into butter by beating, or the cream is delicious served with puddings or stewed fruits.

CRANBERRIES, TO SERVE WITH ROAST TURKEY.

Pick out all the imperfect ones; after washing the berries, place in a porcelain kettle with cold water to cook— the berries must just be covered with the water; put on the fire where they will boil; as soon as the skins commence to burst, add three-fourths of a pound of sugar to every pound of berries; stir the sugar well with the berries and boil briskly a moment, then take from the fire, strain through a colander and pour into a mold; if you do not wish a jelly, strain into a bowl and stir the berries several times with a spoon while they are cooling.

CELERY SAUCE.

Cut up a head of celery, put into a saucepan with enough milk to cover it, cover and cook until tender, then take out the celery and rub it through a sieve. Mix together one flat tablespoonful of butter and one-half tablespoonful of flour; stir this mixture into the milk in which the celery was boiled, add one saltspoonful of salt, a little pepper and one-half cup of cream; put back the celery, let all boil once together and serve.

GERMAN CHERRY SAUCE.

One quart of cherries, pound the cherries in a mortar or wooden bowl until the stones are broken, then boil them until tender with one-half pint of water; rub them through a sieve and boil again with one-half pound of sugar, one tablespoonful of lemon juice, a little of the grated lemon rind, one teaspoonful of cinnamon, and one-fourth teaspoonful of cloves; add one teaspoonful of flour mixed to a smooth paste with a little cold water; stir the sauce until it thickens; strain and serve with the pudding.

DRAWN BUTTER SAUCE.

Take one ounce of butter and stir into it one ounce of flour; let them cook together for a minute, stir all the time; then put in one-half pint of boiling water and one-half teaspoonful of salt; boil this once, then stir into the saucepan another ounce of butter, stir briskly until this butter disappears; when all the butter is in, add the beaten yolks of five eggs; remove the pan from the fire while stirring in the eggs; when they are well mixed return to the fire until they commence to thicken, then add one tablespoonful of lemon juice and a little cayenne. The sauce should be a yellow color and thick like custard.

DUTCH SAUCE.

Put one ounce of butter and one ounce of flour in a saucepan over the fire, and stir constantly until it bubbles; then add gradually one gill of boiling water, remove the sauce from the fire, stir in the yolks of three eggs, one at a time; add one saltspoonful of dry mustard; one tablespoonful of vinegar and three of oil, gradually, drop by drop, stirring constantly till smooth.

DUTCH SAUCE FOR FISH OR MEAT.

One-fourth pound of butter, one tablespoonful of flour; put in a saucepan and let it cook a moment, then add one teacup of broth and cream; add two yolks of eggs, beaten, the juice of one lemon, salt and pepper. Do not boil, keep hot.

EGG BALLS.

Yolks of two hard-boiled eggs, one tablespoonful of melted butter. Make into balls, dredge with flour and fry a few minutes.

EGG SAUCE.

To three yolks of eggs, beaten to a cream, add one large spoonful of melted butter; one tablespoonful of cream, a little salt and pepper, put on the fire and stir carefully until the sauce sets as a cream; do not let it boil.

EPICUREAN SAUCE.

Mix well together one-half pint of mushroom catsup, one-half pint of walnut catsup, two glasses of port wine, two glasses of Indian Soy, three ounces of shallots, one-half ounce of cayenne, one-half ounce of cloves, one and one-half pints of vinegar, one saltspoonful of pepper. Put all these into a large jar that can be tightly covered, shake well every day and at the end of two weeks strain and bottle.

FAIRY BUTTER.

Four ounces of butter, five ounces of powdered sugar, the juice and grated rind of one lemon. Cream the butter, then add the sugar gradually, beating hard and fast until it is very light, then add the lemon; drop from the beater; pile up.

SAUCE FOR FISH AND BROILED LOBSTER.

One-third of a pound of butter; when bubbling hot, add two teaspoonfuls of Worcestershire sauce, one teaspoonful of tomato sauce and two drops of tabasco sauce or a pinch of cayenne.

FORCE MEAT BALLS.

One pound of boiled veal, chop very fine, put in two yolks of eggs, pepper, salt, a pinch of sweet marjoram, a little pinch of cloves and allspice; make into balls and fry brown.

GARLIC SAUCE OR WINE.

Half fill a pint bottle with garlic cloves, then fill the bottle with port wine; in two months pour off the wine and bottle it. It will be very strong, one drop is enough to use at a time.

GERMAN SAUCE.

One-fourth pint of sherry, two yolks of eggs, two tablespoonfuls of sugar. Put the yolks into a basin and whisk well, pour into a saucepan, add the sherry and sugar; let it heat but not boil. Pour round the pudding.

GIBLET GRAVY FOR TURKEY AND CHICKEN.

Put the neck, gizzard and liver with one onion into one and one-half pints of water; boil until the liver and gizzard are tender; remove the onion, chop the gizzard fine, mash the liver with one tablespoonful of butter, two tablespoonfuls of flour, season with pepper and salt. Stir this mixture into the gravy; when it thickens, add the gizzard and serve.

HORSERADISH SAUCE TO SERVE WITH ROAST BEEF—1.

Four tablespoonfuls of grated horseradish, one teaspoonful of sugar, one teaspoonful of salt, one-half teaspoonful of pepper and one teaspoonful of mustard, one tablespoonful of vinegar. Grate the horseradish, mix it with the sugar, salt, pepper and mustard, add the vinegar and three tablespoonfuls of cream and heat all together, do not let it boil, but heat it in the double boiler. This sauce will be found an improvement over cold horseradish sauce. With cold beef serve it cold.

HORSERADISH SAUCE—2.

Two tablespoonfuls of grated horseradish, two tablespoonfuls of whipped cream, one saltspoonful of mustard and one saltspoonful of salt, one tablespoonful of vinegar;

mix well together   A pinch of powdered sage is thought by many to be an improvement.

HOLLANDAISE SAUCE.
For Meats.

One-fourth pound of butter; mix in this one teaspoonful of flour, and the yolks of three eggs well beaten, the juice of one-half a lemon, a little grated nutmeg and one tablespoonful of water; mix together and stir constantly over a slow fire. The sauce must not boil, or it will curdle, and be unfit for use.

HORSERADISH BUTTER.
For Roast Beef.

Grate the horseradish; after which pound well in a mortar; add butter and a little salt.

HORSERADISH VINEGAR.

One-fourth pound of scraped horseradish, one ounce of bruised shallots, one-half teaspoonful of cayenne, one quart of vinegar. Put all these into a bottle, which shake well every day for two weeks, then strain and bottle. It is a good relish with cold meats or a few drops added to a salad is an improvement to the salad.

HARD SAUCE.
For Puddings.

One cup of butter, two cupfuls of sugar; stir together until perfectly creamy, then add one-half a cup of wine and a little lemon juice, or a little nutmeg; beat until it is firm and smooth, then make into a flat ball and keep on the ice until needed.

JELLY SAUCE FOR VENISON.

Take equal quantities of butter and currant jelly; melt the butter, then add the jelly, and when it is melted add one teacup of port or sherry wine. Bring all to a boiling point.

LEMON BUTTER.
For Puddings.

Three lemons, juice and grated rinds—three eggs well beaten, one pound of sugar, one teacup of water, one tablespoonful of melted butter. Beat these all together, then boil for five minutes or until thick. Put into glasses. It will keep.

LEMON SYRUP.

To one pint of strained lemon juice add one and one-fourth pounds of sugar; let it simmer on stove until it is perfectly clear; when cold, bottle and cork tightly.

MAITRE D'HOTEL BUTTER OR SAUCE.

Mix one-fourth pound of butter, two tablespoonfuls of chopped parsely, juice of two lemons, a little salt. This butter will keep and it is most convenient to have it mixed.

MAPLE SYRUP SAUCE.

One-half pound of maple sugar, one-fourth pound of butter, one-half gill of hot water; dissolve the sugar in the hot water, let it simmer a few minutes until clear, add the butter; pour into sauce-boat and serve.

MELTED BUTTER.

Take one tablespoonful of flour, two tablespoonfuls of butter, and not quite half a pint of milk, and a few grains of salt. Mix the flour and a little of the milk smoothly together in a basin, and melt the butter in the saucepan; put the flour paste into the hot butter in the saucepan; stir it over the fire for one minute and then pour in the remainder of the milk; keep stirring one way only over a quick fire; let it boil quickly for a minute or two, and then it will be ready to serve. This sauce is the foundation of many other sauces.

MINT SAUCE, FOR ROAST LAMB—1.

Four tablespoonfuls of chopped mint, two teaspoonfuls of sugar, one tablespoonful of vinegar. Mix these well together; make two hours before dinner.

MINT SAUCE—2.

Take a large bunch of fresh mint, enough to make three tablespoonfuls, chop the rind of a lemon fine and add it to the mint, then add two tablespoonfuls of best vinegar, the juice of the lemon, and dissolve in this as much loaf sugar as it will absorb; let the sauce stand for an hour or two before using.

MONTPELIER BUTTER.

Pick the leaves of a quantity of watercress, mince them as finely as possible, and dry them in a cloth; then mince them still more and dry them again. Then knead them with as much fresh butter as they will take up, adding a very little salt and pepper. Make it up into balls and serve with the cheese course.

MAYONNAISE DRESSING.

One egg, yolk only; put this into a small basin or soup plate, stir with a wooden spoon, and pour into it, drop by drop, the olive oil; after you have used about two tablespoonfuls of oil, you can pour in the oil by the teaspoonful. When a sufficient quantity of mayonnaise is made, add one teaspoonful of vinegar, one teaspoonful of salt and some cayenne. Should the egg break, you must stop at once and take a fresh plate and egg, and commence with the oil drop by drop; if this mixture is all right, you can then add the first mixture to it. Keep on the ice until needed.

MUSTARD SAUCE.

One tablespoonful of butter; when hot, add one tablespoonful of flour; stir until smooth, then add one onion sliced and one half-pint of stock, the grated rind of one lemon, one saltspoonful of salt, a little cayenne, and two tablespoonfuls of vinegar; let these simmer for fifteen minutes, and then add three tablespoonfuls of mustard mixed smooth, with a little water; boil together until smooth, and serve hot.

SWEDISH SAUCE.

For Fish or Salad.

One-half pint of cream, three tablespoonfuls of mayonnaise, one teaspoonful of mustard, which dilute with cold water, one large tablespoonful of grated horseradish, one saltspoonful of salt, one-half saltspoonful of pepper. Whip the cream until it is a stiff froth; then add the mayonnaise and mustard, mix all well together, add the horseradish, salt and pepper, place on ice until required. Serve with cold fish, or with cold asparagus, tomatoes or cauliflower.

ONION COLORING FOR SOUPS AND SAUCES.

One-half pound of onions, cook them in about a cupful of water for ten minutes, then add one-half pound of sugar and simmer all until the mixture is of a very dark brown color; add one gill of boiling vinegar; stir well; when cold bottle it.

ONION SAUCE—1.

Cut in slices six onions, steam them in a covered saucepan with a lump of butter the size of an egg, until they are soft, then add one tablespoonful of flour, one teacup of broth, one tablespoonful of tarragon vinegar, one tablespoonful of sugar, one glass of white wine; stir until the sauce is smooth and thick, then strain and serve.

ONION SAUCE—2.

Peel some onions and put them into a little salt and water, and let them steep for fifteen minutes. Then put them into a saucepan, cover with water, and let them boil till tender. Then drain the onions, chop finely, and rub them through a sieve. Take half a pint of melted butter (see "Melted Butter"), and when it is boiling put in the onions, seasoned with a very little salt and some white pepper, and serve.

ONION JUICE.

Remove the outer skin and press the onion against the grater.

ORANGE SYRUP.

To every pint of orange juice, add one pound of sugar; boil slowly ten minutes, skim carefully; when cold, bottle and cork tightly.

OYSTER SAUCE.

Take half a pint of melted butter (see "Melted Butter"), and put it into the liquor of the oysters, in which liquor the beards of the oysters should be scalded and then strained, add a few drops of essence of anchovy, a teaspoonful of lemon juice, and a dash of cayenne; boil up, and then put in the oysters cooked, but cut in half. A tablespoonful of cream is a great improvement.

PEPPER SAUCE.

Five large heads of cabbage chopped fine, one-half pint of salt; let all stand over night, next day squeeze dry, add twenty-five peppers seeded, twenty-five pickles; mix, sprinkle all with mustard seed, one cup of whole pepper, one tablespoonful of allspice, one tablespoonful of cloves, one pint of vinegar. Boil until the vegetables look clear.

PIQUANT SAUCE.

Use one cup of stock; stir into this one tablespoonful of flour and one tablespoonful of butter, which have been well browned in the saucepan; add two tablespoonfuls of vinegar, one tablespoonful of chopped shallots or onion, one bay leaf, one little bunch of parsley, one saltspoonful of salt; boil rapidly for a few minutes and strain.

POIVARDE SAUCE—1.

Two tablespoonfuls of lean, uncooked ham, chopped fine, two tablespoonfuls of carrots cut in pieces, one teaspoonful of turnips cut fine, two onions cut in small pieces, one blade of celery, one-half a leek, two sprigs of thyme, two bay leaves, two sprigs of parsley, one saltspoonful of pepper, one tablespoonful of butter. Fry all these together for twenty minutes, then add the juice of one lemon, one wine glass of claret, and one pint of stock, one teaspoonful of sugar, a little cayenne. Skim the sauce well and serve with a fillet of beef, fish or rabbits.

POIVARDE SAUCE—2.

Two tablespoonfuls of vinegar, three shallots or two onions, one sprig of thyme, one bay leaf, four cloves, one tablespoonful of chopped parsley, one small carrot sliced, one teaspoonful of pepper; boil these well together, then add one-half pint of broth. Mix one tablespoonful of butter and one tablespoonful of flour together, put in another stew pan, and pour in the contents of the first stew pan slowly, boil together for twenty minutes, then strain and serve.

PUDDING SAUCE—1.

Four tablespoonfuls of sugar, two tablespoonfuls of butter, one tablespoonful of flour. Stir together until creamy, then add the white of one egg beaten stiff, then pour on one gill of boiling hot brandy or water.

PUDDING SAUCE—2.

One cup of butter, two cups of powdered sugar, beat together until very light; add the whites of two eggs unbeaten gradually into the sugar and butter; then put the bowl containing the mixture into a pan of boiling water, beating the mixture all the while until it is very creamy, then add one gill of good brandy.

PUDDING SAUCE—3.

Mix the yolks of two eggs with a heaping tablespoonful of powdered sugar in a saucepan, put over the fire, adding slowly a gill of best brandy. Do not let the mixture boil, but heat hot, stir continually after taking it off the fire, and at the end of five minutes, when it has cooled, add a pint of whipped cream sweetened with two tablespoonfuls of powdered sugar. Beat the sauce well, then put on the ice (to keep it cold). Just before serving, beat sauce thoroughly, adding one-half glass of sherry; then serve.

ROUX, OR WHITE THICKENING.

Melt ten tablespoonfuls of butter over a slow fire and stir into it very gradually thirteen tablespoonfuls of flour, stir until the mixture is thick, but not colored. Placed in a jar it will keep for a long time and is always ready for use, to thicken white sauces. Brown roux is made in the same manner, only the mixture must cook until it is of a brown color.

ROMAINE SAUCE FOR WATERCRESSES.

Grate half an ounce of onion, and use two tablespoonfuls of vinegar to wash it off the grater; to these add a saltspoonful of sugar, a tablespoonful of lemon juice, three tablespoonfuls of olive oil, six capers chopped fine, as much cayenne as can be taken up on the point of a very small pen-knife blade, a level saltspoonful of salt, and a quarter of a saltspoonful of pepper; mix well and use for dressing watercresses, or any other green salad. A few cold boiled potatoes sliced and mixed with this dressing, and a head of lettuce, makes a very nice potato salad.

SAUCE ROBERT FOR STEAKS AND ROAST GOOSE.

Put one tablespoonful of butter into the stew pan with two onions sliced; fry these together until brown; add one tablespoonful of flour, stir well; then add one tablespoonful gravy or stock, let these boil for five minutes, skim off the fat and add one teaspoonful of made mustard, one saltspoonful of salt, a little pepper, one tablespoonful of vinegar, and one-half the juice of a lemon. Boil together and strain over a steak or goose.

SOUBISE SAUCE—1.

Peel and cut in small pieces one Spanish onion, cook in one tablespoonful of butter, and one-half tablespoonful of flour for five minutes—it must not color at all; then add one-half cup of milk and simmer until the onion is tender, then wash through a sieve; add one saltspoonful of salt, one teaspoonful of sugar and two tablespoonfuls of cream; heat all together and serve.

SOUBISE SAUCE—2.

Take four onions and cut them in pieces and boil for twenty minutes or longer in boiling water, then drain. Take one large tablespoonful of butter, put into this the onions, stew for a few minutes, then add one tablespoonful of sugar, one saltspoonful of salt, a little pepper and a little grated nutmeg; mash all through a fine sieve, then add the same amount of cream sauce, and serve over beefsteak or lamb chops.

SAGE AND ONION SAUCE.

Cut three onions into small pieces; fry them with one tablespoonful of butter for twenty minutes; then add one teaspoonful of salt, a little pepper, one teaspoonful of sage chopped fine, two tablespoonfuls of bread crumbs, one-half pint of good stock; stir well together until smooth; cook for fifteen minutes longer, and serve with roast pork, etc.

SAUCE FOR BOILED FISH.

One-half a pound of butter, the juice of one lemon, one saltspoonful of salt, a little pepper; beat these together until smooth on the fire, but do not let the mixture boil. Take from the fire and add the yolks of two eggs well beaten.

TOMATO SAUCE—1.

One tablespoonful of butter, one onion cut in slices, one carrot cut fine, a little thyme, one-half a bay leaf, one stalk of celery cut fine, two sprigs of parsley minced fine, one tablespoonful of boiled ham, also minced fine. Fry the vegetables, herbs, ham and butter together for ten minutes, then add one tablespoonful of flour; when the flour has browned and the sauce thickened, add one can of tomatoes or the same of ripe tomatoes; cook for forty-five minutes, then add one teaspoonful of salt, one saltspoonful of pepper, one tablespoonful of sugar; strain the sauce through a sieve—this sauce will keep for several days if kept in a cold place.

TOMATO SAUCE—2.

Either fresh or canned tomatoes can be used. Take one cup of tomatoes, put them into the stew-pan with one bunch of sweet herbs, one cup of water, one saltspoonful of salt, one-half saltspoonful of pepper; boil together for thirty minutes, then drain and return to the stew pan and add one tablespoonful of butter mixed with one-half tablespoonful of flour; if the sauce is too thick, add a little broth and more boiling water.

SAUCE FOR PLUM PUDDING.

Five eggs beaten separately, five tablespoonfuls of sugar. Beat the yolks with part of the sugar; beat whites very stiff; add to them the rest of the sugar, mix together, and add slowly one-half wine glass of rum, one tablespoonful of brandy and a little nutmeg; beat all the time you are adding the rum, etc.; add one cup of currants and raisins chopped fine. Add liquor when ready to serve.

TARTAR SAUCE.

Put the yolks of two eggs into a basin, stir the yolks, and a saltspoonful of salt, one-half a saltspoonful of pepper, one tablespoonful of vinegar; mix well, and pour in drop by drop one gill of olive oil, then add one teaspoonful of vinegar and one-half teaspoonful of tarragon vinegar. Take a bunch of parsley, boil it five minutes with a little salt and a bit of soda, dry thoroughly by squeezing it in a cloth, chop it, take one teaspoonful of the chopped parsley, add one tablespoonful of chopped capers and little cucumber pickles; mix these with the sauce.

VANILLA SAUCE.

Boil one pint of milk with a piece of vanilla bean and one-half a cup of sugar, add two teaspoonfuls of flour, when the sauce thickens add the yolks of three eggs; remove from the fire and stir in the three whites beaten very stiff with one tablespoonful of powdered sugar—stir these into the sauce just as it is served.

WINE SAUCE—1.

One pint of powdered sugar, one-half pint of soft butter, beaten together until very creamy. Boil two gills of wine (sherry) with one gill of water, pour over the mixture of butter and sugar, add a little grated nutmeg, and one gill of hot sweet cream.

WINE SAUCE FOR PUDDING—2.

One cup of sugar, one-half cup of butter stirred to a cream, one egg well beaten, one-half cup of hot sherry wine. Stir well, keep over hot water till ready to use (in a double boiler). Beat butter and sugar to a cream, add egg well beaten, then boiling wine and it will foam.

WHITE SAUCE—1.

Two tablespoonfuls of butter, one tablespoonful of flour. Melt one-half of the butter; when hot add the flour, stir together for one minute, then add one teacup of boiling water; stir until smooth—boil about two minutes. Remove from the fire, add the rest of the butter; as soon as this is melted, serve.

WHITE SAUCE—2.

One-half pint of cream and milk, one gill of lemon juice, one-half pint of white stock, two ounces of butter, one-half ounce of flour, one stick of celery, one small onion, one small carrot, four mushrooms, one-half ounce of gelatine, salt, bay leaf and pepper. Cut up the vegetables fine, put them with salt, pepper-corns, and bay leaf into a stew-pan with one-half ounce of butter for a few minutes; before the vegetables have browned, mix the flour and the rest of the butter in another stew-pan, and whisk in the cream or milk; when smoothly mixed pour over the vegetables, and let all boil together for ten minutes. Dissolve in the stock one-half ounce of gelatine; mix it with the other ingredients; pour over the pheasant or other game.

WHITE SAUCE WITH MUSHROOMS.

Two ounces of butter, one and one-half ounces of flour; put into a stew-pan, mix well, then add one pint of white stock and stir until it boils, then add six mushrooms, washed and peeled, let all slowly simmer for twenty minutes, take the lid half off the pan, to throw up the butter, which skim off as it rises, strain this into another stew-pan. Put in it one-half pint of cream, and juice of one-half a lemon; mix and let all boil together. Stir while it boils.

THICKENING WITH EGGS.

It must always be remembered that in thickening with eggs any sauce or soup, they must not be allowed to boil after they are added. The boiling point only should be reached.

SAUCE FOR WILD DUCKS.

One tablespoonful of Harvey sauce, one tablespoonful of Worcestershire sauce, one tablespoonful of mushroom sauce, one tablespoonful of port wine, one teaspoonful of currant jelly, one teaspoonful of lemon juice, the grated rind of one-half a lemon. Let these boil together, then add one-half cup of stock and one tablespoonful of flour to thicken.

SALADS.

ASPARAGUS SALAD.

Trim off the hard part of the asparagus, tie into bunches—see that the stalks are of the same length; boil in salted water, drain and cool; when cold, place in the ice-box. Serve when needed, with a French dressing, or with a Mayonnaise dressing.

SALAD OF JERUSALEM ARTICHOKES.

Slice one pint of cold, boiled artichokes and add to them one tablespoonful of finely chopped parsley, one tablespoonful of tarragon vinegar, three tablespoonfuls of olive oil, one teaspoonful of salt, a little cayenne. Pour over the artichokes and let the salad stand an hour before serving.

CALF'S BRAINS AS A SALAD.

Whiten the brains in cold water; stew them in a little water, with one tablespoonful of vinegar, one onion, three cloves, one saltspoonful of salt, three pepper-corns; simmer them for one-half hour, then drain them; when cold, cut in small pieces and pour over them a thick Mayonnaise dressing; garnish with small green pickles.

CHEESE SALAD.

Rub together one-half pound of grated cheese, the yolk of one hard boiled egg and one tablespoonful of olive oil; then add one saltspoonful of cayenne, one teaspoonful of salt, one teaspoonful of sugar, one teaspoonful of made mustard, three drops of onion juice, one tablespoonful of tarragon vinegar. Mix well together; one cupful of minced chicken is an improvement. Eat with bread and butter.

CHICKEN SALAD.

Boil one chicken until tender. Put in the water one onion. When the chicken is cold, cut into small square pieces—the salad made of only the white meat is considered the finest, but if economy is studied, the dark meat is equally good, and the salad liked by many more than when made with the white meat alone. Take celery, cut it in small pieces, add an equal quantity of the chicken—make a mayonnaise dressing—mix carefully with the chicken and celery; garnish with lettuce leaves or with the celery leaves. The water in which the chicken was boiled should be saved for soup. A medium-sized chicken boiled will make enough salad for six people.

SALAD OF CELERIC OR TURNIP-ROOTED CELERY.

Boil the celeric; when cold, take off the skin, cut it in thin slices, dress them with one tablespoonful of vinegar and three tablespoonfuls of olive oil, one teaspoonful of salt and a little pepper, or you can dress them with a mayonnaise.

CAULIFLOWER SALAD.

Prepare the cauliflower the same as for serving as a vegetable; drain carefully and place on the ice for some hours before serving; when required pour over a mayonnaise dressing.

CREAM SALAD DRESSING.

One pint of very thick sour or sweet cream; the yolks of six eggs well beaten, with one tablespoonful of sugar. Add these to the cream, then add one tablespoonful of melted butter, one saltspoonful of pepper, one-half saltspoonful of cayenne, one saltspoonful of mustard, one teaspoonful of salt. Mix all well together and then add slowly four tablespoonfuls of hot cider vinegar. Put the mixture into the double boiler and let it cook until thick; be careful it does not curdle; use when cold on raw cabbage, lettuce or tomatoes, and on cooked cauliflower, beans and potatoes.

ENDIVE.

Serve with either a French or mayonnaise dressing. Is a fall and winter salad; it is a healthy and an excellent salad.

"F. F. V." SALAD.

Ripe tomatoes, celery, green sweet peppers, lettuce. Make a bed of crisp lettuce leaves, on this place the tomatoes whole, carefully peeled. Over the tomatoes put the celery shredded, then the peppers cut finely. Pour over all a dressing of three tablespoonfuls of olive oil, one tablespoonful of vinegar, one teaspoonful of paprika, one teaspoonful of salt.

FRENCH DRESSING FOR SALAD.

One tablespoonful of vinegar, three tablespoonfuls of olive oil, one saltspoonful of salt, one-fourth saltspoonful of pepper, a little cayenne; mix together. This dressing can be varied by using Chili and tarragon vinegar, and by adding a few drops of onion juice.

JARDINIERE SALAD.

Cut into fine pieces, carrots, beets, turnips, potatoes, green peas and beans; boil them together with a little butter in the water until they are tender, then let the vegetables become cold. When needed, pour over a French or mayonnaise dressing.

LETTUCE SALAD.

Lettuce is one of the best and most useful salads, for it can easily be obtained all the year. Wash the lettuce leaves carefully; drain, arrange in salad bowl and pour over either a French or mayonnaise dressing.

LOBSTER SALAD.

Prepare the lobster by boiling as directed. When cold remove the shell, cut the meat into cakes and place on the ice for an hour before serving; make a mayonnaise dressing; pour over the lobster and serve; be careful that the lobster is perfectly fresh if purchased cooked.

MAYONNAISE DRESSING.

One egg, yolk only; be sure that it is perfectly cold. Stir the yolk, if it thickens and does not run over the bottom of the soup plate; stir into it drop by drop some olive oil, then put in the oil by half teaspoonfuls; when as much of the dressing is made as will be needed add one teaspoonful of vinegar or one teaspoonful of lemon juice, one teaspoonful of salt, one-half teaspoonful of pepper, a little cayenne. If desired add another teaspoonful of vinegar. Keep the mayonnaise on ice until it is needed. One teaspoonful of dry mustard may be added to the yolk, if liked.

OYSTER SALAD.

Scald fifty oysters in their own liquor, drain and let them cool, then pour over them a tablespoonful of vinegar, three tablespoonfuls of oil, salt and cayenne, and let them stand two hours; then drain them from the dressing, place them on serving dish, cover with celery cut in small pieces. Pour over all a thick mayonnaise dressing; serve at once.

ORANGE SALAD.

Two oranges, one-fourth pint of oil, one teaspoonful of vinegar, one saltspoonful of pepper, one-half saltspoonful of salt. Cut the oranges into thin slices; remove the rinds; mix the vinegar, pepper, salt and oil together and pour over the oranges. Serve with wild duck.

SWEETBREAD SALAD.

Soak the sweetbreads in salted water for an hour, then drain; remove any strings and blood, then put them into boiling water and cook for fifteen minutes, drain them and let them cool; when ready to serve cut into small pieces, make a mayonnaise dressing. Mix with it the sweetbreads, arrange on lettuce leaves or in a salad dish; the salad can be garnished with slices of hard boiled eggs. Serve very cold.

POTATO SALAD—1.

Boil the potatoes in their skins, remove from the fire before they are quite done; they must not be "mealy" or "floury;" when cold peel and cut them in square pieces as nearly of one size as possible; add a few drops of onion juice, one tablespoonful of chopped parsley, then add a French dressing of three tablespoonfuls of olive oil, and one tablespoonful of vinegar, one teaspoonful of salt, one-half teaspoonful of pepper. Let the dressing stand on the potatoes for half an hour before serving.

POTATO SALAD—2.

Boil the potatoes in their skins, but be careful not to cook them until they break open; when cooked let them become cold before cutting them into small pieces; add one-half tablespoonful of onion chopped fine, one-half tablespoonful of celery chopped fine; mix these all well with the potatoes and pour over a mayonnaise dressing made as follows: Take the yolks of two eggs, stir into them one-half pint of olive oil slowly; when the dressing is smooth and thick, add one tablespoonful of mustard, a little cayenne, one saltspoonful of salt, one tablespoonful of vinegar, or more if the dressing is too thick.

ROMAINE SALAD DRESSING.

Grate half an ounce of onion; mix it with a teaspoonful of lemon juice, a saltspoonful each of salt and powdered sugar, a level saltspoonful each of white pepper and dry mustard, then gradually add three tablespoonfuls of oil and one tablespoonful of vinegar. Use for lettuce or tomato salad.

TOMATO SALAD.

Select small, round, perfect tomatoes, wipe them dry, cut a lid from the top and scoop out a portion of the insides and all the seeds; cut some celery very fine; mix this well with mayonnaise dressing. Fill the tomatoes with this, placing a little of the dressing on the top; put in the ice-box for an hour to chill the tomatoes; serve on lettuce leaves.

SALAD OF TOMATOES WITH CAVIARE.

Take two large tomatoes and slice them, cover the slices with a dressing made of some caviare, highly seasoned with paprika and lemon juice, and pour over a French dressing. Serve on lettuce leaves.

VEGETABLE SALAD.

Wash carefully one beet, one carrot, one onion, one potato, one-half pint of green peas, one-half pint of string beans. Cook these until soft in boiling water with one teaspoonful of butter and a little salt; cook the beet separately; when cold peel and slice the vegetables and mix them together and pour over all a mayonnaise. Do not put the beet with the other vegetables until just before serving; dress the salad with lettuce leaves.

WATERCRESS SALAD.

Take nice young watercress, cleanse thoroughly in salt and water and put in a salad bowl with a few sliced young radishes and four hard boiled eggs cut into half quarters. Make a dressing of one tablespoonful of vinegar and three tablespoonfuls of olive oil, a little salt and cayenne.

WALNUT AND PEAS SALAD.

If fresh peas are used have them cooked cold and carefully drained; if canned peas are used have them rinsed in cold water poured into a colander and drained; the canned peas are already cooked. Shell and blanch the walnuts by letting them remain in boiling water for a few minutes and remove the thin brown skin; this requires time and patience; cut the nuts about the same size as the peas, sprinkle them with salt; mix the nuts and peas together, moisten with a mayonnaise dressing. Keep cool until served.

VINEGAR FOR SALAD.

Mix together four tablespoonfuls of cider vinegar, two tablespoonfuls of tarragon vinegar, two tablespoonfuls of Chili vinegar, one tablespoonful of celery vinegar; put the mixture into a bottle and use one tablespoonful for French salad dressing with the olive oil.

VEGETABLES.

Fresh vegetable, especially of the cabbage tribe, should be put into fast boiling water; salt should be added only towards the end of the cooking, as its earlier application would simply tend to harden the vegetables.

Potatoes should always be put into boiling water. Do not peel potatoes and let them soak for an indefinite time in cold water. Never boil potatoes to be served plain before you need them; never try them with a fork; the fork causes them to break and crumble.

All green vegetables should be cooked in soft water; add a small bit of soda to preserve the green color. Never cover green vegetables.

Garlic is a most excellent condiment.

Always put vegetables into boiling water; never have the vegetables wait for the meat.

ASPARAGUS.

Asparagus of the large or giant variety should be cut of exactly equal lengths and boiled standing tops upward in a deep saucepan; nearly two inches of the heads should be out of the water, the steam sufficing to cook them, as they are the tenderest part of the plant. The stalks can be boiled by this method thirty or forty minutes, thus ensuring a third more of the asparagus delicious.

ASPARAGUS CREAMED.

Cut off the heads of the asparagus; cook them in slightly salted water; when tender, which will be in about twenty minutes, drain off the water and add one cup of cream, one-half tablespoonful of butter, one saltspoonful of salt, and a little pepper; as soon as the cream is hot, serve the asparagus on slices of toast.

GLOBE ARTICHOKES.

The ordinary manner of cooking green artichokes is to boil them in water; when tender, drain them and dish them, and send melted butter or cream sauce to be eaten with them.

JERUSALEM ARTICHOKES STEWED.

Wash the artichokes, cut off the end of each quite flat. Boil them in milk and water and lift them out the moment they are done; drain and place them in the dish in which they are to be served, and serve them with a rich bechamel sauce.

BEETS.

Wash free from dirt, but never peel them before cooking. Be careful not to break the skin for if broken the beets will bleed. Cook young beets about thirty minutes, old beets until they are tender. When cooked peel off the skin, slice the beets in thin slices or chop fine, put over some melted butter, a little salt and pepper and if liked, one tablespoonful of hot vinegar.

BAKED BANANAS.

Peel the bananas, place them in a tin pan with three teaspoonfuls of cold water and one half teaspoonful of butter, drop a little lemon juice over each banana, dredge them with cinnamon and sugar; bake for fifteen minutes, or until they are easily pierced with a fork. Serve at once.

BRUSSELS SPROUTS.

Two quarts of Brussels sprouts, wash them thoroughly, put them into three quarts of boiling water with one tablespoonful of salt; boil them gently until they are tender—this will be in twenty minutes, shake the pan occasionally, then drain them, do not break them; return to the saucepan, add one-half tablespoonful of butter, one teaspoonful of lemon juice, a saltspoonful of salt, one-fourth saltspoonful of pepper; stir over the fire until hot, then serve on hot, buttered toast.

GREEN BEANS CREAMED.

Cut the ends of young green beans and string them carefully. Cut the beans in narrow strips, cook in a saucepan, putting them into boiling water, do not cover the pan, add a pinch of soda; when the beans are tender, drain, put back into the saucepan, add one tablespoonful of butter, one tablespoonful of cream, salt and pepper.

LIMA BEANS—1.

Boil the beans in water; when nearly done let the water simmer away, add one cup of cream or milk, with one tablespoonful of flour and two tablespoonfuls of butter mixed together.

LIMA BEANS—2.

Boil one pint of lima beans for one hour, then drain them, season with a little salt; keep them hot. Make a sauce with one egg beaten light with two tablespoonfuls of cold water, two teaspoonfuls of lemon juice; add one tablespoonful of butter; boil these together until the sauce thickens, then pour it over the beans and serve hot.

BOSTON BAKED BEANS.

Wash the beans and soak them over night in cold water; in the morning put them into cold water and boil until soft, then put them into the bean pot with the same water, some pepper, one pound of salt pork to one quart of beans, one-half cup of molasses. Bake all day; if the water bakes out add more.

BAKED CABBAGE.

Put the cabbage into boiling water until the leaves open out; clean. Take two slices of boiled ham, chop it very fine with a few leaves of the cabbage, add three hard boiled eggs, chopped fine, one teaspoonful of salt, one saltspoonful of pepper, one teaspoonful of mustard, one tablespoonful of melted butter; mix these together, remove the heart of the cabbage and fill in its place the above mixture. Tie up the cabbage and put it into boiling water and cook until tender; when cooked remove the cloth, put the cabbage on a pan, sprinkle over a little flour and one spoonful of melted lard, put into the oven and bake until brown. Serve with a sauce poured over it; for the sauce, take one tablespoonful of butter, melt it in the saucepan, when hot stir in one tablespoonful of flour; as soon as the sauce thickens add two tablespoonfuls of hot milk; stir well and pour over the cabbage and then put slices of hard boiled eggs over all.

BOILED CABBAGE.

Wash and quarter the cabbage not quite into four pieces; keep it so it will not fall apart. Then have four quarts of boiling water and add to it one-half teaspoonful of soda, one heaping teaspoonful of salt, boil the cabbage in this with the cover on ten minutes, then remove the cover and boil twenty minutes. Serve with a sauce as for cauliflower. Cabbage cooked exactly as in this recipe, will be found digestible, and there will be no odor in the house from the cooking of it.

CABBAGE WITH BUTTER.

Boil a cabbage in two quarts of water for an hour, then chop it fine, put it into the saucepan with four ounces of butter, a little salt and pepper and one teacup of vinegar; let it become very hot, and serve.

CABBAGE COLD SLAW.

Three well-beaten eggs, four tablespoonfuls of cream, one tablespoonful of mustard, one tablespoonful of slightly melted butter. Mix well together, then add six tablespoonfuls of vinegar, a little cayenne, one teaspoonful of salt, one-fourth teaspoonful of pepper; place the mixture in a bowl over boiling water and stir until it thickens; pour over the cabbage—which should be chopped fine.

ESCALLOPED CABBAGE.

Boil a firm head of cabbage until it is tender and set it aside; when it is cool chop it fine; add two well-beaten eggs, one ounce of butter, three tablespoonfuls of cream, a little salt and pepper; bake one-half hour in a moderate oven.

CABBAGE OR HOT SLAW.

Chop fine a head of good, firm cabbage, cook in saucepan with salted water until tender, then drain it from the water, return to the saucepan and add one-half cupful of vinegar, one teaspoonful sugar, one tablespoonful butter, salt and pepper—let it cook in this for ten minutes.

CARDOONS BOILED.

Cut away the coarse outside of the cardoon, wash it free from sand, lay in cold water to harden; then boil in milk and water till tender, drain it on the back of a sieve. Cut each stalk in two; place them in a vegetable dish and pour white sauce over them.

CARROTS A LA MAITRE D'HOTEL.

Scrape, wash and scald the carrots in boiling water; cook them in hot water, with salt and a piece of butter the size of a small egg. When cooked, remove and put them to drain. Mix in a stewpan another piece of butter, one tablespoonful of chopped parsley, one chopped shallot, one teaspoonful of lemon juice, and pepper and salt to taste. Put in the carrots, toss them up for two minutes, and serve them on fried bread.

STEWED CARROTS IN THEIR OWN JUICE.

Wash the carrots very clean, scrape them and cut in thick slices, put them in boiling water slightly salted, just enough to cover them, boil gently until tender, then boil them rapidly to reduce the water; when only about one tablespoonful is left, put with the carrots one-half tablespoonful of butter rolled in flour, a little salt and pepper, stir for a moment, then add one spoonful of minced parsley, one teaspoonful of cream, and serve at once.

BAKED CORN.

Eighteen ears of corn, cut down the middle of each grain, scrape the cob well, add a teaspoonful of salt, a little pepper, one tablespoonful of sugar; beat one egg into one cup of cream and two tablespoonfuls of flour, add to the corn, put the mixture into the baking pan and bake for forty-five minutes; serve it in the same pan.

BOILED GREEN CORN.

Remove the husks and the fine silk from the ears, put the corn into boiling water enough to cover it and boil until tender—young corn will cook in ten minutes. Take from the water, spread a napkin on a dish and put the corn on it; fold over the napkin and serve at once.

CREAMED CORN.

Cut the corn from the cob, cut only the outer part of the grain, then scrape the cob clean; cook the first part in a little milk for forty minutes, add the part scraped from the cob, and cook together for five minutes; season with one tablespoonful of butter, a little salt and pepper.

GREEN CORN CAKE.

Cut the grains from the corn cob, then scrape the cob well, add one tablespoonful of melted butter, one tablespoonful of flour, salt and pepper. Have the frying pan hot and lightly greased with butter, pile the corn on it, brown, then turn it over and brown the other side.

GREEN CORN CAKES.

Grate the corn, scrape well the cob. For twelve ears take three eggs, beat them well and add to the corn one teaspoonful of salt. Mix well together and fry like griddle cakes. These cakes will be found very delicate. Serve with meat.

ESCALLOPED CORN.

One can of corn or one pint fresh corn, season highly; add one egg, two spoonfuls of cream; place in baking dish, cover with cracker crumbs and bits of butter. Bake ten minutes, just to brown nicely for luncheon. The corn, if fresh, must first be boiled until tender.

CORN PUDDING.

Scrape with a knife two dozen ears of corn, cut the grains and then scrape the cobs well. Melt one-half pound of butter; stir into the corn and add one pint of milk, the yolks of three eggs well beaten, one teaspoonful of salt, one saltspoonful of pepper, then add the whites beaten stiff. Pour the mixture into a baking dish and bake in a moderate oven for one hour and a quarter unless the corn is old, when a longer time will be necessary.

CORN FRITTERS.

One pint of corn, either fresh or canned. Make a batter of four eggs, one cup of milk, one teaspoonful of baking powder, one cup of flour, one teaspoonful of salt;

mix these well together until light. Have the fat deep and boiling, then drop the mixture in spoonfuls into it and fry until the fritters are a light brown.

STEWED CELERY.

Take the outer stalks of celery, cut in pieces two inches in length, boil in milk until tender, add a little salt and pepper; when cooked drain from the milk, put into the milk one teaspoonful of butter and one teaspoonful of flour mixed together, stir until the milk thickens and then pour over the celery.

CAULIFLOWERS BOILED.

Choose white, firm and small grained cauliflowers; trim off the leaves and stalk; wash them well in cold water, in which put one tablespoonful of vinegar—by using this, any insect in the cauliflower will be sure to come out. Put the cauliflower in boiling water for five minutes, remove, cool and drain, then boil again in two quarts of water with one teaspoonful of salt. You can tell if the cauliflower is done, if when you pinch a small piece, it is tender, though still firm. Serve with a white sauce, or sauce for cauliflower.

CAULIFLOWER WITH CHEESE.

Cook the cauliflower in salted water; when tender, drain from the water, put into a porcelain dish which will stand the heat of the oven; cover with white sauce, then put two tablespoonfuls of grated cheese over it and some fine bread crumbs and bits of butter; when brown, serve hot.

CUCUMBERS.

It is a mistake to soak cucumbers in salted water to draw out the indigestible part; it surely renders them unpalatable and wilts them. To prepare the cucumber properly is to cut off the rind, then cut the cucumber into thin slices and place them in an earthern bowl with ice-water. Let them stand at least one hour before serving, they will then be crisp and the poisonous substance (to some) will be extracted.

CUCUMBERS FRIED.

Peel the cucumbers, cut in slices one-fourth of an inch in thickness, dip each slice in beaten egg and then into bread crumbs or into flour; fry brown the same as egg plant.

CUCUMBERS—FOR FISH.

Peel the cucumbers, then place in water for one hour, grate them, removing first the seeds, add to the pulp a French salad dressing; this preparation of cucumbers is very nice served with fish.

DRESSED CUCUMBERS.

Take cucumbers, pare and chop them into small pieces. Take half the quantity of young onions and cut them fine; add one tablespoonful of lemon juice, a trifle of cayenne, and a glass of sherry or Madeira and a dessertspoonful of Chili vinegar. This is very good with any roast meat.

FRIED EGG PLANT.

Cut the egg plant into slices one-fifth of an inch in thickness, sprinkle them with salt, pile them on each other and place a weight on the top; leave them for three hours, then rinse and dry the slices, dip them into beaten egg and then into flour, fry them in hot lard; serve hot.

STUFFED EGG PLANT—1.

Wash and dry one large egg plant, cut off the top like a lid; scoop out the inside of the egg plant, season it with salt and pepper; take one onion, peel and chop it very fine, put it into the saucepan with one tablespoonful of butter, cook these together for five minutes, do not brown; add a few mushrooms chopped fine, one ounce of sausage meat; cook all these together, carefully stirring all the time. Let the mixture cool, then fill the egg plant, tie on the lid, cover the egg plant with buttered paper; cook in a hot oven for twenty minutes.

STUFFED EGG PLANT—2.

Scoop out the inside of a gourd shaped egg plant, put this into the saucepan with one tablespoonful of butter, a little salt and pepper, and one cup of milk or cream, cook it well, then return the mixture to the shell of the egg plant, dip it in egg then in bread crumbs, and bake in the oven until it is browned.

KOHLRABI OR CABBAGE TURNIP.

Peel the turnips, cut them into small pieces, boil them until tender in salted water; boil the green leaves of the tops, and when they are done, strain and chop them fine like spinach and return to the stewpan with a little butter, season with salt and pepper. Put the turnips into the center of a dish, pour over a little melted butter, dish the greens around the turnips and serve hot.

BAKED MUSHROOMS.

Toast for each person a slice of bread and spread over it some cream. Lay on each slice of toast, with the head down, one mushroom, if large; if small, two or three mushrooms; fill in each cup with as much cream as it will hold, with a bit of butter and a little salt and pepper. Place over the dish a closely-fitting cover; the mushrooms should be in a shallow dish. Bake in a moderate oven for fifteen minutes; do not remove the cover until just before serving. Serve in the same dish, if possible, in which the mushrooms are baked.

MUSHROOMS WITH BUTTER.

Cut the stems from the mushrooms, clean them with a piece of flannel and some salt; if necessary to wash them, dry thoroughly after. To one part of mushrooms put one and one-half tablespoonfuls of butter into the saucepan; when hot put in the mushrooms and shake them in the butter until they begin to brown; in five minutes add one saltspoonful of salt and a little pepper, stew them until tender, remove from the pan and serve on hot toast. If any butter remains in the stewpan, put it into a small cup and keep for a steak or some chops the next day; it will have a delicious flavor.

MUSHROOMS STEWED—1.

Take two tablespoonfuls of butter, one-half teaspoonful of pepper, one fourth teaspoonful of cayenne. Mix together into a paste, put in saucepan two tablespoonfuls of butter; when it is hot put in the mushrooms which have been peeled, place on each mushroom a little of the paste; as soon as a brown sauce comes from the mushrooms, they are cooked and should be served at once on hot toast.

STEWED MUSHROOMS—2.

Cut off the stems and boil in a cup of beef stock for twenty minutes and strain. Take one quart of mushrooms and strip off the skins, put into the stock and stew gently, add one-half cup of cream, one teaspoonful of butter, and thicken with a little flour, salt and pepper. Cook all about half an hour.

ONIONS.

Old onions are better steamed; new onions stewed.

ONIONS WITH CREAM.

Parboil the onions, slice and spread them in layers in a baking dish with bits of butter; first onions, then bread crumbs and so on until the dish is full; last add enough cream to fill the dish. Bake one-half hour. To parboil, put the onions into boiling water for ten minutes, then drain.

ONION CUSTARD.

Peel and slice twelve small-sized onions, fry them in one tablespoonful of butter, drain them well from the butter, then mince them very fine, add to them four eggs beaten lightly and one pint of milk; season the whole with one-fourth teaspoonful of grated nutmeg, a little salt and cayenne. Pour the mixture into a baking dish and bake for fifteen minutes. Serve hot with meat or poultry.

ONION FRITTERS.

Chop up two large onions, make a batter with one tablespoonful of flour, one egg, one-half cup of milk, one teaspoonful of salt, one-half teaspoonful of pepper; mix all well together, drop a spoonful at a time into a pan of boiling lard.

FRIED ONIONS.

Two quarts of sliced onions, put them into cold water for ten minutes, drain. Put two tablespoonfuls of butter or fat into the skillet; when hot, add the onions, one teaspoonful of salt and one-half teaspoonful of pepper; cover for ten minutes, then remove the cover and cook for twenty minutes or longer.

ONIONS IN GRAVY.

Cook the onions in salted water until tender; mix one tablespoonful of flour, one tablespoonful of butter over the fire until they are brown, then add one wine glass of claret, one cup of gravy; serve hot.

ONIONS STEAMED.

Put the onions into a baking dish, cover it with a plate and let them steam in a hot oven for three hours, then pour over them some melted butter, salt and pepper.

STUFFED ONIONS.

Take a large Spanish onion, scoop out the centre, peel and parboil it; fill the centre with forcemeat and place it in a stew-pan; cover it with slices of bacon, sprinkle with salt and sugar and cook over a quick fire. When done, remove the onions, reduce the sauce and pour it over them and serve. The forcemeat can be made of chicken, ham, parsley and mushrooms, and some chopped suet, all finely minced together, with pepper and salt to taste.

BAKED SPANISH ONIONS.

Take a large onion; wash it clean; take a corer and remove the core and put in its place some butter, pepper and salt, and let it bake with a thin piece of paper round it for an hour, or till done, in a slow oven. When done, peel it and put it into a vegetable dish, and pour over some good brown gravy.

SPANISH ONIONS WITH MAITRE D'HOTEL BUTTER.

Peel the onions, put them in cold water with one teaspoonful of salt, let them boil once, then remove, wash in cold water and put them into the stew-pan with plenty of boiling water, boil gently for three hours; when tender, drain them and put on each a bit of maitre d'hotel butter.

OKRA.

Boil the young pods in salted, hot water; when cooked, drain and dress them with some butter, pepper and salt.

FRIED PARSLEY.

Wash the parsley, dry thoroughly in a cloth, then put in hot, boiling fat and let it remain until crisp; shake from the fat, sprinkle with salt, and use. To prepare parsley for sprinkling over any preparations, chop the parsley very fine, wash, drain, place in corner of a clean napkin and squeeze dry, then the parsley will be found very light and dry.

PARSNIP BALLS.

Boil six parsnips, let them get cold, then peel and grate them; beat two eggs until light, mix them with the grated parsnip and one tablespoonful of flour, one teaspoonful of salt, one-half teaspoonful of pepper; make the mixture into small flat balls, have some lard boiling hot, drop the balls into it until they are brown; serve hot with fried parsley.

PARSNIPS BOILED.

Boil the parsnips, then slice them and put over a dressing of one cup of cream, one tablespoonful of butter, salt and pepper; if cream is not obtainable one cup of sweet milk and two tablespoonfuls of butter mixed with one tablespoonful of flour.

PARSNIP FRITTERS.

Take three large parsnips, cook until tender, peel and mash them smooth; add one teaspoonful of flour, one egg well beaten, one teaspoonful of salt; make the mixture into small cakes, and fry them on both sides in good butter; pile them on a hot dish and serve.

GREEN PEAS.

If the peas are young and freshly gathered the very best way to cook them is to boil them in water, slightly salted; do not cover the saucepan; when cooked drain from the water, add a tablespoonful of butter and a little pepper. A sprig of mint is considered by many a valuable addition. If the peas are a little old cook them in a little water, add one tablespoonful of butter, a little salt and one teaspoonful of sugar; when served, add one tablespoonful of cream or one tablespoonful of butter.

DRIED PEAS.

Wash and pick them over carefully, put into boiling water and let them boil until soft, then drain off the water and put with the peas a piece of butter the size of an egg, a chopped onion, a little salt and pepper, and stew until the onion is cooked, then serve.

GREEN PEPPER CROQUETTES.

Select good-sized, firm sweet peppers, wash them, cut a small hole at the stem and remove all the seeds, then put the peppers in a stew-pan in a little boiling water to par-boil them, remove and let them cool. Stuff each pepper with a forcemeat, made with cold chicken, veal or sweet-breads minced fine and mixed with some bread crumbs, and seasoned with a little salt and a few drops of onion juice. Put the peppers when stuffed into a pan with a very little water to prevent burning; put bits of butter over the peppers; when nicely browned remove from the pan and serve over the peppers some White sauce.

GREEN PEPPERS FOR WINTER USE.

Put the peppers on the back of the stove or in a cool oven, turn them until they are cooked enough to crack the skins, then throw them into a bowl of hot water and with a knife scrape and peel them, cut them open, remove the seeds, rinse in cold water, drain them and pack into glass jars, pour boiling vinegar over them and a little salt, and seal.

BOILED POTATOES.

Potatoes should be very carefully boiled; and if not used as soon as they are done, should be kept hot and dry, by pouring off the water, covering them with a dry cloth, and setting them on the back of the stove. After washing them thoroughly, pare them entirely, or take off one ring around each; if they are new put them over the fire in hot water; if they are old, put them on in cold water; in either case, add a tablespoonful of salt, and boil them from fifteen to thirty minutes, as they require, until you can pierce them easily with a fork, then drain off the water, cover them with a clean, dry towel, and set them on the back of the fire until you are ready to use them.

POTATOES A L'ANNA.

Cut up some raw potatoes very fine, put them in cold water for six hours, then drain them, season with salt and pepper, put them into a well-buttered dish, sprinkle bread crumbs on top, add enough melted butter to cover them; bake in a very hot oven for one-half hour or until they are well browned. If baked in a porcelain dish they can be served in it, a folded napkin being put around the dish, or they can be put on a hot dish.

POTATO BALLS.

Boil four large potatoes; when hot mash and add to them one tablespoonful of chopped parsley, one egg well beaten, one teaspoonful of salt, one-half teaspoonful of pepper, a little grated nutmeg and a little cayenne. Mix these well together and roll into balls, dip them in beaten egg, then into fine bread or cracker crumbs; be sure the crumbs are fine, and fry in deep boiling fat; drain from the fat and keep hot until served.

BAKED POTATOES.

Choose large and smooth potatoes, put them in the oven; when they are half done take each one in a kitchen towel and press it hard; return to oven; bake one hour.

COLD BOILED POTATOES.

All potatoes that are intended to be boiled and then made into different preparations should be boiled in their skins and not quite cooked; set away and allowed to get cold in their skins. This plan makes a great difference in the successful preparation of potatoes, and should be followed.

POTATOES CADEAU.

Boil four large Irish potatoes in their skins and let them become cold; it is best to boil them the day before using; grate the potatoes, add one egg beaten until light, one tablespoonful of flour, a little salt. Make the mixture into balls and roll them in flour. Have two kettles on the stove, one half full of boiling water, the other with boiling lard; put the balls first into the boiling water, as soon as they rise on the surface, take from the water and drop into the lard, as soon as the balls are brown they are cooked.

POTATOES WITH CHOCOLATE.

Slice the cooked potatoes, put a layer of potatoes in a porcelain dish, which you can serve them in; then a layer of sugar and butter, then a layer of potatoes, then a little more sugar and butter, then one tablespoonful grated chocolate dissolved in one cup of milk; pour this over the potatoes and bake for twenty minutes.

CREAMED POTATOES.

Boil some potatoes; when done remove from the fire and beat them until they are soft and creamy, then beat in the yolks of two eggs, a little salt and pepper, one tablespoonful of melted butter and two tablespoonfuls of cream; lastly, add the whites beaten very stiff; put the mixture in the saucepan and let it become very hot.

POTATO CAKES.

One-half pound of flour, one-half a pound of mashed potatoes, six eggs, two teaspoonfuls of baking powder, one tablespoonful of sugar, one-half teaspoonful of salt. Sift the flour, baking powder, sugar and salt into a bowl, then add the eggs well beaten, then enough sweet milk to make a light batter, lastly add the potatoes; mix well and let all stand for one-half hour before baking, bake on well greased griddle like batter cakes. These cakes are very nice served with afternoon tea.

POTATO CROQUETTES.

Take two cups of mashed potatoes, add to them a few drops of onion juice, the yolks of two eggs well beaten, one teaspoonful of salt, two tablespoonfuls of cream, one tablespoonful of butter, a little cayenne. Stir all these ingredients well together in the saucepan; when hot remove from the fire and let the mixture cool; when cold form into balls, dip these first into beaten eggs, then into very fine cracker or bread crumbs; see that the balls are smooth, place in the ice-box for an hour or more. When required fry them in very hot deep fat. It is best to use the frying basket; when the balls are of a brown color drain from the fat on brown paper. Keep them hot until served.

POTATOES CRUMBED.

Peel and boil the potatoes; when they are cooked but not broken, split them in halves, season with salt and pepper, pour over them some melted butter, then dip each piece in browned bread crumbs, place them in a buttered tin and bake for fifteen minutes in a hot oven.

ESCALLOPED POTATOES.

Pare, wash and slice enough potatoes to nearly fill the baking dish; season the potatoes with salt and pepper; add little bits of butter all through the dish, then pour over the potatoes enough milk, or better, cream, to fill up the dish; put one tablespoonful of butter on top of the dish; bake. Keep the dish covered until the potatoes are nearly done, then uncover and let them brown.

FRENCH FRIED POTATOES.

Peel the potatoes, cut them in narrow strips, soak in ice water one hour, drain and dry, have ready a kettle of deep lard; when boiling drop in the potatoes a few at a time and let them brown, sprinkle salt over them when they are removed from the fat, drain on wire dish or on filtering paper; serve in a hot dish.

FRIED POTATOES—1.

Take six good potatoes, peel and slice them about one-fourth of an inch in thickness. Have two pans of fat, either clarified beef suet or lard; cook the potatoes in one for a few minutes, then remove them with a skimmer and put them into the other pan; the fats must be very hot. The potatoes will swell and be much lighter from the double frying.

FRIED POTATOES—2.

Peel the potatoes, slice them lengthwise about one-eighth of an inch thick, place in cold water for a few minutes, then drain and fry them in hot fat for six minutes, remove from the fat, let them cool. Keep the fat hot (it must be deep fat), and just before serving the potatoes plunge them into the boiling fat for five minutes; this will cause them to swell; then remove from the fat, drain them, sprinkle with salt and serve at once.

POTATOES FRIED WITH PARSLEY.

One pound of potatoes, two ounces of butter, two teaspoonfuls of chopped parsley, pepper and salt. Scrape and boil the potatoes; let them get cold. Put the butter into the frying pan; when melted put in the potatoes and fry a pale gold; add the parsley about five minutes before serving; sprinkle with pepper and salt.

HASHED BROWN POTATOES.

Six potatoes cut fine. Take two tablespoonfuls of onions cut fine and one tablespoonful of parsley chopped fine; put these into hot lard and fry them; as soon as the onions commence to brown add the potatoes, stirring all together; press the mixture down on the pan, let it brown, then stir again, so as to mix the crust well; when the potatoes are well mixed with the crust add one tablespoonful of butter; press the potatoes well on the pan so that they will have a good brown crust; turn them out on a platter, the crust side up.

POTATO KLOSSE.

Take about six baked potatoes and scoop out the floury part till there are about six ounces. Beat one tablespoonful of butter to a cream and mix it with the potato flour; add the well beaten yolks of two eggs, a grate of nutmeg and a little pepper and salt to taste. Beat the mixture thoroughly and mold it into small balls. Drop these in boiling salt and water, and be careful to do this with a metal spoon, and to dip it into boiling water each time it is used. Or they may be made with two ounces of finely-grated bread crumbs and one ounce of Parmesan, the white of one of the eggs, then molded and boiled as above. Sprinkle fried bread crumbs over when dishing them up.

POTATOES A LA MAITRE D'HOTEL.

Wash half a dozen potatoes; boil them in salt and water; when done drain and let them cool. Then peel and cut the potatoes into thick slices; put into a saucepan one and one-half ounces of butter, a little pepper and salt to taste, four tablespoonfuls of good gravy and one tablespoonful of minced parsley, mix all well together; put in the potatoes; shake them well in the sauce to cover them, and when quite hot through, squeeze in one tablespoonful of lemon juice and serve.

POTATO CAKES.

Take a tablespoonful of warm mashed potatoes in the palm of your hand, make it into a ball, then with a teaspoon take out the center; fill this cavity with minced onion and celery, which has been previously cooked tender in butter; add a teaspoonful of grated cheese; cover the cavity with the mashed potato, dip each ball into melted butter and egg; place in a shallow pan and bake in a hot oven until a nice brown. Serve on hot platter; garnish with parsley.

POTATO LOAVES.

These are very nice when served with roast beef. Take mashed potatoes and mix them with some finely chopped onions, a little pepper and salt; beat these well and add one tablespoonful of melted butter. Make into little loaves and place in the pan with the roast of beef; the gravy from the beef gives a very good flavor to the potato loaves.

LYONNAISE POTATOES.

Two tablespoonfuls of good beef dripping or butter made very hot in the frying pan, when hot add one tablespoonful of minced onion; let this fry until brown, and then put in two cupfuls of cold boiled potatoes cut into small dice; stir well together until the butter is well absorbed, then add one teaspoonful of salt, one-half saltspoon of pepper and two tablespoonfuls of finely chopped parsley.

PRINCESS POTATOES.

Boil the desired quantity of potatoes; while yet hot, mash them perfectly smooth and spread about half an inch thick on a platter and set aside to cool; when desired to use, cut the mixture into strips an inch wide and two inches long; dip these strips into melted butter and then into well beaten egg, place them on a pan and bake until brown in a hot oven.

POTATO PUFF.

To two cupfuls of cold mashed potato add two tablespoonfuls of melted butter, beating well together, then add two eggs beaten very light and one teacupful of cream or milk, a little salt and pepper; beat well and put into a baking dish and bake in a quick oven until it is brown; this will be in about fifteen minutes.

ROAST POTATOES WITH MEAT.

Have the potatoes of uniform size; peel, wash clean and lay them in the pan with the meat about one hour before the meat is done. Serve with the roast.

POTATO RISSOLES.

Two pounds of potatoes, one-fourth pound of butter, pepper and salt; two eggs, dried crumbs, one-fourth pint of milk. Boil your potatoes in their skins, skin them and mash them with the butter; add the seasoning and milk. Make into balls, brush over with yolk of egg and crumbs. Fry three minutes in boiling fat in a frying basket.

SARATOGA POTATOES.

Slice three potatoes as thin as possible, throw them into a bowl of ice-water, keep them in the ice-water for two or three hours. When ready to use the potatoes, have the kettle of fat very hot; you must have deep fat, at least four inches deep. Dry the potatoes by putting a few at a time in a clean coarse towel, drop them into the boiling fat, a few at a time. Stir, to prevent them from sticking together. The moment they are of a light yellow color remove with the skimmer; drain on brown paper. These potatoes should never be greasy, and they will not be if the fat is at the right temperature and care is used.

POTATO SNOW.

Have some very mealy potatoes; boil; when cooked drain and keep them hot; heat the colander and pass the potatoes through; do not crush the snow as it falls into the dish, which must be hot. Potatoes look most tempting prepared in this way.

POTATO SOUFFLE.

Take two cups of mashed potatoes (free from lumps), add one teaspoonful of salt and one-half teaspoonful of white pepper, two tablespoonfuls of melted butter; beat these together until the mixture is light, then add the yolks of two eggs beaten light, five tablespoonfuls of cream. Beat the two whites until light, stir them into the mixture, place this upon a tin, pile up in a rough mould and place in the oven until it is brown.

STEWED POTATOES—1.

Take cold, boiled potatoes, slice them thinly, place in a shallow but wide saucepan with some butter—for five potatoes two tablespoonfuls; then cover the potatoes with cream or milk; if milk is used add one more spoonful of butter, season with salt and white pepper. Let them simmer on the back of the range for two hours; if the cream or milk cooks into the potatoes, leaving them dry, add some more. Serve hot.

STEWED POTATOES—2.

Boil the potatoes in their skins; when almost cooked remove from the fire; when cold peel them and cut into pieces about the size of dice. Have a large saucepan, broad at the bottom; place in this one-half pound of butter when melted, but not at all brown, stir in the potatoes; season with one teaspoonful of salt and one-half teaspoonful of white pepper; stir the potatoes and butter well together; when thoroughly mixed pour over one pint of good cream in which you have stirred one teaspoonful of flour. Heat all well together and serve.

POTATO TURNOVERS.

Boil the potatoes; mash and add one-half teacup of milk, one satspoonful of salt, one-half tablespoonful of melted butter, one egg well beaten and enough flour to enable you to roll out the potato mixture like pastry; roll it out one-half inch in thickness; cut into oval-shaped pieces; cover one-half of each with some minced, cold meat of any kind that you may have; season the meat with a little salt and pepper and a few drops of onion juice; lay over the other half of the potato pastry, pinch the edges together and bake until a light brown in the oven.

BROILED SWEET POTATOES.

Boil the potatoes; when cold, peel them and cut in slices one inch in thickness; dip each in melted butter; put in the double broiler and let them broil until a light brown. Pour a little melted butter over them when cooked.

BAKED SWEET POTATOES—1.

Bake them in their skins, having first carefully washed them.

BAKED SWEET POTATGES—2.

Parboil the potatoes, when cool remove the skins, slice the potatoes and bake them in the oven until they are browned.

CANDIED SWEET POTATOES—1.

Parboil the sweet potatoes; peel and slice them in pieces about one-half inch thick; grease a shallow earthenware dish, and put in a layer of potatoes; then sprinkle over some sugar and a little cinnamon, and a little melted butter, then another layer of potatoes, and so on until the dish is full; add lastly a cup of hot water or milk; then add some bits of butter on the top and bake in a slow oven until well browned, and serve on the same dish in which they are baked.

CANDIED SWEET POTATOES—2.

Cut the cold cooked sweet potatoes into slices about an inch thick; have some melted butter in which you have dissolved a tablespoonful of sugar; dip each slice of potato into this liquid and lay them on a pan; cook them for about fifteen minutes in a hot oven; serve hot.

SPINACH—1.

There is no vegetable cooked which will show the difference between a careful housewife and a careless one more than spinach. To have spinach at its best, wash it well in two waters and be sure you have removed all sand; cut off the roots and stems, drain the leaves, put them into a large kettle containing one quart of boiling water and one tablespoonful of salt; toss and turn the leaves for ten minutes; remove from the pot, drain them in a colander; when dry, chop them very fine, or press them through a coarse sieve; put the mixture into a saucepan with one tablespoonful of butter, two tablespoonfuls of cream, a saltspoonful of salt, a little pepper; stir constantly until very hot and serve; put sliced hard-boiled eggs on top.

SPINACH—2.

Cook as spinach No. 1, then fry one tablespoonful of onion chopped fine, one tablespoonful of cream or milk, one tablespoonful of butter, salt and pepper. Stir well together and re-heat.

SALSIFY BOILED—1.

Scrape the roots, cut the salsify into small slices, boil in salted water until tender, then drain and put back into the pan with one tablespoonful of cream or milk, one tablespoonful of butter, one tablespoonful of flour, a little salt and pepper; when the sauce has thickened, serve hot.

SALSIFY BOILED—2.

One bundle of salsify, one-half pint of cream, pepper and salt, one lemon, one ounce of butter. Scrape the roots very gently to get off the outer skin and quickly throw them into vinegar and water or they will become black. Boil them in enough water to cover them; drain, add the butter, the juice of the lemon, pepper and salt, and allow to boil till tender. Boil the cream, add to it one gill of the water used for boiling the salsify; pour over the vegetables and serve.

SALSIFY CAKES.

Scrape the roots thoroughly and let them lay in cold water for ten minutes, then boil them until tender, drain and mash them to a smooth paste, add a little milk, one tablespoonful of melted butter, one egg beaten light; mix well together, add a little salt and pepper. Make into small flat cakes, roll these in flour and fry in a pan with a little butter.

TO PICKLE SAUER KRAUT.

Select firm, white cabbages, leave out the outer leaves and stalks, begin at the top of the head to cut across in narrow strips using a large knife; have a small oak barrel or pickling jar or tub, cover the bottom with clean cabbage leaves, throw in the cabbage as fast as it is shredded, sprinkle with salt; stamp it down hard with a club; when all is closely packed, strew more salt on top, cover with some cabbage leaves and then with a clean linen cloth. Put on a cover that will fit closely and on this a heavy stone.

Do not put the kraut in too cool a place or fermentation will not begin. When it has begun small white globules will form on the brine, which should appear in two or three days; if they do not, boil some salt and water, cool and pour over the cabbage.

A large handful of salt is enough for a firkin of cut cabbage; too much salt prevents fermentation. In two weeks the cloth over the kraut must be taken off and washed and the leaves renewed, then cover again—the washing of the cloth must be done every week.

In three weeks it will be ready for use, and will keep good for a year.

SAUER KRAUT COOKED.

One tablespoonful of butter; melt this in a saucepan, then put in half as much sauer kraut as needed, and a piece of pork, bacon, ham or sausage; lay over this the rest of the kraut, but in a glass of vinegar, a little water; cover all closely and stew gently until the kraut is soft and yellow. Remove the meat when it is done; dredge in a little flour; cook one-half hour longer; put back the meat to heat thoroughly; stir the kraut and serve.

Sauer kraut is equally good warmed over, and it should be cooked three hours the first time. A little onion can be added if liked.

SUMMER SQUASH STEAMED.

Cut the squash into four pieces, place in a steamer over boiling water, steam for forty-five minutes, or until the squash is tender. Serve with a little melted butter, seasoned with salt and pepper, or else mash through the colander, and then add a little butter, salt and pepper.

SUMMER SQUASH.

Peel them, unless they are very young and tender, take out the seeds and boil until tender, then drain and mash soft and smooth, add two teaspoonfuls of butter, one tablespoonful of cream (if you have it), some salt and pepper, and serve hot.

WINTER SQUASH.

Pare the squash, take out the seeds, cut into pieces and cook until tender, drain and press it through the colander, add one tablespoonful of butter, some salt and pepper—always let the squash lie in cold water an hour before cooking.

SQUASH GRIDDLE CAKES.

One egg, one pint of milk, one and one-half cups of squash, boiled and strained, one pinch of salt, flour enough to make a batter, one-half teaspoonful of soda.

TOMATOES STUFFED WITH BRAINS.

Take ripe tomatoes; remove the core and seeds, season the insides with a little salt and pepper.

Put one tablespoonful of butter mixed with one tablespoonful of flour in the saucepan; when hot and smooth add one tablespoonful of cream, a little cayenne and one teacup of sheep's or calf's brains, which have been cooked and cut into fine pieces; mix well together and then stuff the tomatoes with this mixture; put some bread crumbs on the top and bake for fifteen minutes in a brisk oven. Serve the tomatoes on rounds of fried bread; garnish with water-cress or parsley.

TOMATOES WITH CHICKEN.

Remove the core and seeds from the tomatoes, season the inside with a little olive oil and tarragon vinegar, minced onion and salt. Chop some cold chicken very fine, season with cayenne and salt, one tablespoonful of cream and one teaspoonful of melted butter mixed well together: fill the tomatoes, put a few bread crumbs on the top and a bit of butter. Bake in a hot oven for fifteen minutes and serve on lettuce leaves.

DEVILLED TOMATOES.

Cut three large, firm tomatoes in slices one-half an inch thick. Make a mixture of one tablespoonful of butter, one tablespoonful of vinegar, the yolk of one hard boiled egg, one teaspoonful of sugar, one teaspoonful of mustard, one teaspoonful of salt, one-half teaspoonful of pepper; beat this mixture until it is smooth, then heat it to the bolling point, no longer; take from the fire and pour it over one egg which has been well beaten, put this over a tin containing hot water while you broil the tomatoes, then put the tomatoes on a hot dish and pour over them the dressing.

FRIED TOMATOES—1.

Slice with the skins on, some ripe tomatoes, fry them in the pan with a little butter, or beef dripping, until thoroughly cooked; skim the tomatoes out of the pan and place on slices of dry toast: then put in the pan one tablespoonful of butter, one tablespoonful of flour, one tablespoonful of cream, one saltspoonful of salt, a little pepper; cook until the sauce has thickened, then remove the pan from the fire and put in one wine glassful of white wine, stir the sauce thoroughly, then pour over the tomatoes.

FRIED TOMATOES—2.

Four large tomatoes, do not peel them, cut them in four pieces, then dip them in flour, fry them in butter or beef drippings, until they are brown and cooked, then take them from the pan and place them on a platter and put them into the oven, while you prepare the dressing. Put one cup of sweet cream, a little salt and pepper and one teaspoonful of flour into the pan in which the tomatoes were fried; stir until it boils, then strain it over the tomatoes; serve.

TOMATO AU GRATIN.

Cut some ripe tomatoes in slices, place them in a china baking dish in layers with some chopped onions and bread crumbs, pepper and salt, and a little gravy between each layer; cover the top with a layer of bread crumbs, and a few lumps of butter. Bake for about twenty minutes.

TOMATO PILAU.

Cut three slices of salt pork into small pieces, fry until brown in the frying pan, then add one chopped onion, cook five minutes, then pour in one quart of stewed tomatoes, and one teaspoonful of salt; when the mixture is boiling, add one pint of cooked rice, and a little cayenne.

STEWED TOMATOES.

Pour boiling water over the tomatoes, if fresh ones are used, to remove the skins; cut the tomatoes into pieces; stew for thirty minutes, then add one tablespoonful of butter and a little salt and pepper, and one small pinch of soda.

STUFFED TOMATOES.

Select firm, round tomatoes, cut a lid from the top; scoop out all the seeds and much of the inside of the tomatoes; make a filling of one cup of bread crumbs, one tablespoonful of melted butter, one saltspoonful of salt, a little cayenne, one-half teaspoonful of sweet herbs. Mix well together and fill the tomatoes, bake for one-half hour and serve. Use the tomatoes which were left for a tomato sauce.

TURNIPS STEWED IN BUTTER.

Take some young turnips, wash and dry them, pare and slice them half an inch thick, and divide them into dice. Now dissolve one ounce of butter for each half pound of turnips, and stew them gently in this for nearly an hour. When half cooked, add salt and white pepper and one teaspoonful of sugar. These can be served by themselves or dished up in the center of an entree.

TURNIPS WITH BREAD CRUMBS.

Prepare as for "turnips and peas," fill the turnip cups with bread crumbs, which have been soaked in cream, and seasoned with salt and pepper.

TURNIPS STEWED IN GRAVY.

Wash and peel the turnips, cut them in thin slices, boil for five minutes in boiling water, then drain off the water, and put over the turnips one pint of stock or gravy and one teaspoonful of sugar, one saltspoonful of salt, a little pepper, and boil together until the turnips are tender. Serve hot.

TURNIPS MASHED.

Wash and peel the turnips, cook in boiling water until tender, then mash them through a colander, return to the stew-pan and add one-fourth teacup of milk, one tablespoonful of butter, one saltspoonful of salt, one teaspoonful of sugar, a little pepper; stir together until hot and serve.

TURNIPS AND PEAS.

Boil the turnips, which should be the white ones, until tender in salted water, then take from the fire, place for five minutes in cold water; when cool scoop out the inside, leaving cups of the turnips; fill the cups with green peas which have been boiled, seasoned with a little salt and pepper, and a tablespoonful of cream; re-heat the turnip-cups, add a little butter to the peas, fill the cups and serve.

In cooking turnips always add two lumps or one tablespoonful of sugar to the water; the sugar will correct the bitterness which sometimes spoils this excellent vegetable.

VEGETABLE MARROW (BOSTON SQUASH) BOILED.

Take the marrow, peel and remove the seed part, cut into two pieces about two inches wide, cook these in boiling slightly salted water until they are tender, which will take fifteen minutes, then drain and place on slices of buttered toast and pour over melted butter seasoned with salt and pepper.

VEGETABLE MARROW STUFFED.

Peel the marrow carefully, cut off a slice at the ends and scoop out the insides. Cook the marrow slowly fifteen minutes in a stew pan with plenty of boiling, salted water, remove carefully and place in a basin and cover with cold water. Then mix together two tablespoonfuls of cold chicken or veal pounded smooth in the mortar and one tablespoonful of thick cream sauce (see cream sauce), two raw yolks of eggs, a little cayenne; drain the marrow, stuff with this mixture, roll in flour, then into beaten egg, then into bread crumbs and fry in boiling fat until a light brown color. Serve hot, garnished with parsley.

RICE, ETC.

TO BOIL RICE.

One quart of water with one teaspoonful of salt. When boiling hard, put in one pint of well-washed rice. As soon as the water boils hard again, remove to the back of the range and let the rice cook slowly; when all the water is boiled away, cover the rice until it is perfectly cooked, do not stir at all—be careful not to burn the rice.

The addition of a little lemon juice to the water in which rice is boiled will increase the whiteness, and the grains will readily separate.

RICE CROQUETTES WITH MEAT.

Boil the rice until quite soft and tender; while warm add an egg well beaten, a teaspoonful of butter, and salt to taste, and half a teacupful of any kind of cold meat, ham or tongue, chopped fine. When cold, make into croquettes, cover with beaten egg and bread crumbs, and fry in hot dripping-pan till browned.

RICE CROQUETTES.

One-fourth pound of rice well-washed and dried, one pint of milk; boil them together until the rice is perfectly tender. A thin rind of lemon cooked with the rice is an addition. When the rice is rather dry and tender add one tablespoonful of sugar, one teaspoonful of butter, one teaspoonful of salt, a little pepper and a little nutmeg. Stir together and spread on a dish to cool; when cold form into croquettes; dip each one in beaten egg, then into fine crumbs, either of bread or crackers; put on the ice for an hour or more, then fry in deep hot fat until a light brown color, and serve at once.

RICE CROQUETTES WITH JAM.

Prepare the rice as for plain croquettes. Take each croquette when ready to fry, make a hole in the center and fill it with some jam, either peach or apricot, cover it over with rice, dip each croquette into beaten egg, then into fine bread crumbs, and fry in deep, hot fat.

RISOTTO MILANESE.

One-half glass of sherry, one-fourth teaspoonful of Indian saffron dissolved in one-half a cup of stock, one and one-half cups of rice, one teaspoonful of grated cheese, one cup of butter, one-half an onion, one tablespoonful of salad oil, one quart of stock. Cut the onion fine, cook well in the butter and oil until of a golden color, mix it in the rice, add the wine, then one-half the stock (one pint), add the rest of the stock, a little at a time until the rice is done and the mixture thickens—it must boil fast and hard; when almost done, add the saffron and last the cheese; after removing it from the stove add a piece of butter. The Risotto should be a trifle thicker than a puree.

RICE CASSEROLE.

Wash two pounds of rice in water twice; drain and put into a stewpan with two quarts of water, one saltspoonful of salt; when the water boils, cover the rice with some thin slices of salt pork and let it simmer slowly until cooked; when the rice is cooked, pound it in a mortar, gather it into balls and mold it into the shape of a casserole, then brush the casserole over with a brush dipped in melted butter, and put it into the oven until it is slightly brown, then trim it and take out some of the rice inside and fill the casserole with any preparation you wish, sweetbreads, game, chicken, fish, etc.

RICE AND CHEESE.

One pint of cold, boiled rice, and one cupful of grated cheese, add to the cheese a little cayenne and soda the size of a pea. Put first a layer of rice in a buttered pudding dish, then a layer of cheese; when the dish is full, put a thin layer of powdered cracker crumbs and bits of butter and over the whole pour the following mixture: One cupful of milk, one egg well beaten into it, one saltspoonful of dry mustard, one-half teaspoonful of salt, a little cayenne; all well mixed together. Bake twenty-five minutes in a hot oven, and serve very hot.

SWEET RICE.
A PORTUGESE RECIPE.

Wash thoroughly, then drain and dry half a pound of rice, stew it with three pints of milk for thirty minutes, then add one-half pound of sugar, a little salt; boil together until the rice is tender, then add two tablespoonfuls of blanched almonds chopped fine. Put the rice mixture into shallow dishes and shake until the surface is smooth, then sift over thickly some powdered cinnamon, which will give it the appearance of a freshly baked cake. Serve cold. It will remain good for several days. If desired richer, one-third cream may be used in the place of the milk.

SAVORY RICE.

Put one-fourth pound of rice in fast boiling, salted water; when half cooked, pour off the water and replace it with three-fourths pint of good stock, and cook until the rice is done. Then add salt, pepper, two ounces of freshly grated cheese and one egg well beaten. Pour this all into a buttered dish, and bake or brown in oven.

RICE SOCLES.

Wash one pound of rice; put it in a stewpan with half a gallon of water and a little salt; boil on a very slow fire. When the rice is done pound it in a mortar, and mold it to the required shape. For hot dishes the socle should be egged over and put in the oven to color it. For cold dishes, spread the rice over with Montpelier butter.

TIMBALE OF RICE.

One teacupful of rice, one pound of any cooked meat, one egg, two tablespoonfuls of bread crumbs, one-half a small onion, one-fourth pint of stock, salt and pepper, one teaspoonful of chopped parsley, one ounce of butter. Boil the rice till tender, put on a sieve to drain. Chop the meat fine, season with onions chopped fine, parsley, pepper and salt, add the bread crumbs and egg, mix well; then the stock. Butter a mold, line with the rice, put in the meat, cover the top with rice, and steam three-quarters of an hour; turn out and pour tomato sauce round the dish.

.COLD WINE RICE.

One pound of rice boiled with one pound of sugar, and one-half pint of white wine, a little lemon rind or orange rind boiled with the rice; when cooked place in a mold and let it become cold. Serve with cream or a little orange juice.

MACARONI A LA BRIGNOLI.

Cut one onion in slices and fry with one-half teaspoonful of butter, then put in a saucepan with one pint of tomatoes, a few sprigs of parsley, one-half a garlic clove, and one teaspoonful of mushroom powder, and one tablespoonful of butter; let these stew gently for two and one-half hours. While this is cooking, take one-fourth of a pound of macaroni, cover with boiling water, add one tablespoonful of salt; when cooked, drain and put it into cold water; when the sauce is ready, drain the macaroni from the water, put it in a dish, sprinkle over it one tablespoonful of Parmesan cheese and then the sauce; place in the oven for a few minutes to re-heat the macaroni.

ITALIAN MACARONI—1.

Cook the large macaroni until soft; throw into cold water, where let it remain until ready to prepare the dish.

Take some rough pieces from the leg of veal, fry until quite brown, not burned; put one pint of water in a saucepan, add one pepper, leek, garlic and one-half a bay leaf. Let all simmer a long time, strain; cook the macaroni in the stock about a half hour, add mushrooms sliced. Put some butter in a small saucepan and when it melts, add what flour you think it will need to thicken; dip the sauce from the macaroni, add it slowly to the flour stirring all the time; then pour it over the macaroni, being careful not to break the macaroni. Just before serving, strew with chopped parsley; then having the macaroni in the dish in which it is to be served, scatter Parmesan cheese over all and serve very hot.

ITALIAN MACARONI—2.

Place in a quart stew-pan a pint and a half of boiling water, put into this four ounces of macaroni broken into four inch pieces, seasoned with salt and pepper, and boil gently for twenty minutes, then drain from the water in a colander; wipe out the stew-pan, and return the macaroni into it with a half pint of good stock; let it simmer gently until all the stock is absorbed by the macaroni—this will take about twenty minutes. Grate one ounce of Parmesan and one ounce of Swiss cheese or two ounces of good York State cheese; put one-half of the cheese into the stew-pan, stirring well into the macaroni; when this half of the cheese is dissolved, add the balance with one tablespoonful of butter, some salt and a little cayenne. Serve in a hot, deep dish.

MACARONI QUENELLES.

Take one ounce of macaroni, four ounces of bread crumbs, two eggs, half a pint of milk, a teaspoonful of minced parsley, a pinch of mixed herbs, a dust of cayenne, and salt to taste, two ounces of melted butter and two spoonfuls of chopped ham; boil the macaroni till cooked, cut it into small pieces, boil the milk and pour on the bread crumbs and soak for five minutes, add the macaroni, herbs, eggs, melted butter and ham, steam in a well buttered basin for an hour, and serve with brown mushroom sauce over it.

MACARONI WITH TOMATO SAUCE.

Boil a pound of macaroni with a piece of butter the size of an egg, an onion, two cloves, and some salt; when done, drain the macaroni and place it in a saucepan with five ounces of grated Swiss cheese, five ounces of Parmesan cheese, one teaspoonful black pepper, and six tablespoonfuls of cream; stir over the fire until the cheese becomes thick and stringy. Dish up in a pyramid and cover with thick tomato sauce.

SPAGHETTI AND CHEESE.

One-fourth of a pound of spaghetti, one-half pint of milk, three tablespoonfuls of butter, two eggs, yolks, one-half cup of grated cheese, one saltspoonful of salt, a little pepper and a little cayenne. Break the spaghetti into pieces, wash it in cold water, boil it with two quarts of water gently for two hours, then pour off the water and put the spaghetti into a dish and pour over the sauce and bake in the oven for five minutes.

Make the sauce by boiling the milk, cheese and butter together, add the salt and pepper, then the yolks well beaten, stir together and then pour it over the spaghetti, and serve hot.

SPAGHETTI WITH TOMATO SAUCE.

Boil the spaghetti in either salted water, or in beef stock till tender, serve with grated Parmesan cheese, and tomato sauce. For the sauce, take one can of tomatoes, boil them down until very thick with one onion chopped fine, and one bay leaf; when cooked, strain, return to the pan, and add one tablespoonful of butter, a little salt and cayenne. Put a layer of the spaghetti into the baking dish, cover with part of the sauce, then the rest of the spaghetti and the sauce; cover with Parmesan cheese; put a few bits of butter on the cheese, bake until it is a light brown color.

SAVORY VERMICELLI.

Boil one pint of milk; when boiled, put in three tablespoonfuls of vermicelli. Let it simmer for five minutes, then add three eggs; beat up all together with two tablespoonfuls of cream, a little salt, white pepper, and a small onion. Butter a mold and stick it all over with small neatly cut pieces of ham and tongue. Pour in the mixture. Then bake it, and serve it, when turned out, with savory gravy or tomato sauce.

HOMINY.

Soak the large hominy over night; to one quart add two quarts of water, boil slowly until perfectly soft, drain off all water, put into vegetable dish, and mix butter, pepper and salt with it. Serve hot.

COLD HOMINY FRIED.

Cut the cooked hominy in thin slices; put one tablespoonful of butter in the pan; when hot, put in the hominy, fry on both sides. Used as a vegetable, or served with syrup.

HOMINY CROQUETTES.

Take one cupful of cold boiled hominy, add one teacupful of milk, stir this well into the hominy, add one teaspoonful of sugar and one well-beaten egg and a little salt. Make the mixture into croquettes, dip them in beaten egg, then in fine bread crumbs. Put on the ice for an hour or more; when needed, fry them in deep hot fat.

SMALL HOMINY OR GRITS.

Soak the hominy over night, boil in a little salted water, stir very frequently—it should be as thick as mush. It can be eaten as a breakfast dish with cream and sugar, or as a vegetable with butter, salt and pepper with it. Serve hot. Any left over is very nice, cut in slices and fried in a little butter.

CHEESE PREPARATIONS.

CHEESE.

Cheese is regarded as a most important article of food; it contains more nutritious material than any other food that is ordinarily obtainable. Mr. W. Matthieu Williams, in his "Chemistry of Cookery," says: "All that is required to render it, next to bread, the staple food of the world, is scientific cookery." Mr. Williams advises the use of a very little bicarbonate of potash in all cheese dishes.

AIGRETTES OF PARMESAN.

One-fourth pint of water, two ounces of butter, two ounces of flour, two ounces of grated cheese (Parmesan), two eggs, one-fourth ounce pepper and salt. Put the water into the saucepan with the butter, let it boil, shake in the flour, cook well; add the cheese, the eggs, well beaten, one at a time. Have ready some boiling fat and drop in about a dessert-spoonful of the mixture at a time; fry a golden brown, and serve very hot.

CHEESE BALLS.

Two cups of grated cheese, the whites of two eggs beaten very light, one tablespoonful of cream, one saltspoonful of salt, a little cayenne, five drops of Worcestershire sauce. Mix all these together, then make into small balls, dip them in beaten egg and fine bread crumbs; fry in hot deep lard.

CHEESELETS.

A saucer three-fourths full of grated cheese, mix with it the whites of three eggs beaten stiff, add a pinch of salt, a few drops of Worcestershire sauce. Form into balls, roll in cracker crumbs (very fine), drop in boiling lard. To be made during the dinner and served directly with the salad.

CHEESE CUSTARDS.

Take two ounces of grated cheese, three teaspoonfuls of milk or cream, one egg well beaten, a little cayenne and salt to taste. Beat all well together, bake in a small dish in a gentle oven for fifteen or twenty minutes and serve very hot.

COTTAGE CHEESE.

Take sour milk, put it on the range until the milk crinkles, then put it in a colander and drain off all the whey; beat the cheese until very light, add a little cream and salt, and make into balls and pour over them some rich cream.

CHEESE FONDUE—1.

The fondue must be baked in the dish in which it is served—a small silver dish or a French porcelain one is suitable. Mix one tablespoonful of butter and one tablespoonful of flour in the saucepan, stir until they bubble, then add one gill of rich milk; this will make a thick white sauce; stir constantly to prevent burning; when smooth, stir into the sauce three tablespoonfuls of grated cheese (good York State cheese), one small saltspoonful of salt, a little cayenne. Turn the mixture into a bowl, stir in the well-beaten yolks of two eggs; whip the whites of three eggs very stiff and stir them in very gently at the last. Butter the dish in which the fondue is to be baked; the fondue must half fill it. Bake until it is a golden brown in hot oven. Serve at once.

CHEESE FONDUE—2.

One cup of bread crumbs fine and dry, two cups of milk, one-half pound of cheese grated, three eggs, whipped very light, one tablespoonful of melted butter, pepper and salt, a pinch of soda dissolved in a little hot water and stirred into the milk. Soak the crumbs in the milk, beat the eggs and stir into the crumbs and milk, then add the cheese. Butter the baking dish, pour the mixture into it, strew some dry crumbs on the top, and bake in a hot oven.

A very little soda should be put in all cheese preparations.

KLUSKIS OF CREAM CHEESE.

Take half a pound of fresh butter, six eggs, six tablespoonfuls of cream cheese, a pinch of powdered sugar, salt, and sufficient grated bread crumbs and cream to make a paste ; mix well together and roll into balls ; poach them in boiling salt and water, drain, and serve them with poivrade sauce.

CHEESE MUFF.

One and one-half ounces of butter, four ounces of grated cheese, one teaspoonful of salt, one-half teaspoonful of pepper, four eggs. Put the cheese and the butter in a saucepan on the fire ; when they melt, add the eggs well beaten, and the salt and pepper. Stir and cook until you can push it up into a soft, muff-shaped form. Serve at once.

AN ENGLISH MONKEY.

Soak one cupful of bread crumbs in one cupful of milk for fifteen minutes. Melt one tablespoonful of butter and one cupful of cheese broken into bits, stir together until melted ; add the crumbs and one egg well beaten, one-half teaspoonful of salt, a little cayenne, one piece of bi-carbonate of soda the size of a pea. Cook for five minutes ; serve on crackers.

CHEESE PUDDING.

Soak six slices of bread, buttered, in a batter made of two eggs, beaten into a large cup of milk ; then place the slices of soaked bread in a pudding dish, covering each with a thick layer of grated cheese ; fill the dish with these layers, pour over all any batter remaining. This is a most delicate as well as a very nutritious dish.

ROASTED CHEESE.

One-fourth pound of cheese cut fine, mash it well and add to it the yolks of two eggs, two tablespoonfuls of butter, one very small teaspoonful of mustard, one-third teaspoonful of salt, a little cayenne. Spread the mixture on slices of nice toast, place in oven for a few minutes and serve at once.

RAMAKINS.

Four ounces of grated cheese, two ounces of bread without crust, one-third of a teaspoonful of mustard, one-third of a teaspoonful of salt, two eggs, one-half gill of milk. Crumb the bread into the milk and boil until soft, then add the mustard, salt, pepper, cheese and the yolks of the eggs beaten thoroughly, then stir in the whites beaten to a stiff froth. Bake in shallow pan, or in paper cases; bake fifteen minutes.

STEWED CHEESE.

Two tablespoonfuls of grated cheese, four tablespoonfuls of cream, one tablespoonful of butter, one egg, a little cayenne; melt the butter in the saucepan or in the chafing dish, then stir in the cream, then the cheese, lastly the eggs well beaten; stir until the mixture is smooth; serve on hot toast.

CHEESE STRAWS.

Roll out scraps of cold puff paste dough very thin, sprinkle with grated cheese and a little cayenne, roll the paste several times and sprinkle with the cheese and pepper each time, then put the paste away to harden on the ice; when needed, roll out thinly and cut with a pastry cutter into strips five inches long and about a quarter of an inch wide. Bake quickly and serve piled up like straws.

CHEESE SOUFFLE—1.

Six ounces of rich cheese, one teaspoonful of mustard, one saltspoonful of white pepper, a little cayenne, two ounces of butter, one-sixth of a grated nutmeg, two tablespoonfuls of flour, one gill of milk, six eggs. Put the cheese into the saucepan with the mustard, peppers, nutmeg, butter, flour and milk; stir all until it looks like rich, smooth cream—it must not boil; then add the yolks well beaten, then the whites well beaten; put into a pudding dish and bake for twenty minutes; serve at once, or fill little paper cases or the small porcelain ones with the mixture and bake for fifteen minutes.

CHEESE SOUFFLE—2.

Two tablespoonfuls of butter, one tablespoonful of flour, one-half cup of milk, one cup of grated cheese, three eggs, one-half teaspoonful salt, a little cayenne. Put the butter into the saucepan, when it is hot add the flour, stir until they are perfectly smooth but not browned, then add the milk and other ingredients; cook for twenty minutes, then add the yolks of the eggs well beaten, then the cheese; when all looks smooth and well blended, set away to cool; when cold add the whites of the eggs beaten to a stiff froth; turn all into a buttered dish, and bake for twenty-five minutes. Serve at once and in the dish it is baked in.

CHEESE CROQUETTES.

One coffeecupful of milk, two large tablespoonfuls of flour, lump of butter the size of a walnut, one-fourth teaspoonful of salt, a pinch of mustard, one pinch of cayenne, one pinch of pepper, one egg, three-fourths of a coffeecupful of Gruyere cheese grated, one-fourth of a coffeecupful of American cheese grated. Heat the milk; when hot, stir into the flour which has been previously mixed into a paste with a little of the cold milk, then add butter, mix together, take from the fire and add one egg beaten light, the salt, pepper, cayenne, mustard, beat all thoroughly, then add the cheese, and when the batter is mixed place in the ice box. Form into croquettes, dip each in egg and bread crumbs, place again in ice-box for several hours; when wanted to use, fry quickly in deep, hot fat and serve at once.

CURDS WITH CREAM.

Four quarts of sour milk, drain in a cheese cloth bag until the whey is all out, then beat the curd well, add a little salt and a few spoonfuls of cream; form into small, flat balls; pour rich, sweet cream over them with a little grated nutmeg.

PARMESAN CROQUETTES.

Four ounces of Parmesan, one ounce of flour, one ounce of mashed potatoes, two ounces of butter, one-fourth pint of cream, one-fourth pint of milk, two eggs, a pinch of unmixed mustard, a pinch of salt, a pinch of cayenne, one ounce of bread crumbs.

Mix one ounce of flour with two ounces of butter in a sauce pan, stir for five minutes and add the milk and potato and cheese; stir thoroughly together; add the seasoning and the cream; allow to boil; then take off the fire, and stir in gradually the well beaten yolks of two eggs; allow to get cold and hard, then make up into balls the size of a small walnut, egg and bread crumb, and fry in boiling lard in a frying basket; allow to drain, then pile up high in a small silver dish, and ornament with pickled chillies and mustard and cress.

CHEESE TOAST.

Put one-half ounce of butter into sauce pan; when hot add four ounces of good cheese, beat it thoroughly until it it is melted, then add one half pint of cream and two eggs, add a little salt and a small pinch of soda; serve at once on toast.

WELSH RAREBIT—1.

The secret of making Welsh rarebit digestible, is to add paprika to the cheese. One pound of full cream American cheese, one teaspoonful of butter, when hot stir in the cheese; add slowly as it melts, two spoonfuls of ale; when smooth, put in the paprika. Put on hot toast.

WELSH RAREBIT—2.

To four tablespoonfuls of sherry, add butter the size of a butternut; when melted, add one coffeecupful of grated cheese, then four tablespoonsfuls of milk, and a little cayenne; boil gently for a few minutes; then pour over the hot toast, buttered on one side and the crust taken off. For other Welsh rarebits see chafing-dish recipes.

EGGS.

Eggs contain all that is required for the building up of the body.

EGG BALLS.

Boil four eggs until they are hard, then put into cold water for a little while, remove the shells and take the yolks, pound them smooth, add one teaspoonful of salt, one-fourth teaspoonful of pepper, a little cayenne and one yolk of raw egg. Make the mixture into small balls, roll them in flour, fry them with a little butter until they are a delicate brown; serve with mock turtle soup or other soups.

BAKED EGGS—1.

Put some good gravy into a shallow baking dish. Break four eggs or as many as are required into this, salt them, and sprinkle some bread crumbs over them, and bake for five minutes in a quick oven. Take up the eggs carefully one by one, and lay upon little rounds of fried bread. Add to the gravy a little cream and some very finely chopped parsley and onion; put into a saucepan and boil up quickly and pour over the eggs.

BAKED EGGS—2.

Spread a thick layer of fresh butter on a tin or fireproof china dish, sprinkle with salt, and break the eggs carefully onto it, one at a time; pour some cream over them, season with salt, pepper and one grate of nutmeg; place a few small lumps of butter over all, bake in the oven for four minutes.

BAKED EGGS—3.

Boil eggs until hard, then put them into cold water; when cold remove the shells, chop the eggs very fine, add one saltspoonful of salt, one saltspoonful of pepper; stir together; put the eggs into a porcelain dish; first put a layer of breadcrumbs, then a layer of the eggs, then bread crumbs, eggs, or until the dish is full; then put bits of butter over the top with some bread crumbs; lastly pour over all one cup of cream; bake fifteen minutes.

EGGS AND CHEESE.

Take the small china dishes that will stand the heat; place in each a bit of butter, a little chopped parsley, break over a fresh egg, sprinkle on the top of the egg some grated cheese—American cheese is excellent for this, a few bread crumbs and a little salt and pepper; bake in a hot oven for three minutes, and serve in the same dish in which they are baked.

EGGS WITH CREAM—1.

Poach eggs in boiling water, allowing one for each person to be served; trim them and dish on a slice of bread; pour over some hot cream sauce; sprinkle some chopped parsley or truffles over, and place around the eggs slices of hot, fried bacon cut thin and rolled.

EGGS WITH CREAM—2.

Cover the bottom of a porcelain plate with cream; break on this the eggs carefully; let them bake for four minutes; sprinkle a little salt and pepper and a bit of butter on each egg, and serve in the same dish in which they are baked.

EGG CROQUETTES.

One ounce of butter, one pint of flour, one pint of boiling water, five eggs. Mix the flour with the water in a saucepan; when well cooked take it off the fire and cool the mixture; when cold add the eggs one by one, beat the batter very hard before the eggs are put in, and after, drop the batter in little bits like eggs, into deep boiling lard.

DEVILLED EGGS.

Take as many eggs as there are persons to be served; break them into the saucepan and fry them until the whites are firm; be careful not to break the yolks; trim the eggs nicely and place them on a hot dish; pour over them this sauce, which should be ready at the same time the eggs are to be served. Put into a stewpan one tablespoonful of butter, two tablespoonfuls of cream, a little cayenne, one saltspoonful of salt, one teaspoonful of French mustard, one-fourth teaspoonful of English mustard, one tablespooonful of tomato catsup, the yolks of two raw eggs. Stir together on the fire until the sauce thickens, add one tablespoonful of finely minced cold ham, and one green pepper cut very fine (if convenient); serve.

FRIED EGGS—1.

When the frying pan is hot put in a little butter, then place the pan on a cooler part of the stove, break into the pan, one at a time, the eggs; if the eggs are put into the pan when it is very hot they they will burst and crack.

FRIED EGGS—2.

One tablespoonful of olive oil, put into the saucepan; when hot, drop gently into it the eggs. As soon as the eggs are cooked, carefully remove from the oil; the whites should have a yellow edge. It is very necessary that the eggs for frying should be most carefully put into the pan so as not to break the yolks. In place of the oil, butter can be used. Serve very hot; sprinkle over the yolks a litttle salt and pepper.

EGGS IN A NEST.

Toast some slices of bread a dainty brown and pare off the crust, leaving an oval of toast; on this put a big teaspoonful of white of egg beaten to a stiff froth; drop the yolk in the center, with pepper, salt and a tiny bit of butter, and set in the oven until it becomes a golden brown.

EGGS ON THE PLATE.

Rub the plate well with butter, sprinkle a little salt and pepper over, then break the eggs carefully; do not break the yolks; put bits of butter on the eggs, and put one spoonful of cream for each egg; put the plate on a tin containing a little hot water. and stand in the oven for five minutes, and serve hot

POACHED EGGS.

A wide and shallow pan is the best for poaching eggs in; half fill the pan with boiling water slightly salted; break the eggs carefully into a saucer separately and slide them into the water; let them simmer for two minutes, then let the water boil for another minute; this detaches the eggs from the pan; then remove the eggs with a pancake turner; place them on slices of hot toast or on minced meat or fish.

Eggs can be poached in milk; all eggs for poaching must be perfectly fresh.

Three drops of Worcestershire sauce on each egg just before it is quite cooked, is a great addition to a poached egg.

POACHED EGGS WITH ANCHOVY PASTE.

Make six slices of toast, butter and spread over them some anchovy paste and place in the oven for a few minutes. Poach six eggs and place an egg on each piece of toast, add a very little salt and pepper to each top and serve very hot.

PLAIN OMELETTE.

Beat three eggs lightly with a little salt and pepper, add three tablespoonfuls of hot water. Put a little butter in the omelette pan; when hot, pour in the eggs, stir continually with a fork so that all may cook evenly; the omelette must cook quickly; when the eggs are set, run the knife under the omelette which is nearest the handle of the pan; turn this half over on the other half; take a hot plate and place it on the edge of the pan and flop the omelette on to it This is a plain omelette; all other varieties are made by adding the ingredients after the eggs are put into the pan.

OMELETTE CELESTINE.

One-half a pint of milk, boil with it two tablespoonfuls of rice flour, four ounces of sugar, one teaspoonful of vanilla extract, simmer for ten minutes, stirring constantly, add then the yolks of three eggs mixed with a little milk, and one-half tablespoonful of butter, then add the whites beaten light, and divide the mixture, making two omelettes; put one-half in the pan, having a little hot butter in the pan; when the omelette is ready to fold, put over it one tablespoonful of marmalade, fold over the omelette and serve hot.

SPANISH OMELETTE.

One large tomato cut in pieces, one small green pepper cut in pieces, one small onion sliced, one teaspoonful of parsley chopped fine, one teaspoonful of celery chopped fine, half a can of mushrooms cut in pieces. Cook these together for a few minutes, then put with the omelette when it is in the pan.

ORANGE OMELETTE.

For three eggs use the thinly-grated rind of one orange and three tablespoonfuls of the juice. Beat the yolks until light, add three tablespoonfuls of fine sugar, then the juice and rind of the orange; beat the whites of the eggs until light, fold them in the mixture and then all into an omelette pan, cook until set, then place in a moderate oven and lightly brown. Serve on a hot dish.

STUFFED EGGS.

Boil as many eggs as you require until they are hard; put them in cold water, when cold remove the shells, cut the eggs in halves; cut with a warm, sharp knife; remove the yolks, mash them into a smooth paste, with one tablespoonful of olive oil, or two tablespoonfuls of melted butter; one saltspoonful of salt, one-half saltspoonful of cayenne, one-fourth saltspoonful of mustard. Mix these all together until smooth, then fill in the eggs and press the two halves together; place upon a bed of lettuce leaves. If desired, a mayonnaise sauce can be poured over the eggs.

SCOTCH EGGS.

Boil one-half dozen eggs twenty minutes and then drop them into cold water. Chop very fine, enough lean cooked ham to make one cupful. Cook one-third of a cup of stale bread crumbs in the same amount of milk and stir until it is a smooth paste. Take it from the fire and mix the prepared ham with the paste. Add half a teaspoonful of made mustard and half a saltspoonful of paprika; lastly stir in a beaten egg and mix well. Remove the shells from the boiled eggs and cover the eggs with a thick coating of this mixture. With a spoon cover the outside of this mixture with a partly beaten egg and then roll them in fine bread crumbs. Lay the prepared eggs in a frying basket and put them in a cold place until required; then fry them in hot lard to a nice brown and let them drain on brown paper in the mouth of the oven, where they will remain hot. Cut some rather thin slices of bread and with a biscuit cutter make them into round pieces. Toast and butter these slices of bread and lay them on a hot platter. With a sharp knife cut each egg into halves lengthwise and lay them upon the toast with the cut side down. Garnish the dish with watercresses and serve them with the eggs. A bechamel or cream sauce is often served with the eggs in place of the cresses.

SWISS EGGS.

Spread two ounces of butter on a dish, and lay on it six thin slices of Swiss cheese; break six eggs upon this, keeping the yolks whole. Sprinkle over some salt and pepper. Mix a teaspoonful of chopped parsley and two ounces of grated Swiss cheese together and strew over them. Bake in a very quick oven for about five minutes.

EGGS A LA TRIPE.

Allow one egg to each person to be served. Boil them for eight minutes, then slice them, using a warm, wet knife for the purpose. Butter a porcelain dish, put in the bottom a layer of cream sauce, then a layer of the sliced eggs, sprinkle over them a little finely chopped onion or shallot, some chopped parsley; continue these layers until the dish is full, having the cream sauce for the last layer, put over some fine bread crumbs and some bits of butter. Place the dish in a tin half filled with boiling water and put into the oven for fifteen minutes, then take from the oven, sprinkle over the top some hard-boiled yolk of egg, which has been passed through a fine sieve, and serve.

SAVORIES.

Savories are served with the salad course at dinner or at luncheon.

SAVORIES.
(ANCHOVIES.)

Take two hard boiled eggs, mash the yolks with one saltspoonful of salt, two mustard spoonfuls of French mustard; rub the whole together, then add slowly two tablespoonfuls of olive oil, two tablespoonfuls of tarragon vinegar, stir all one way until all are blended smoothly, then add two filletted anchovies, which have been well pounded; lastly add one-half gill of whipped cream and spread the mixture on thinly cut brown bread.

ANCHOVY STRAWS.

Take "anchovies in oil," dry them and cut into long, thin strips; roll each strip in pastry and fry in deep, hot fat; pile them two by two over each other and serve hot.

ANCHOVY TOAST.

Toast thin slices of bread, butter them and spread over some anchovy paste; serve hot.

A SAVORY WITH BACON.

Among the many excellent ways of serving bacon the following is one of the best. The bacon may be prepared and can be easily cooked the last moment over the fire in a frying pan; or if desired it may be cooked upon the table in a chafing dish. Skin and bone some sardines; add to them some paprika, a little chopped parsley (or lemon juice may be used in place of parsley), and some butter. Rub these ingredients together, making them into a smooth paste. Spread this paste upon thin slices of bacon and roll each slice up in a close roll and fasten it with a little wooden toothpick. Lay the prepared slices in a hot frying pan and cook quickly. Serve very hot.

CAVIARE CANAPES—1.

Cut some slices of bread one-fourth inch thick, cut with the two-inch cutter into rounds. Fry in hot fat until both sides are brown. To one-fourth cup of butter made soft and creamy, add one teaspoonful of salt, one teaspoonful of paprika and one teaspoonful of watercress. Make into balls and let them become hard; when needed, spread on the bread slices and then put on a layer of caviare and squeeze a little lemon juice over all. To prepare the cress, wash and drain, then chop very fine, then squeeze it dry in a cloth.

CAVIARE CANAPES—2.

Cut some slices of bread a quarter of an inch thick, cut them out with a plain two-inch cutter and fry these rounds in a little butter till of a light golden color. When cold spread them over with Montpelier butter and place a layer of caviare on the top. Squeeze lemon over them and serve.

CRACKERS.

Hot crackers always make a good relish. Butter them and then cover thickly with fine grated cheese. Place them in a baking pan and sprinkle a little sherry over them. Bake in a hot oven until slightly browned and serve at once.

EGG SAVORY.

Cook half a can of tomatoes eight minutes with a teaspoonful of chopped parsley and a teaspoonful of chopped onion; add five eggs after beating them a little, and stir all together briskly until consistency of scrambled eggs. Add cayenne pepper and salt to taste. Thin slices of green pepper are an addition. Serve on square pieces of hot toast, from which the crusts have been removed, and spread with anchovy paste; then serve immediately.

GASCONY BUTTER.

Take equal quantities of parsley picked from the stalk and parboiled, of boned and pounded anchovies, and of fresh butter. Mix the ingredients well together and pass them through a hair sieve; shape the butter into little balls and put on the ice for one hour. These are nice little relishes for breakfast or lunch.

HAM BUTTER.

Pound together one hard-boiled yolk of egg, two tablespoonfuls of cooked ham, two tablespoonfuls of butter, a little cayenne. Mix until smooth. This butter is very nice spread on hot toast for breakfast or to use as a savory.

OLIVE CUSTARDS.

Take one ounce of grated cheese to one egg well beaten; mix this over the fire until it becomes a very thick custard; fry some neat little rounds of bread in butter, spread them very thinly with anchovy paste and pour on each a small quantity of the custard. Stone some olives, and put one in the middle of each round.

PUFF PASTE STRAWS WITH BLOATER PASTE.

One-fourth of a pound of flour, rub into it one tablespoonful of bloater paste, a little cayenne, one-half cup of cold water; make into a smooth paste, roll it out and put on on it one-fourth of a pound of butter, fold it up and roll out six times, lastly roll out to one-eighth of an inch in thickness; cut it into strips two inches long and one inch wide and bake in a moderate oven for fifteen minutes; take out and spread over them some bloater paste, and over that some whipped cream seasoned with a little salt and cayenne.

SARDINE BUTTER.

Remove the skins and bones from eight sardines; put into a mortar and pound until smooth, two tablespoonfuls of parsley chopped very fine, four ounces of butter; pound these with the sardines. This butter is very appetizing spread on hot toast.

BROILED SARDINES ON TOAST.

Broil the sardines; have some small slices of hot toast; place a sardine on each piece and pour over them a sauce made with the oil in which the sardines were packed, and one spoonful of paprika heated together.

SARDINES WITH CHEESE.

Take small sardines, drain them from the oil, remove the skin and tip of the tail, and put over the fish a sprinkle of cheese grated fine. Make some slices of toast a little larger than the sardines, butter them and put the sardines on, place in the oven to warm, but not to become crisp, and serve hot.

ICED SAVORY SOUFFLE.

This dish can be made of almost any kind of fish, chicken or game; it is excellent with lobster meat. Cut up the lobster or whatever it may be, into very small pieces; let it soak in mayonnaise sauce for two or three hours. Have some well-flavored aspic jelly and whip it till it is frothy. Put some of this at the bottom of the dish it is to be served in, then place a layer of the lobster and fill it up with aspic and lobster alternately till the mold is nearly full; place a stiff band of paper round, and fill it with whipped aspic. Put it on ice for two hours, take off the paper and serve.

SAVORY.
CHEESE, EGGS AND TOMATOES.

One cup of tomatoes, two eggs, two tablespoonfuls of grated cheese, one-half teaspoonful of salt, a little cayenne, a little mustard, one teaspoonful of lemon juice, one teaspoonful of sugar, butter the size of an egg, and hot toast. Beat the eggs; mix in the cheese, seasoning, tomatoes, melt the butter; when hot stir all the ingredients together and heat until very hot, but not boiling. Serve on slices of hot toast.

SAVORY.
CHEESE AND EGGS.

Cut six slices of bread, remove the crusts, fry them until a light brown in hot fat; keep them warm while you beat together two ounces of cheese cut fine, one ounce of butter and the yolk of one egg; when the butter and cheese are melted, stir in the yolk, add salt and pepper and a little nutmeg, spread the mixture on the bread and serve at once.

SAVORY BUTTER.

Pound to a paste four ounces of rich cheese with a small piece of butter (this varies with the dryness of the cheese), a couple of spoonfuls of vinegar from pickled walnuts, a good dash of cayenne, a dessertspoonful of essence of anchovy and the same of mustard. This mixture, if heated over the fire, makes a delicious savory toast.

A SAVORY OF SEMOLINA.

Two tablespoonfuls of semolina; stir into one pint of boiling milk, with a little salt, until it has the thickness of cream. Boil carefully (as milk is quick to burn) until it has the taste of being thoroughly cooked. In the meantime beat the eggs, whites and yolks separately, about four to a pint of new milk. Stir in the yolks, keeping the saucepan a little longer on the fire; follow with the whites and pour into a large shallow vessel. Place in a cool place for several hours until thoroughly set, when the semolina should be cut into pieces a couple of inches square, sprinkled over with grated cheese, and baked quickly in a hot oven.

SCOTCH WOODCOCK.

Eight hard-boiled eggs, chop them fine; one cup of milk, when boiling stir into it one tablespoonful of flour well mixed into two tablespoonfuls of butter, add one tablespoonful of anchovy paste, a little cayenne and a little salt; stir in the eggs, heat for one minute, then pour the mixture on to pieces of hot toast and serve at once.

CATSUPS AND PICKLES.

A FINE CATSUP.

Put into a wide-mouth glass bottle one pint of vinegar, one dozen skinned shallots, slightly bruised, one gill of red wine which has been made hot, one dozen blanched and filleted anchovies which have been heated with the wine. When the mixture is cold add one gill of red wine, three blades of mace, one piece of ginger root, one dozen cloves, one dozen pepper corns, one dessertspoonful of grated horseradish, the rind of one lemon, one grated nutmeg; close the bottle tightly, shake it several times each day for a week; if you have any mushroom catsup add one tablespoonful. It will keep for years if well sealed and kept in a dry place.

BENGAL CHUTNEY.

One pound of brown sugar, one half pound of salt, one-half pound of ground mustard seed, one-fourth pound of garlic, one-fourth pound of onions, one-fourth pound of ginger (ground), one-half pound of raisins, one ounce of cayenne, three pints of best cider vinegar, fifteen large sour apples, thirteen ripe tomatoes. Garlic, raisins, onions all to be chopped fine, apples, and tomatoes and all boiled in the vinegar until quite soft, then mash and mix all well together; when cold, cork tight.

CUCUMBER PICKLES.

First, make a strong brine and scald the brine for four mornings, and pour over the pickles hot each day. Second, make a fresh brine, scald for five mornings, then put the pickles into cold water, adding a little piece of alum, for twenty-four hours. Scald the vinegar, add red peppers, a stick of horseradish, cloves, cinnamon, mace, mustard seed and sugar. For five hundred pickles take three pounds of sugar.

CHILI PICKLES.

Thirty ripe tomatoes, seven green peppers, ten onions, fifteen tablespoonfuls of white sugar, seven cups of cider vinegar, five small tablespoonfuls of salt. Chop the tomatoes, peppers and onions fine; cook all one and one-half hours.

DELICIOUS PICKLES.

Three quarts of ripe tomatoes, three quarts of green tomatoes, two red peppers, two green peppers (take out the seeds from the peppers), three heads of celery, three onions, one cup of grated horseradish. Chop all the vegetables, put them in a large bowl, sprinkle over them some salt, let them stand over night; in the morning drain off the water, then take one quart of vinegar, two pounds of brown sugar, one-half cup of mustard seed, two tablespoonfuls of celery salt, one tablespoonful of powdered cinnamon, one-half tablespoonful of powdered cloves, one tablespoonful of allspice, one tablespoonful of ginger. Boil all until the vegetables are perfectly soft.

EAST INDIA CATSUP.

One-half bushel of green tomatoes cut fine, ten pounds of brown sugar, ten lemons cut fine, one ounce of white ginger root cut fine. Boil all down to two gallons and bottle.

GRAPE CATSUP.

Pick six pounds of grapes from the stems, put in a kettle and cover with water. Let this boil, then strain. To the juice add one pound of sugar, one pint of vinegar, and one teaspoonful each of cloves, salt and cinnamon. Boil until thick, and bottle.

GOVERNOR'S PICKLE.

One peck of green tomatoes sliced thin; one layer of tomatoes with a layer of salt—use a cupful; let all stand over night, pour off the liquor; then place tomatoes in a kettle, with enough vinegar to cover them, and six red peppers cut up, four large onions cut fine, one large cup of sugar, one teaspoonful of cloves, one teaspoonful of allspice, one teaspoonful of cayenne, one teaspoonful of white pepper corns tied in a little bag; let all simmer until soft, then put into jars and keep air tight. Have the spices ground, and remove the whole pepper corns.

KITCHEN PEPPER.

One ounce of ginger, one ounce of cinnamon, one ounce of pepper, one-half ounce of allspice, one-half ounce of nutmeg, ten cloves, six ounces of salt; mix and bottle.

LEMON CATSUP.

Six lemons, cut them into quarters and remove the seeds and put them into a small stone jar. Take one quart of vinegar in which put two shallots slightly bruised, three blades of mace, one nutmeg, twelve pepper corns, one teaspoonful of cayenne, one teaspoonful of salt. Boil these together and then pour over the lemons, cover the jar closely; let it stand in a warm place; stir it occasionally, and sometimes place it on the back of the range to warm, not cook; after three weeks, strain and bottle. This is an excellent sauce for fish and white meats and will keep for years.

HOW TO MIX MUSTARD.

Mustard should be mixed with water that has been boiled and then cooled. Put the mustard in a cup, add a pinch of salt; mix into it gradually, carefully rubbing down the lumps, enough water to make a smooth paste that will drop from the spoon.

CUCUMBER CATSUP.

Three dozen large green cucumbers, three small onions, one teacupful of salt. Cut the cucumbers lengthwise, and scrape out the seeds, then chop the cucumbers fine and drain for twelve hours, then add one fourth cupful of pepper, one cup mustard seeds, cover with vinegar and seal tight.

MIXED PICKLES.

Eight large green peppers; take out the seeds and slice them fine, three hundred small cucumbers, eight large heads of cauliflower, six heads of white cabbage cut fine, two quarts of onions sliced fine, two horse radish roots grated, three quarts of green tomatoes cut fine. Put all the ingredients into a brine strong enough to bear an egg for nearly four hours, then drain for three hours, then sprinkle in one-half pound mustard seed, one-fourth pound of celery seed, two teaspoonfuls of cayenne, two tablespoonfuls of black pepper, then pour this over the vegetables. Put two gallons of vinegar on to boil, pour this over the vegetables when cold and stir into the vinegar one pint of prepared mustard.

PEPPER CATSUP.

Four dozen peppers, boil them in two quarts of vinegar until soft, then strain and add one tablespoonful of salt, one tablespoonful of cloves, three tablespoonsfuls of horseradish grated, three garlics and five onions chopped fine. Boil one-half hour, add a little cold vinegar, and bottle.

RASPBERRY VINEGAR.

Two quarts of berries, put into a stone jar and pour over one quart of best vinegar; after twenty-four hours, strain and pour the syrup over two fresh quarts of berries, then let it stand twenty four hours; add one pound of sugar to every pint of juice, boil, cork and seal tightly.

SWEET CHERRY PICKLES.

Three pints of seeded cherries, two pints of white sugar, one-half pint of vinegar, one tablespoonful of powdered cinnamon; boil together for one hour, then seal in mason jars.

SWEET PEACH PICKLE.

Seven pounds of peaches, three and one-half pounds of sugar, one quart of vinegar, one ounce of allspice, one ounce of whole cloves, two ounces of stick cinnamon; tie the spices together in a bag. Scald the vinegar, sugar and spices and pour over the peaches; repeat this for three mornings.

SWEET PEAR PICKLE.

Eight pounds of pears, eight pounds of granulated sugar, one-half pound of candied ginger, four lemons. Boil the lemons whole in clear water until soft. Peel the pears, chop them fine, put the sugar and pears in the preserving kettle with the water from the boiled lemons and cook for one hour, then add the ginger cut fine and the lemons chopped fine; remove the seeds. Cook for one hour or until the mixture is thick as marmalade.

SWEET PICKLED PINEAPPLE.

Pare and cut the fruit into small square pieces. To each pound of fruit allow three-fourths pound of sugar; let the sugar stand on the fruit until it is dissolved, then put into the kettle and cook until the fruit is tender; skim out the fruit, add one pint of vinegar to the syrup, a few blades of mace, whole cloves and allspice tied in a bag; cook the syrup until it is thick, then put back the fruit and boil all together for a half hour. Put into jars, seal while hot.

TOMATO CATSUP—1.

One gallon of tomatoes, four tablespoonfuls of salt, two tablespoonfuls of pepper, three tablespoonfuls of mustard, one-half tablespoonful of ground allspice, one-half tablespoonful of ground cloves, one-half tablespoonful of cayenne, one tablespoonful of cinnamon, one pint of vinegar. Boil two hours, or longer if necessary, to thoroughly cook the juice down, so that it will not be watery; add the vinegar when the catsup is nearly done. After the tomatoes are cooked, before any spices are added, let them drain through a flour sack for several hours; in this way all of the water is taken out.

TOMATO CATSUP—2.

One bushel of ripe tomatoes, one-half gallon of vinegar, one-half pound of sugar, one-half pint of salt, one and one-half ounces of pepper, one and one-half ounces of allspice, two ounces of mustard, one ounce of ginger, one-half ounce of cloves, one-half ounce of cayenne, one-half ounce of asafaetida, one pint of alcohol. Put tomatoes on to boil for one half hour, then strain; return juice to kettle, and boil down to one and one-half gallons, add vinegar, boil down; add sugar, spices, etc. Mix the asafaetida in a cup, add a little of the juice to it and mix well; strain into the kettle, stir continually until all boils, take from the fire and add the alcohol. Bottle and seal while hot. It takes five hours boiling.

TOMATO PICKLE.

Twenty-four tomatoes, thirteen onions, eight green peppers, four cups of vinegar, eight tablespoonfuls of sugar, five tablespoonfuls of salt, one tablespoonful of cinnamon, one tablespoonful of allspice, two tablespoonfuls of celery salt. Boil all two hours, adding a little vinegar the last hour.

TOMATO SOY.

One peck of green tomatoes, one-half pint of salt, eight small onions sliced, one ounce of ground cloves, one ounce of ground allspice, one ounce of ground pepper, one-fourth pound of mustard seed, two full tablespoonfuls of ground mustard, one teaspoonful of cayenne. Slice the tomatoes and onions into an earthen vessel, between each layer sprinkle some salt and let it remain over night. Next day put in kettle, with the layers previously drained from the salted water; sprinkle over the spices and cover all with good cider vinegar and cook slowly for six hours.

SWEET TOMATO PICKLE.

One peck of green tomatoes sliced, twelve onions sliced thinly, then sprinkle with one cup of salt and let all stand over night. In the morning drain, and add to the tomatoes one cabbage sliced as for cold slaw; add two quarts of water and one quart of vinegar, boil fifteen minutes; throw this vinegar and water away. Add to the pickle two pounds of sugar, two quarts of vinegar, two tablespoonfuls of ground cloves, two tablespoonfuls of allspice, two tablespoonfuls of ginger, one-half pound of mustard seed, two tablespoonfuls of whole cloves, two tablespoonfuls of cinnamon, one teaspoonful of cayenne, six large red and green peppers sliced thin. Boil fifteen minutes or until the pickle looks clear.

WINE CATSUP.

Boil two pecks of tomatoes; when perfectly soft, mash through a sieve and add six ounces of cloves, three ounces of pepper, four nutmegs grated; boil together one hour, then add one quart of port wine and bottle.

A FEW BREAKFAST DISHES.

"A LITTLE BREAKFAST DISH."

Cut two long slices of cold meat and three of bread, buttered thickly, the same size and shape; season the meat with pepper, salt and a little chopped parsley, or if veal is used, a little chopped ham, then lay one slice of the bread between two of the meat, and have the other two slices outside; fasten together with little wooden skewers. Put into a hot oven, baste with butter thoroughly, so that the bread is crisp and brown; serve hot.

BREAKFAST CUSTARD.

One-half pint of sweet milk, two eggs if large ones, if not three eggs. Beat the eggs together until light, stir into the milk, add a little pinch of salt; butter a pint bowl, pour in the mixture, and set the bowl in a tin of hot water, place in hot oven and bake for twenty minutes. Have a hot plate, turn the custard on this and pour over it a tomato sauce, or a sauce made of mushrooms, or a cream sauce.

COLD MEAT BALLS.

Chop the meat fine, season with salt and pepper; make the meat into balls or flat cakes, fry them in a little butter or dripping. Fry some salt pork or bacon cut in thin slices and place around the balls.

CROQUETTES.

Stir into a cup of milk enough crustless bread to make a nice consistency (as glutinous as possible); add to this a cupful of cold meat of any kind, chopped fine. Season with a little chopped onion, chopped parsley, a piece of butter, salt and pepper. A few sliced mushrooms and some chopped truffles are, of course, an addition. This should be prepared in the afternoon and allowed to remain in the ice chest until it is very cold. An hour before breakfast, remove from the ice and form the mixture into any desired shape, dip each croquette into the beaten yolk of an egg and then in bread crumbs, and place in the frying basket and put it back on the ice and do not again remove it until the fat is at the boiling point. By plunging the partly frozen forms into the intense heat, a coating, as it were, is formed, whereby the desired moisture inside is obtained as well as the possibility of maintaining the outward shapeliness.

DRIED BEEF WITH EGGS.

One-fourth pound of thinly sliced dried beef—shred it and let it lie in cold water for about fifteen minutes, then drain and cover the beef with milk, about one pint; put on the stove, and when it begins to simmer, add one teaspoonful of flour, dissolved in one tablespoonful of cold milk; one tablespoonful of butter, a little salt and pepper. As soon as the flour has cooked, break into the saucepan three eggs without beating, stir all rapidly until the eggs are cooked. Have several slices of hot toast ready, well buttered, and serve the beef, etc., on the toast—this will be enough for five half slices of toast.

EGG TOAST.

Six slices of bread, one egg, one cupful of milk, one saltspoonful of salt. Beat the egg until light, add to the milk, also add the salt. Dip the slices of bread in the mixture, then have the griddle hot, grease it with a little butter and fry the toast on both sides. Serve hot.

FRIZZLED BEEF.

Shred the dried beef into little pieces, carefully removing all fat, strings and sinews; if the beef is very salt, freshen it by standing it in cold water for fifteen minutes, draining after. Put one tablespoonful of butter in the saucepan; when hot, put in the beef and fry it for five minutes, then add one tablespoonful of flour dissolved in one cup of cream or milk; as soon as the flour is cooked, serve.

STEWED KIDNEY.

Cut the kidney into small pieces about the size of a cherry, put into a colander and let cold water run over it while in the colander, then put on a plate to drain; put a piece of butter the size of a walnut in a pot, and sprinkle flour on the bottom of the pot, and stir the flour and butter together with a spoon until brown, then sprinkle flour on the kidney in the colander, stirring them together well, then put the kidney into the hot pot on the stove, stirring it until it is well mixed, then pour hot water on it two inches deep; it must boil three hours to make it tender. Then take another piece of butter the same size, mix one tablespoonful of flour, pepper and salt with it to a paste, and stir it into the kidney, a little at a time and let it boil fifteen minutes; while cooking it requires watching or it will burn.

SAVORY MOLDS.

Mince half a pound of underdone beef or mutton as finely as possible and put it into a basin with half its weight of bread crumbs, one ounce of butter broken into small pieces, a tablespoonful of finely minced onion, a teaspoonful of mixed powdered herbs and a good seasoning of salt and pepper. Mix these ingredients thoroughly, moisten with one beaten egg and fill in some small, well-buttered molds; bake in a moderate oven for half an hour, and turn out carefully; insert a small sprig of parsley in the top of each, and pour a little brown gravy round the meat.

"MY DEVIL."

One tablespoonful of Worcestershire sauce, three mustardspoonfuls of mustard, one saltspoonful of salt, one-half saltspoonful of black pepper, one-fourth saltspoonful of cayenne pepper, one teaspoonful of vinegar, a few drops of "Soy." one small teaspoonful of brown sugar, a squeeze of lemon, one glass of port wine. Mix all well together—fry the meat (turkey legs generally) in a frying pan with a little butter; when almost ready, pour sauce over; boil up and serve.

PORK TENDERLOINS.

Broil the tenderloins and serve with melted butter poured over them, a little salt and pepper; serve very hot—very nice for breakfast.

CALCUTTA TOAST.

Put one tablespoonful of butter into the saucepan over boiling water; as it melts, stir in two eggs, a little cayenne, one-half teaspoonful of essence of anchovy and a few chopped capers; stir until the eggs are cooked; then spread the mixture on hot buttered toast. Serve hot.

TOMATO TOAST.

Boil one-half can of tomatoes or six fresh ones for fifteen minutes, then add one saltspoonful of salt, a little pepper, one-half tablespoonful of butter, one-half tablespoonful of flour mixed together; when the mixture is thick and smooth, pour over some pieces of hot, buttered toast. Serve at once.

VEAL SEFTON.

Put one pint of strong, rich veal stock or gravy boiling hot, on to six fresh eggs, well beaten; sprinkle in a little grated lemon peel, a dust of cayenne, salt and mace, then two ounces of melted butter. Bake slowly in buttered cups, turn out and serve with a good, rich gravy, or a tomato sauce.

VIRGINIA WHITE PUDDINGS.

One pint of fresh beef suet chopped fine and free from strings or skin, one pint of flour, one teacupful of corn meal, one teaspoonful of salt, one teaspoonful of pepper. Mix all well together, fill small cotton bags with this mixture, allowing a little space for the puddings to swell. Tie very tightly and boil for six hours, keeping the puddings well covered with water. When cold, hang in a cool, dry place; when required for use, remove the bag and slice the pudding in thin slices and fry in a little butter. Serve very hot.

TRIPE.

TO PREPARE TRIPE.

When the tripe comes from the butchers, scrape it well, then put it on to boil in cold water; as soon as it boils drain off the water and replace with more cold water—boil for four hours; add to the water one onion, one teaspoonful of salt, a little cayenne, six pepper-corns and two cloves tied in a little bag, one bay leaf, one tablespoonful of vinegar; when the tripe is cooked it is ready to be used for any of the various preparations of tripe.

CREAMED TRIPE.

Prepare the trip as directed. Cut the tripe into small pieces; put one tablespoonful of butter into the stew-pan; when it is hot add one tablespoonful of flour, stir together; when smooth add one teaspoonful of salt, a little cayenne, a little nutmeg, one-half pint of cream and the tripe, and cook for five minutes.

TRIPE CUTLETS.

Prepare the tripe as directed. Cut the tripe into pieces large enough for one portion; dip each cutlet into beaten egg, then into fine bread crumbs—have the crumbs seasoned with salt and pepper, a little cayenne and a very little nutmeg, then into the egg again. Take one tablespoonful of butter, place in a pan; when hot, put in the cutlets, brown and turn—they are cooked as soon as they are brown. Serve hot.

FRIED TRIPE.

Prepare the tripe as directed. Cut the tripe into small pieces, dip them in beaten egg, then into bread crumbs; fry in deep hot fat.

TRIPE A LA MODE.

Cook the tripe for four hours and let it cool; take one slice of bacon, one onion, one garlic clove, one teaspoonful of butter, one-half teaspoonful of sugar; fry together until brown, add one teacup of stock, boil once, then strain and add one teacup of tomatoes, one-half teaspoonful of salt. Take two teaspoonfuls of butter in the saucepan, when hot add one tablespoonful of flour, when smooth add the sauce, stirring all the time, then add the tripe which should be cut in small pieces two inches square; cook long enough to thoroughly season the tripe; just before serving add one yolk of an egg, beaten with one tablespoonful of cream.

TRIPE AND OYSTERS.

One pound of tripe, one quart of oysters. Cut the tripe into inch pieces; drain the oysters, cook the tripe in boiling water for five minutes; put the oysters in a pan and let them just come to the boiling point, then drain them. Make a white sauce of two tablespoonfuls of butter, two tablespoonfuls of flour; when hot, add one cup of cream; when smooth, add the tripe and oysters, seasoned with salt and pepper.

TRIPE.

It may not be generally known that stewed tripe is the most easily digested of all solid animal food; it is fully digested in one hour after being eaten.

FRYING.

In frying be sure that the pan is perfectly clean. To fry well the fat must always be very hot. To test this throw into the pan a bit of bread; if it turns a light brown at once the fat is in a proper condition.

Do not be afraid to put one or two pounds of fat into your frying pan; it can be used over and over again, provided it is strained each time.

To Clarify Dripping—When poured from the meat pan it should be put into a bowl, pour into it some boiling water and a little salt, and stir well; when it is cold remove from the bowl—the water and sediment will be at the bottom. Scrape the cake of dripping, put it into some more boiling water until it melts, then stir well and let it cool; place in a crock and it will keep for weeks in cool weather.

All the fats skimmed from boiled meats, soups, etc., should be treated in the same way and then added to the general crock.

Fat for Frying—The light colored drippings of roast meat and the fat taken off from broths or beef suet chopped fine and melted down without browning. As soon as the bottom of the stew-pan can be seen through the suet is done.

Olive oil of the best quality is tasteless, and is the best of all frying media.

FRYING MIXTURE.

A mixture of one-half lard and one-half beef suet is a good frying medium.

BEEF SUET DRIPPING.

Prepare the dripping by putting into a basin and pouring boiling water over it, stirring well to wash the suet from all impurities, then let it cool—all the impurities will settle with the water at the bottom of the basin; when cold, place on fire; when hot, remove the dripping and put it away in a cool place. Beef dripping is preferable to other dripping for cooking.

Frying once understood is a very easy process; to have the operation successful the fat must be deep and very hot; when the smoke comes from the center of the fat, a bit of bread thrown into it at this stage must color at once. The time for frying any article must be very short, two minutes being, in nearly every case quite enough. A kettle which has suspended from the handle a basket which can be filled with the articles to be fried and then let down into the fat is the best possible arrangement for frying.

FRYING BATTER.

Mix together in a bowl four tablespoonfuls of flour, one of olive oil, a saltspoonful of salt, the yolks of two eggs and enough cold water to make a stiff batter, about half a pint; the batter should be stiff enough to hold on its surface the drops from the mixing spoon. Just before using the batter add to it the whites of the two eggs beaten to a stiff froth. This batter may be used with any kind of fruit, or with chopped oysters or clams, to make oyster and clam fritters.

FRYING MEDIUM.

Equal quantities of butter and beef suet make an excellent frying medium. Boil the beef suet in plenty of hot water, strain, melt the butter, pour the suet and butter together and let them cool. Keep in a cool, dry place.

TO RENDER LARD.

Cut the fresh lard into small pieces, let it melt slowly over a moderate fire, as it melts pour it off and strain it into small crocks,—cover with oiled paper when cold.

CHAFING DISH.

CHICKEN CREAMED.

One pint of cooked chicken, twelve mushrooms chopped fine, one tablespoonful of butter, one teaspoonful of flour, one teacupful of milk or cream. Put the butter into the blazer, when hot stir in the flour until smooth; add the milk, then let the mushrooms cook in this for five minutes; season the chicken with a little salt and pepper, add to the sauce and cook for three minutes. Serve from the chafing dish.

COLD CHICKEN OR COLD GAME.

Cut into small pieces cold cooked chicken or cold game; season with salt and pepper; put into chafing dish, one teacupful of stock; when hot, add the chicken or game, one tablespoonful of butter, and one small cup of currant jelly; as soon as the preparation is hot, serve.

CHEESE FONDUE.

Two eggs, one tablespoonful of butter, one cup of fresh milk, one cup of fine bread crumbs, two cups of grated cheese, one saltspoonful of dry mustard, a little cayenne. Put butter into the chafing dish, when melted add the milk, crumbs, cheese and stir constantly, and just before serving add two well-beaten eggs. This fondue can be cooked on the stove as well.

EGGS SCRAMBLED.

Beat the eggs together a little; add to six eggs, eight tablespoonfuls of ice-water, one saltspoonful of salt, a little pepper and one tablespoonful of butter; melt the butter in the chafing dish; when hot, put in the eggs mixed with water; stir constantly until they are cooked. Cream can be used instead of the ice-water, using four tablespoonfuls.

EGGS SCRAMBLED WITH TOMATOES.

Cook the same as for scrambled eggs, only omit the ice water, and add one cup of tomatoes.

CHOCOLATE CARAMELS, TO MAKE IN A CHAFING-DISH.

Take one-third of a cake of Baker's chocolate, two cups of granulated sugar, half a cup of sweet milk, one tablespoonful of butter, one tablespoonful vanilla. Boil all these together (excepting the vanilla), for fifteen minutes, or until the mixture on the sides of the pan becomes sugary, then pour in the vanilla, remove from the fire and pour on buttered plates. Cut into squares before the mixture is cold.

EGGS A LA GOLDEN ROD.

One dozen hard-boiled eggs, chop whites and grate yolks. Make a sauce by blending two tablespoonfuls of butter and two heaping tablespoonfuls of flour and pouring over this a pint of hot milk; when thickened stir in the chopped whites, season with salt. Have ready, rounds of toast slightly buttered; pour mixture on the toast, then sprinkle over the grated yolks. Garnish with bacon cut in ribbons, and crisped in hot spider.

FISH DINNER.
(SO CALLED.)

The following quantity of ingredients is supposed to be used for one person, doubled for two, etc., but I have found it too much; however, you can easily judge for yourself: One cooked white potato, one cooked beet (same size), one hard-boiled egg, one tablespoonful of cooked codfish, either fresh or salt, small piece of cooked carrot, one cucumber pickle, two tablespoonfuls of olive oil, according to taste, one-half tablespoonful of butter, one-half tablespoonful of flour; mix together and stir well into the mixture one teaspoonful of mixed mustard, one-half saltspoonful of cayenne pepper, one saltspoonful of salt, provided fresh fish is used. Heat together in chafing dish.

CALF'S HEAD TERRAPIN.

One pint of cold calf's head cut into small pieces, one cup of the water in which the head was cooked, one-half a a teacupful of cream, one-half teaspoonful of salt, a little cayenne, two tablespoonfuls of sherry, the yolks of two eggs, one tablespoonful of butter and one tablespoonful of flour. Put the stock into the stewpan or chafing dish ; beat the flour and butter well together and stir into the boiling stock ; stir constantly until thick and smooth ; add the meat, salt and pepper and cook for five minutes, then remove from the fire or put out the lamp of the chafing dish and add the sherry. Cold chicken, turkey, game and veal are all very good treated in this manner.

COLD ROAST BEEF.

Six slices of rare roast beef, six tablespoonfuls of tomatoes, one-half teacup of gravy, one onion chopped fine, one tablespoonful of butter, one tablespoonful of Worcestershire sauce, one teaspoonful mustard, salt and a little cayenne. Put the butter into the blazer with the onion, stew for about five minutes, then add the tomatoes and the gravy, sauce, mustard, salt and pepper; when the mixture is smooth add the beef. As soon as the beef is hot it is ready to serve. Any rare cooked meat can be treated in the same way.

LIVER.

Slice a calf's liver one-fourth of an inch in thickness, dip each slice in flour, in which mix some salt and pepper and a little cayenne. Put in the chafing dish two tablespoonfuls of butter ; when hot, put in the slices of liver, cook these for five minutes, then turn them, cook three minutes longer, then add one wine glass of sherry or port wine ; let this boil once, then serve.

LOBSTER CREAMED.

Have the meat of the lobster cut into small pieces. Put into the chafing dish one cup of cream ; rub together one teaspoonful of flour and two tablespoonfuls of butter, stir into the hot cream and boil for five minutes, then add the lobster and one saltspoonful of salt, a little cayenne, and the yolks of two eggs well beaten ; lastly, just before serving, add one glass of sherry.

MACARONI.

One-half package of macaroni or spaghetti, one-half cup of Parmesan cheese grated fine, one-half cup of melted butter. Cook the macaroni for ninety minutes. Put it into a very hot dish (silver, if possible). After it has been cooked, add salt and red pepper, spread it over the cheese and pour on the butter, mixing it well, then cover for five minutes and eat at once; it should be quite stringy.

CREAMED HAM.

Cook one cup of finely chopped boiled ham and one pint of cream together; when hot, stir in quickly, two well-beaten eggs, a little pepper; stir constantly.

CREAMED OYSTERS.

One pint of oysters; drain them. Put into the blazer one tablespoonful of flour, one tablespoonful of butter; stir these until they bubble, then add one cup of cream or milk; keep stirring until you have a thick, smooth sauce; add one pint of solid oysters, season with salt, pepper and a little grated nutmeg. Clams can be cooked in the same way.

OYSTERS WITH CELERY.

One quart of oysters; drain them from the liquor; have the chafing dish hot, put in one tablespoonful of butter; when hot, add one-half tablespoonful of flour, one-half teaspoonful of salt, one-fourth teaspoonful of pepper, one-fourth saltspoonful of cayenne. Stir together until smooth, then add one tablespoonful of celery chopped very fine and one tablespoonful of finely-chopped parsley; then the oysters; stir well, and cook until the edges of the oysters curl.

OYSTERS AND SHERRY.

Put one quart of oysters into the chafing dish with a little of their liquor, one tablespoonful of butter, three stalks of celery cut fine, a little salt and pepper; when the oysters begin to curl, add one tablespoonful of sherry wine for each portion, and one extra spoonful for the dish.

PANNED OYSTERS.

Put one tablespoonful of butter into the chafing dish; when melted, pour in one pint of oysters from which all the liquor has been drained; cook them until the edges "ruffle," then add two tablespoonfuls of sherry, a little cayenne and one saltspoonful of salt. Serve on hot buttered toast. The sherry may be omitted if desired.

SQUIZZLED OYSTERS.

Drain the oysters, have the blazer hot, put in two ounces of butter; when it is hot put in the oysters, with a little pepper and salt. As soon as the oysters are puffed, add one gill of cream; let all boil up, serve at once on hot toast.

CREAMED SWEETBREADS—1.

Two sweetbreads, cooked, cut in small pieces; one tablespoonful of butter put in blazer; when hot stir into it one tablespoonful of flour; when cooked smooth add the sweetbreads, one cup of milk or cream, a little mace, salt and pepper; cook for five minutes, serve at once.

CREAMED SWEETBREADS—2.

Two pounds of sweetbreads, parboil the sweetbreads in a little water, put them after this into cold water for a few minutes, then remove the skin and any hard parts. Put in the chafing dish one tablespoonful of butter and one tablespoonful of flour; when smooth put in two tablespoonfuls of cream, a little salt, pepper and a very little nutmeg; rub until a perfectly smooth paste; add a little cream and the yolks of two hard-boiled eggs; add the sweetbreads; cut into small pieces; let the mixture boil once. serve from the dish.

SQUABS STEWED.

Prepare two squabs as for broiling; melt two tablespoonfuls of butter in the chafing dish; when hot put in the squabs, cook for ten minutes, then turn and cook for five minutes, add one teaspoonful of salt, a little pepper and cayenne.

SALMI OF TONGUE.

Put into the chafing dish two tablespoonfuls of butter; when brown add two tablespoonfuls of flour, then add one pint of stock or water, one pint of cold tongue cut in small pieces (either salt or smoked tongue), one dozen olives, stoned and cut in pieces, pepper, salt, one tablespoonful of Worcestershire sauce. Let all boil up, then put out flame and add two tablespoonfuls of sherry or Madeira.

STEWED TOMATOES WITH EGGS.

One pint of tomatoes; as soon as the tomatoes commence to boil, add one tablespoonful of butter, some salt and pepper, then add three well beaten eggs, one small pinch of soda; as soon as the mixture has thickened pour out and serve on thin slices of toast.

VENISON STEAK.

Take two pounds of venison steak, cut into portions, about enough for each person to be served. Put into the chafing dish two tablespoonfuls of butter, one teaspoonful of salt, one teaspoonful of lemon juice, and one tablespoonful of currant jelly (the lemon juice may be omitted). Stir this mixture until it is hot, then add the venison and cook for five or six minutes,—if wanted very rare, four minutes will answer; add at the last two tablespoonfuls of port or sherry wine if desired. Slices of venison are very nice warmed in the chafing dish with the gravy left from the roast of a previous meal.

WELSH RAREBIT.

Melt one tablespoonful of butter in the chafing dish; when hot add three teacupfuls of cheese (American) cut in small pieces, a little cayenne, and about one-third of a pint of beer, or the same amount of cream; stir constantly; when melted, pour the mixture on toast. Poached eggs can be added after the cheese is melted and poured on the toast, and the mixture is then called a golden buck, one egg to each slice of toast.

BREADS, BISCUITS, ETC.

BREAD—1.

Take five quarts of flour and one tablespoonful of salt, use one cake of compressed yeast dissolved in a teacup of warm water; add two quarts of milk and water, or of milk only, or water only, warm enough to melt in it one tablespoonful of butter; mix these all well together and then let the mixture raise,—this will take from three to four hours; then knead in five additional quarts of flour thoroughly into a dough,—leave this to raise for one and one-half to two and one-half hours; then knead the dough again thoroughly and make it into loaves for baking; let it raise in the tins; when light, bake. This recipe makes twelve pounds of bread.

BREAD—2.

Sift three sifters full of flour into the bread pan, add one tablespoonful of sugar, one teaspoonful of salt, add luke warm water or milk, or half milk and half water, in which has been melted one tablespoonful of butter, one cake of compressed yeast. Stir well together, beating hard. Set to raise for two and one-half hours, or two hours; then knead until it does not adhere to the board; make into loaves, put into pans, let it raise again one hour or one and one-half hours. Bake forty-five minutes.

BOSTON BROWN BREAD.

Mix two cups of Indian meal, two cups of rye meal, one cup of sweet milk, one cup of sour milk, one cup of molasses, one teaspoonful of soda, a little salt; add soda last. Boil three hours in a mold.

BROWN BREAD.

One cup of hot water, three tablespoonfuls of molasses, a teaspoonful of salt. Stir into this enough graham flour to make a stiff mixture, add one-half cake of yeast; let all raise over night, next morning stir down the dough, and let it rise again in the pans before baking; as soon as it is light, bake : do not knead it at all.

COFFEE BREAD.

One quart of flour, one pint of milk, one-half cup of butter melted in the milk, two eggs, two-thirds of a cup of sugar, one-half a yeast cake dissolved in a little warm water, Mix together, and let it raise; when light, push it down in the pan; when again light, knead it, and add, if desired a cup of stoned raisins or currants; put into the pans and when light bake. When done pour over a little thick syrup made of sugar and water mixed.

CRACKLING BREAD.

One and one-half cups of corn meal, three-fourths of a cup of flour, one-half teaspoonful of soda, one saltspoonful of salt, sour milk enough to make the batter; stir into the batter one cupful of crackling (the little brown scraps left when lard is made). make into a loaf, and bake in a hot oven.

BREAD PUFFS.

If the bread is light at breakfast or luncheon time, have some hot lard in a deep kettle; pull up some of the dough quite thin, cut in two inch squares or lengths, drop them into the lard and fry. They are eaten at the table like biscuits, with butter.

RYE AND INDIAN BREAD.

Take one pint of Indian meal, scald it with enough boiling water to make it moist; let this remain a few minutes, then add cold water enough to make a batter; add one-half teaspoonful of salt, one-half yeast cake, dissolved in a little warm water, one-half cup of molasses, one-half teaspoonful of soda dissolved in the molasses and one pint of rye meal. Beat all together very well, put to rise over night; next morning stir the dough down and make into a loaf—put into a buttered and floured pan, sprinkle a little flour over the loaf and let it rise again; when light bake for two hours.

WHOLE WHEAT BREAD.

One pint of milk, one pint of boiling water, mix together and let it become luke warm. Then add one yeast cake dissolved in two tablespoonfuls of tepid water, one tablespoonful of salt—if home made yeast is used, take one cupful, add flour enough to make a batter, beating well for fifteen minutes, then let the batter rise; when light add flour enough to make a dough stiff enough to mold. Mold, make into loaves and let them rise, when light bake one hour.

SOUFFLE BREAD.

Three eggs; mix the yolks of the eggs with three tablespoonfuls of flour, and to this mixture add one dessertspoonful of melted butter and enough milk to make a thick batter; mix this well together, then add one teaspoonful of sugar and one saltspoonful of salt, then add the three whites beaten very light, add one teaspoonful of baking powder mixed with a teaspoonful of flour. Have the frying pan very hot, put in one tablespoonful of butter, pour in the batter which should be about as thick as sponge cake batter; cover the pan and put it on the back part of the range, if the fire is very hot; when the bread has risen very lightly, put it into the oven, removing the cover of the pan and let it brown; it will take about fifteen minutes. Turn it out of the pan carefully. Serve hot.

THIRD BREAD.

One cup of white flour, one cup of rye flour, one cup of yellow corn meal, one teaspoonful of salt, three tablespoonfuls of sugar, one-half cake compressed yeast. Mix with milk (scalded and cooled), until it is thick enough to make into a loaf, let it rise until it cracks; put into the pan, when well risen; bake one hour.

BAKING POWDER BISCUITS.

Two quarts of sifted flour, in which rub two spoonfuls of butter, or butter and lard mixed; one teaspoonful salt, and two teaspoonfuls of baking powder. Add enough milk to make a soft dough, roll the dough to half an inch in thickness and cut into small biscuits, and bake in hot oven.

SPLIT BISCUITS.

One pint of sweet milk, one egg, three tablespoonfuls of melted butter, two teaspoonfuls of sugar, one-half cake of compressed yeast. Heat the milk, but do not let it boil, pour it on the beaten egg, add melted butter, sugar, a little salt and flour enough to make a stiff sponge. Set in a warm place to rise; when light knead in flour enough to make a stiff dough; let rise again, then divide the dough into two parts and roll out separately; spread over one-half of it some melted butter so that every atom of the surface is thoroughly greased, then lay the other half over the buttered one, and roll till an inch thick. Cut in small biscuits with a tin cutter (one-fourth pound baking powder box can be used), let rise; when light, bake. Should be very light and puffy. Mix at nine in the morning if you want them for supper. Do not bake till after you begin to eat supper, so that they may be hot.

MILK BISCUITS—1.

One pint of milk, with it it put one tablespoonful of butter, one tablespoonful of sugar; heat these together, then add flour to make a batter like bread; add one-half cake of compressed yeast. Mix very soft, let this rise, then roll it out, do not knead any more. Cut into biscuits and let them rise, spread a little butter on each biscuit and bake.

MILK BISCUITS—2.

Scald one cup of milk and let it cool; then add one tablespoonful of butter, one teaspoonful of sugar (if you like them sweetened), a little salt, one-half cake of compressed yeast, about two cups of flour. Let rise two hours, then add the white of one egg beaten to a stiff froth, rise again; when light, make into biscuits; when light, bake about ten minutes in a hot oven.

SOUR MILK BISCUITS.

Two quarts of flour, four teaspoonfuls of baking powder sifted into it, then rub in one tablespoonful of butter, mix with one bowl of sour milk in which put one teaspoonful of soda dissolved in a little warm water. Have the dough as soft as it possibly can be handled · bake in a quick oven.

BUTTERED CAKES.

One pound of flour, sift this into a basin, make a hollow in the center and mix in it one cake of compressed yeast dissolved in one-half teacup of warm milk, then put the sponge to rise in a warm place; when the sponge has risen to twice its original size, add one-half tablespoonful of sugar, one-half teaspoonful of salt, four tablespoonfuls of butter, and one-half teacup of milk; mix these well into the sponge, and then add six eggs, mixing each egg separately; work these to a smooth paste and put it in a bowl, lightly covered, to rise for three hours in a warm place; then sprinkle the pasteboard with flour, place the dough on it, divide into small portions, make into small cakes, place on the baking tins one and one-half inch space between each; brush them over with egg and let them rise for one hour, then bake in hot oven; when baked, split them open without separating entirely; place a little butter in each, and serve hot.

BUCKWHEAT CAKES—1.

One quart of buckwheat flour, one tablespoonful of wheat flour, mix these into a batter with one pint of lukewarm water; dissolve one cake of compressed yeast in a little warm water and add to the batter (or one teacupful of home-made yeast can be used); add one teaspoonful of salt. Beat the batter well and put in a warm place to rise. Start the batter the noon before the cakes are needed, as it requires to rise several times and be stirred down each time to make really good cakes. Next morning if the batter is oo thick, thin it with a little warm water; add two tablespoonfuls of cream if convenient and two tablespoonfuls of molasses and one-half a teaspoonful of soda dissolved in a little warm water. Keep one cupful of the batter to start the next cakes with. In winter, batter can be kept for several weeks.

BUCKWHEAT CAKES—2.

Two quarts of hot water, enough buckwheat flour to make with the water a stiff batter. Add one-half a cup of wheat flour to the buckwheat; one saltspoonful of salt, dissolve one cake of compressed yeast in a little water, add to the batter; or one scant teacupful of home made yeast. Mix batter on the afternoon before the cakes are required for breakfast. Next morning add a spoonful of common molasses, also a spoonful of melted butter and one-half teaspoonful of soda dissolved in warm water. If the batter is too thick, thin it with either warm milk or water.

BRIOCHE.

Take of your bread sponge which is made of potatoes and no milk, as much sponge as when flour is added, will make a lump the size of a large orange; let this rise.

Put eight eggs into a basin with one pound of butter, one teaspoonful of salt, one teaspoonful of sugar; beat all these together until smooth, then add to the lump of dough as it has risen; work these together for a long time, put to rise again, work it well, put to rise the second time and work it; then the third time; make into cakes like little pin-cushions and bake in a hot oven. If the cakes are for tea, do not add the eggs until noon; keep the dough cool, add very little flour, as the secret is to keep the cakes very soft. The whole process takes seven hours.

BUNS.

One-half pound of flour in which work one-half pound of butter, then add two tablespoonfuls of sugar, a little salt, a little nutmeg. Boil one teacup of milk, in which dissolve one-third teaspoonful of soda, pour over the flour mixture, and then add two eggs well beaten, leaving out one white; when the white is well mixed, grease a baking tin and drop on the buns with a spoon and bake in a moderate oven.

ENGLISH BUNS.

Mix one and one-half pints of sweet milk and one yeast cake, dissolve in half a cup of tepid water, with flour enough to make a thick batter. Set this mixture in a warm place and let it rise over night. In the morning add one cup of sugar, half a cup of melted butter, one saltspoonful of salt, half a nutmeg grated, and just enough flour to make a batter that can be handled; knead well and let the dough rise four or five hours. Roll it out to three-quarters of an inch thick, and cut into round cakes. Lay them in rows on a buttered biscuit pan, and when the buns have stood in the pans half an hour, make a cross with a knife upon the top of each one. Place the pans in a moderate oven and bake the buns a light brown. Beat the white of an egg stiff and add to the egg a little powdered sugar, and lightly cover the tops of the buns when they are taken from the oven.

ENGLISH HOT CROSS BUNS.

Sift into a large bowl one quart of flour, half a cup of sugar and one-half a teaspoonful of salt; dissolve one-fourth of a cup of butter in a generous half pint of warm milk, and add to the dry ingredients, with the yolks of two beaten eggs; add half a yeast cake dissolved in a little water, half a nutmeg grated and the whites of the two eggs beaten stiff; this should make a very soft dough; cover the bowl with a clean cloth, place it where it will keep warm, and let it rise over night. In the morning take pieces of the dough the size of an egg, and with a little flour, mold them into round cakes an inch in thickness. Place them on a buttered tin, leaving a little space between. Cover the tins and set in a warm place for the buns to rise; they should be double their original size. With a sharp knife cut a cross in the center of each bun. Bake them in a moderate oven about a half hour. When the buns are baked brush the tops with a syrup made of sugar and water.

BUNS FOR GOOD FRIDAY.

Two quarts of flour, one quart of warm milk, one-fourth pound of butter, one-half cup of yeast. Mix and let raise four hours, then add four eggs, one-half pound of sugar, one teacup of currants, let all rise in the dough for two hours; when very light, cut them into small buns; brush the tops with a little mixed milk and molasses. Let the buns rise after they are made into small one. Bake twenty minutes.

KARLSBADEN KIPFEL (Buns).

One and one-eighth pounds of flour, one gill of sweet milk, one-half a yeast cake, dissolved in a little warm water; make these into a sponge and let it rise; when it has risen, add one teaspoonful of salt and enough flour to make a dough; work this until it is very light, then add six ounces of butter, work this into the dough, let it raise for fifteen minutes, then make the dough into small buns; put them on the baking tin and let them rise; when light, bake in a moderate oven.

Karlsbad Rolls are made in the same manner, only two and one-half ounces of butter are added to the dough, making eight and one-half ounces in all.

CORN AND RICE PONE.

One cup of milk, two eggs, one and one-half cups of boiled rice, one and one-half cups of corn meal, one teaspoonful of sugar, one saltspoonful of salt, one and one-half tablespoonfuls of melted butter. Beat the rice into the milk until the grains are well separated, then stir this mixture into the corn meal, beat until perfectly smooth, then add the eggs well beaten, then the salt, butter and sugar. Bake twenty minutes.

VIRGINIA CORN CAKE.

Sift into a large pan one quart of corn meal. Boil one pint of milk, pour over the meal with one-fourth pound of butter and one saltspoon of salt, stir these well together and let all cool. Then beat four eggs very light and when the mixture is cool, stir them into it. Bake in shallow tins, in a hot oven for twenty minutes. Serve hot.

ASH CAKES—VIRGINIA.

Wet corn meal with enough water to make a soft dough, add a little salt, let it stand for an hour or so and then make into small cakes; put these on the clean hot hearth and cover with hot wood ashes—it will take about an hour to bake them. Dust off the ashes before serving.

CORN MEAL BREAD.

Two cups of wheat flour, one cup of corn meal, one cup of sweet milk, four eggs, one teaspoonful of salt, two tablespoonfuls of sugar, four tablespoonfuls of butter-melted, three teaspoonfuls of baking powder; beat the eggs until light

CORN CAKE.

Have a hot oven, Scald one large teacup of corn meal with one pint of milk, add butter the size of a walnut, add a little salt while the mush is hot; when it is cold add the yolks of four eggs, then the whites. Bake twenty minutes. Beat the whites very light and stir into the mixture gently.

CORN MEAL CAKES—1.

One pint of corn meal, scald it with hot water (about one cupful), add one tablespoonful of butter, one saltspoonful of salt, two eggs well beaten, and a very small cup of cream; grease a tin pan and bake the mixture as jumbles or drop cakes.

CORN MEAL CAKES—2.

One cup of corn meal, one cup of boiling water, one tablespoonful of butter, a pinch of salt; stir meal into the boiling water, add the butter and salt, spread the mixture on a buttered tin very thin, bake in a hot oven.

CUSTARD BREAD—VIRGINIA.

Two cups of cold boiled rice, one cup of corn meal, two eggs, two tablespoonfuls of melted butter, salt, enough milk to make it all a very soft batter. Bake one-half hour.

VIRGINIA CORN MUFFINS.

Three eggs, three teacups of flour, three teacups of corn meal, three tablespoonfuls of melted butter and lard (half butter and half lard is best), one saltspoonful of salt, one small teaspoonful of soda dissolved in a little warm water, enough sour milk to mix the whole into a thick batter, but not stiff enough to drop from the spoon. Bake in small rings or tins in the oven. This same recipe made thinner makes very nice waffles.

CORN PONE.

Two coffeecups of meal, one quart of milk, four eggs, one tablespoonful of melted butter, one teaspoonful of salt, one teaspoonful of sugar. Beat the eggs thoroughly, add butter, sugar, salt and meal. Scald the milk, pour hot over the mixture. Pour at once into the "Turk's Head" or pan. Bake quickly.

CRUMPETS.

One pint of milk, one teaspoonful of salt, four ounces of butter, one-half yeast cake, three cups of flour. Scald the milk, let it stand until luke warm, then add salt, then flour; beat vigorously, then the butter melted, then the yeast: beat again, cover and stand in a warm place until very light. Grease the rings, place on a hot griddle, fill each ring one-half full. Bake until brown, then turn. When wanted, toast on both sides, butter nicely and serve on a hot plate.

DROP FRITTERS.

One pint of boiling milk, one pint of flour, three eggs, salt. Pour the boiling milk on the flour, beat until very smooth, add salt, when cool add the eggs beaten separately. Drop by spoonfuls into hot deep fat and fry.

GRIDDLE CAKES OF STALE BREAD.

To one pint of stale bread crumbs add one quart of boiling milk, one tablespoonful of melted butter, one teaspoonful of salt. Soak the crumbs in the milk, then beat the mixture until it is smooth, add the yolks of two eggs, then enough flour to make the batter stiff enough to bake, sift into the flour two teaspoonfuls of baking powder, then add the two whites beaten light. Have your griddle very hot and greased with a slice of salt pork.

VIRGINIA HOE CAKE.

Three eggs, one cup of corn meal, one pint of milk, wo tablespoonfuls of melted lard or butter, one teaspoonful of salt; mix these all well together, have your griddle hot. butter slightly; bake the mixture in large cakes, turn and brown. In making hoe cake, beat the meal and milk together for at least ten minutes before adding the eggs, etc.

LAPLAND CAKES.

Lapland cakes are a peculiar, delicate, delicious cake of the popover kind. They are made with a much larger quantity of eggs than the ordinary wheat popovers. Beat the yolks of five eggs thoroughly with the patent egg-beater and stir them into a pint of sweet cream. Do not use a heavy cream for this purpose, but a light quality. Pour the mixture on a pint and a quarter of pastry flour sifted with half a teaspoonful of salt; beat the batter well with a patent egg-beater and fold in carefully the whites of five eggs beaten to a stiff froth. Fill buttered cups of stoneware half full and bake the cakes three-quarters of an hour in a quick oven.

MUFFINS.

One pint of milk, one-half cake of yeast, two tablespoonfuls of butter, one teaspoonful of salt, about three cups of flour. Scald the milk, add butter and salt. When luke warm, add yeast dissolved in one-fourth cup of luke warm water. Stir in enough flour to make a thick batter, cover well; put in a warm place; let rise two and one-half hours, then stir and put a big spoonful in greased muffin rings about half full. Turn when brown. Then split and toast and butter well—you can do this the next day, for the ones left.

RYE MEAL MUFFINS.

Two cups of rye meal, one-half cup of molasses, one teaspoonful of salaratus dissolved in one cup of sour milk, one egg well beaten; bake in muffin rings.

QUICK WHEAT FLOUR MUFFINS.

One large tablespoonful of butter, two cups of sweet milk, four whites of eggs, one teaspoonful of baking powder, two cups of flour, a little salt. Bake in muffin rings on the griddle, which has been rubbed with a little butter, the griddle must be hot; turn the muffins with cake turner.

CORN MEAL MUSH.

One quart of boiling water; stir into this one and one-fourth pints of corn meal mixed smooth with one pint of cold water, two tablespoonfuls of salt; stir until the mush is well cooked. If required for fried mush, fill little cans (those that come with baking powder in them are very nice), as the mush can then be cut in round slices for frying; when cold, slice; dip each slice in bread crumbs and beaten egg and fry in deep, hot fat.

ADIRONDACK PANCAKES.

One quart of sour milk, add flour enough to make a thick batter. Let this stand twenty-four hours; add then two eggs well beaten, a little salt, one-half teaspoonful of soda, dissolve soda in one tablespoonful of warm water; bake on hot, greased griddle.

PAN-CAKES.

One quart of sour milk, one-half teaspoonful of soda, one teaspoonful of salt, four eggs; stir together, thicken with flour until a good batter is made, then stir in the yolks of the eggs well beaten, and then the whites beaten stiff, add the whites very carefully. For waffles, same batter, only add two tablespoonfuls of melted butter.

POPOVERS—1.

Pastry flour is the most desirable, but the best bread flour will do. Sift two cups of flour with half a teaspoonful of salt. Add gradually two cups of milk, and when a smooth batter has been obtained mix in two eggs without separating the whites and yolks. Add a teaspoonful of butter, melted. Beat the batter thoroughly; pour it at once into the cups of stoneware, well buttered. Do not fill the cups more than half full. Bake the cakes in a quick oven until, true to their name, they rise far above the edges of the cups and hang over them in a rich, brown crust. These cakes are nice for breakfast when served with either maple syrup or cream sauce; or may be eaten like a muffin, with butter. They are often served as a plain dessert with sweetened cream.

POPOVERS—2.

One pint of milk, one pint of flour, two eggs. Beat eggs separately and add milk and flour; mix thoroughly and add one saltspoonful of salt. Bake in small pans, and fill half full; the pans must be hot when the mixture is put in.

GRAHAM POPOVERS.

Half a pint of sifted Graham flour, half a pint of sifted wheat flour, one tablespoonful of sugar, half a teaspoonful of salt, and a teaspoonful of butter, melted. Beat the whites and yolks together and beat the batter vigorously with a patent egg-beater. Pour the batter into buttered cups of stoneware. They should rise, like all popovers, to four times their original size. If they are baked in an ordinary muffin pan or even in a heated iron gem pan, they will not rise in this way. Wheat popovers are light and about double in bulk baked in gem pans; in stone cups they are four times the bulk.

RYE POPOVERS.

Rye meal from which Boston brown bread is made, is used, not rye flour. Mix an even cup and a half of rye meal with an even cup of wheat flour; add a tablespoonful of sugar and half a teaspoonful of salt. Pour over these dry ingredients a pint of milk, mixing it to a smooth batter. Add three eggs, whites and yolks together. Beat the batter thoroughly and pour into a dozen stoneware cups well buttered. Bake the cakes in an oven that is very hot for the first twenty minutes; then reduce the heat and bake them from twenty to thirty minutes longer.

PARKER HOUSE ROLLS.

Two quarts of flour, one teaspoonful of salt, one-half cake of yeast, one-fourth teacup of sugar, one-half teacup of lard, one pint of milk. Boil the milk, melt it in the lard, sift the flour into a deep basin, make a hole in the center, stir in the yeast, dissolved in a little water, then put in the milk after it is cool; let it stand over night without mixing; in the morning mix well and let it rise, and when light, work it together again; when light, roll out the dough until one-half inch thick, cut into biscuits or rolls, fold together and let them rise again.

STEPHAINE ROLLS.

One pint of milk, boiled and made into a custard with three eggs; one tablespoonful of sugar. Let all cool, then add one and one-half pints of flour, one-half cup of yeast; when it rises, add one tablespoonful of melted butter, one and one-half pints more flour, teaspoonful of salt; let rise again, roll out, bake one-half hour.

RYE PUFFS FOR BREAKFAST.

Add a cupful and a half of milk to one egg, whipped up in a tablespoonful of sugar; stir in two cupfuls of rye flour, thoroughly mixed with half a cupful of wheat flour. Into this flour put one and one-half teaspoonfuls of baking powder, sifted three times with the flour. Beat the batter hard for a minute before pouring it into the greased gem pans. Bake in a quick oven.

RICE CRUMPETS.

Scald a pint of milk and when luke warm add half a cake of compressed yeast, dissolved in half a cup of water; stir in a cup of freshly-cooked rice that has been well beaten while warm to break the grains; four ounces of melted butter, salt and three half pints of sifted flour; beat hard, cover and stand in a warm place until light. They will require not more than three hours to rise. Grease large muffin rings and bake on hot griddle. Butter and serve quickly.

RAISED SCONES.

Take dough prepared for raised biscuits; when light, roll about an inch thick, sprinkle thickly with currants, pressing them into the dough. Bake in a round tin; score almost through the dough in four parts and slightly wet these cuttings to prevent their adhering. Pour melted sugar on the outside.

SCONES.

Make a soda biscuit dough, roll out to one inch in thickness, cut in four parts nearly to the bottom, sprinkle over currants or very small raisins, put melted sugar on top. Eat either hot or cold.

SHORT CAKES.
HAM OR OYSTERS.

One pint flour, two teaspoonfuls baking powder, one-half teaspoonful salt; wet with milk just so that the dough can be rolled out, and add two tablespoonfuls of melted butter; mix this in well, then put on a floured board and divide; roll out thin in two parts the size of a pie plate, spread each part with a little melted butter, put them together and bake in a quick oven for twenty minutes. Separate the cakes, and serve either creamed ham on the lower cake or oysters, cover with the other half.

SODA BISCUIT.

One quart of flour, two teaspoonfuls of baking powder, a lump of butter and lard the size of an egg, one pint of milk. Rub the butter and lard into the flour, add one teaspoonful of salt, then put in the milk gradually, roll out the dough about an inch thick, cut with small biscuit cutter and bake in hot oven for ten minutes; the quicker the biscuits are put together, the lighter they will be.

SALLY LUNN.

One large cup of mashed potatoes, one pint of milk, one pint of water, four eggs, one piece of butter the size of a walnut, a little salt, two tablespoonfuls of yeast. Mix to a thick batter and let rise before baking.

TEA CAKES.

Two pounds of flour, one-fourth pound of shortening (butter or lard), one cake of yeast, one egg beaten into the dissolved yeast. Make into dough, with warm milk; let rise. Make into flat cakes, let them rise, then bake in hot oven.

BOSTON TEA CAKES.

Two cups of flour, two eggs, one cup of sweet milk, one tablespoonful of melted butter, one teaspoonful of soda, two teaspoonfuls of cream tartar. Mix and bake quickly.

WAFFLES WITH RICE.

One quart of flour, one quart of sour milk, one teaspoonful of soda, four eggs, one tablespoonful of melted butter, three tablespoonfuls of boiled rice. Put the flour in a bowl, stir into it the milk, in which dissolve the soda, then add the melted butter, then the eggs well beaten, lastly add the rice. Have the waffle iron hot and greased with a little piece of salt pork. Sweet milk can be used, the soda omitted and one teaspoonful of baking powder substituted.

RAISED WAFFLES.

One pint of rich, sweet milk, warm; mix enough flour into the milk to make a batter as thick as for griddle cakes, add one-half cake of yeast dissolved in a little warm water, one-half teaspoonful of salt; beat well and let the mixture rise over night; do not stir it in the morning, but bake in hot, greased waffle irons.

VIRGINIA WAFFLES—1.

One teaspoonful of salt, one-half pint of flour, one pint of sweet milk, two eggs, one teaspoonful of baking powder;

stir milk and yolks together (beat the eggs separately), then add slowly the flour, in which sift the baking powder; lastly, fold in the beaten whites. Have waffle irons hot and greased with a bit of salt pork or butter.

VIRGINIA WAFFLES—2.

One quart of sour milk or buttermilk, one-fourth pound of melted butter, six eggs, two cups of flour, one teaspoonful of soda, one teaspoonful of salt. Put the milk into a bowl, add the butter melted, then the flour gradually, dissolve the soda in the milk, add the eggs well beaten, then the salt, beat all well together; have the waffle iron hot and greased with a little piece of salt pork.

YEAST—1.

Three large potatoes, cook them in one quart of water, when cooked mash very fine, put with them one-half cup of white sugar, two tablespoonfuls of salt, a little cold water, add one-third cake of compressed yeast; when the quart of water has cooled, add the potatoes, etc. Set in a cool place in summer, a warm place in winter. It will be ready for use in twenty-four hours. When fresh yeast is needed, and you already have some liquid yeast, one teacup of the liquid is used in place of the compressed yeast.

YEAST—2.

Five potatoes, boil until tender in one quart of water; boil one handful of hops for a few minutes, put them into hot potato water; mash, strain over enough flour to make a good batter; when cool add two yeast cakes well dissolved, two tablespoonfuls of salt, two tablespoonfuls of sugar, one tablespoonful of ginger. Use one-half teacupful for bread.

CAKES.

GENERAL DIRECTIONS FOR CAKE MAKING.

All materials for cake must be of the very best. Before commencing, see that the oven is right for properly baking the cake—one very good test for the right heat, is to place in the mouth of the oven a little flour; if it browns in five minutes, the heat is right. Another is to hold the bare hand without being inconvenienced in the oven for one second; if the oven is too hot the cake will rise and then fall; if a piece of white paper colors a light brown in five minutes after it is put in the oven, the oven is right for all rich cakes. Cake made without butter, or with very little butter, requires a hotter oven than a rich cake; thin cakes require a hot oven. Never jar the oven while the cake is baking. Before commencing to mix the batter, have all the materials ready; the pans greased, the flour sifted twice, the granulated sugar sifted, the eggs counted and separated. First cream the butter, and add to it the sugar gradually. When these are light add the yolks well beaten. Where there is not enough butter to make the mixture creamy, add a part of the yolks, and after, the balance. Then add the milk, then the flour, measured after sifting, and in it sift the baking powder, then add the flavoring and one saltspoonful of salt; lastly the whites beaten until stiff. These should be folded into the batter. In mixing cake an upward beating motion is better than stirring, as more air is introduced into the mixture. If the cake is not to be iced, a thin sprinkle of powdered sugar over the batter, just before baking, and when in tins will give a smooth surface. Sponge cake should have coarse granulated sugar sprinkled over the batter. To know if the cake is done stick a broom straw into the cake, if it comes out clean, the cake is done. All fruit should be lightly floured, and stirred into the batter at the last.

MEASUREMENTS.

Exactness in measuring is absolutely necessary.

When a receipt calls for a "cupful of anything," it means one-half a pint, tin measures holding just this amount can be purchased at any house furnishing store.

Loaf cakes require about an hour to bake. Layer cakes and small cakes about twenty-five minutes.

ALMOND CAKE.
ONE HOUR TO BAKE.

One pound of flour, one pound of sugar, one pound of seeded raisins chopped, three-fourth pound of butter, one cup of thin sour cream, four eggs, one nutmeg, rind and juice of one lemon, one teaspoonful of cloves, one teaspoonful of soda, one wine glass of wine or brandy, one cup of almonds blanched and chopped fine. Beat butter and sugar together, add the milk eggs beaten separately, spices, lemon, cream, soda, dissolved in a little warm water; the wine, flour and almonds. Bake in three tins; when baked, ice with the following mixture: Two eggs, whites only, the juice of one lemon, one cocoanut grated, one pound of raisins, one cup of blanched and chopped almonds; beat the eggs with one-half teacup of sugar, add the lemon juice then add a little more sugar—just enough to enable you to spread the mixture on the cakes; then put on this frosting the grated cocoanut, then a layer of the raisins, put the raisins into boiling water a minute before using them; then a layer of the almonds, then a layer of the frosting.

ANGEL CAKE.
ONE HOUR TO BAKE.

Beat the whites of eleven eggs to a stiff froth; sift into them a little at a time, ten ounces, or one and one-half tumblers of powdered sugar, mixing carefully and lightly then sift five ounces, or one tumbler of flour four times, add a level teaspoonful of cream of tartar to the flour, sift it again, and then sift into the eggs and sugar a little at a time, mixing it carefully and lightly; when all the flour is used, add a teaspoonful of vanilla essence to the cake and put it into a new tin cake pan or mold, not buttered or lined. Bake it in a moderate oven about three-quarters of an hour, testing it with a broom straw; when the straw comes out clean, the cake is done. Let the cake cool gradually in the mouth of the oven with the door open. When the cake is quite cold loosen it from the sides of the pan with a knife and turn it out. The success of this delicious depends upon preserving its lightness. If the eggs are beaten quite stiff, and the flour and sugar very carefully sifted and stirred in, it will be light. Do not open the oven for fifteen minutes after the cake has been put into it.

BLACK CAKE.

Bake Black Cake in a porcelain baking dish, if possible. The cake baked in a tin often becomes very dry and hard outside, from the long time necessary to properly bake it.

Put into the crock with black cake, a thick slice of bread; when very stale, another slice; this will keep the black cake fresh and moist.

BLACK CAKE—1.

One pound of sugar, one pound of butter, one pound of flour, four pounds of raisins, four pounds of currants, one pound of citron, twelve eggs, two wine glasses of wine, two wine glasses of brandy, one tablespoonful of cloves, cinnamon, molasses, one nutmeg. Bake three hours.

Mix the butter and sugar together until light, then add the yolks of the eggs beaten light, then the flour, then the whites beaten very stiff, then the fruit (retain a little of the flour to sprinkle over the fruit), then the spice and liquor.

BLACK CAKE—2.

Five pounds of raisins stoned, three pounds of currants, two pounds of citron chopped fine, one pound of butter, one pound of sugar, one pound of flour, ten eggs, two ounces of cinnamon, three nutmegs, one ounce of cloves, one ounce of mace, two glasses of whiskey, two glasses of wine. This recipe makes three loaves; bake four hours. Mix the butter and sugar together until light, then add the yolks of the eggs beaten light, then the flour, then the whites beaten very stiff, then the fruit (retain a little of the flour to sprinkle over the fruit), then the spice and liquor.

CARAMEL CAKE.

Make a custard of eight tablespoonsfuls of grated chocolate, yolk of one egg, one-half cup of sweet milk, one cup of sugar; boil all together and add one tablespoonful of vanilla when cold.

PART SECOND.

One cup of brown sugar, one-half cup of butter; yolks of two eggs, one-half cup of sweet milk, two and one-half cups of flour, two teaspoonfuls of baking powder; beat well together, and then add the custard and beaten whites of three eggs. Bake in layers and put together with caramel filling.

CARAMEL FILLING.

Three cups of brown sugar, two cups of cream, two tablespoonfuls of butter; cook until thick, and try in water. Water can be used instead of cream.

BREAD CAKE.

One cup of butter, two cups of powdered sugar; work these together until very light, then add two tablespoonfuls sweet cream, three eggs well beaten. Take two cups of very light bread dough, work into it with your hand until all is mixed smoothly, the above mixture, then add one pound of stoned raisins, one-half teaspoonful of cloves, one teaspoonful of cinnamon, one-half a nutmeg, one small teaspoonful of soda dissolved in a little water, one glass of brandy; let all raise twenty minutes before baking.

BLUEBERRY OR WORTLEBERRY CAKES.

One-half cup of butter, one and one-half cups of sugar, four cups of flour, one cup of milk, two eggs, one teaspoonful of saleratus, two teaspoonfuls of cream of tartar, two cups of berries. Mix butter and sugar together, add the eggs beaten together, then the milk, then the saleratus dissolved in a little milk, then the flour, in which sift the cream of tartar, lastly add the blue berries. Bake in a shallow tin and serve warm.

BRANDY SNAPS.

One pound of flour, three-fourths pound of sugar, one pint of molasses, five ounces of butter, one-fourth ounce of powdered ginger. Make the molasses hot, melt the butter in it, mix the flour, ginger and sugar in a basin, stir the molasses and butter into it. Leave this mixture until the next day, then roll out very thin, cut into rounds, and bake on well-floured tin.

CHOCOLATE CUSTARD CAKE.

Break two eggs in a large cup, and fill the cup with cream, and beat well together. Mix one cup of sugar, one tablespoonful of butter, one and one-half cups of flour, two teaspoonfuls of baking powder, well together, then add the cream and eggs, bake in two tins, like jelly cake; when baked put between the layers a thick chocolate custard.

For the custard take half pint of milk, one square of chocolate grated, one teaspoonful of cornstarch, two eggs, put the milk in the double boiler; when boiling add the cornstarch dissolved and a little cold milk, the eggs well-beaten, half a saltspoonful of salt, and the chocolate; stir carefully; when thick remove from fire, add half teaspoonful of vanilla. When cold, spread on the cake.

CHOCOLATE CAKE.

One cup of butter, two cups of sugar, three cups of flour, one cup of milk, six eggs, whites only, three teaspoonfuls baking powder, one teaspoonful vanilla. Mix the butter and sugar together until very light, then add the beaten whites, then the flour and baking powder, and the milk and vanilla, bake in jelly cake tins.

CHOCOLATE FILLING.

One-half cake of bakers' chocolate, one-half pint of milk, one egg, two cups of sugar; stir the grated chocolate melted, into the milk, then the sugar and egg; let it thicken on the fire. When cool, spread on the cake.

CHOCOLATE COOKIES.

Two and one-half cups of powdered sugar, three-fourths cup of flour, one bar Bakers' chocolate melted, four eggs, one and one-half teaspoonfuls of baking powder; bake in long pan in a slow oven and when done, cut into squares. When spreading the batter it will facilitate matters to wet the knife frequently in hot water to prevent the dough adhering to it. The cookies are better the second day.

CLOVE CAKE.

One and one-fourth pounds of flour, one pound of sugar, one-half pound of butter, one teaspoonful of soda, four eggs, one teacup of cream, one tablespoonful of cloves, two tablespoonfuls of cinnamon, one tablespoonful of nutmeg, two wine glasses of wine. Mix the butter and sugar together, then the yolks well beaten, then the cream and soda, then the flour, spices, wine and flour. Bake one hour.

COCOANUT CAKE.

One pound of grated cocoanut, one pound of sugar, one-half pound of butter, one-half pound of flour, six eggs, two teaspoonfuls of baking powder; mix butter and sugar together, until light; then add the yolks, well beaten, then the flour, in which put the baking powder; then add the grated cocoanut; lastly the whites beaten until stiff; bake in shallow tins, ice when cold; reserve one-fourth of the cocoanut to put into the icing.

CUP CAKE.

One cup of butter, two cups of sugar, three cups of flour, four eggs, one cup milk, two teaspoonfuls of baking powder, one nutmeg, two tablespoonfuls of brandy; beat butter and sugar together, add the eggs; then the milk, powder, spice, flour, brandy.

LITTLE CUP CAKES.

One cup of sugar, one-fourth cup of butter, two eggs, one-half cup of milk, one and one half cups of flour, one teaspoonful of baking powder, a little salt, flavor with vanilla or lemon. Beat butter and sugar together, add the yolks, then the milk, then one-half the flour with the baking powder, then the whites well beaten, with the balance of the flour; bake in little tins, and ice the cakes.

CUSTARD CAKE.

Seven tablespoonfuls melted butter, two cups of sugar, one-half cup of flour, two teaspoonfuls baking powder, one-half cup of corn-starch, one-half cup of milk, four eggs, juice of one lemon. Mix butter and sugar together, add the yolks well beaten, then add the flour in which you put the baking powder, then add corn starch, then the milk, then the whites well beaten, then the lemon. Bake in jelly cake tins.

CUSTARD FOR CAKE.

One cup sweet milk, two tablespoonfuls sugar, one tablespoonful corn-starch, two eggs, flavor with vanilla. Make the custard in a double boiler; when cool, put on the cake layers.

COLD WATER CAKE.

One cup of butter, two cups of sugar, three and three-fourths cups of flour, two cups of raisins chopped fine, one cup of cold water, three eggs, one teaspoonful of cloves, one teaspoonful of soda sifted into the flour. Stir butter and sugar together, then add the spices, then the yolks, then the flour, then the water, last of all the whites, beaten very light. Bake one and one-half hours.

COOKIES.

Mix a scant teaspoonful of soda with one-half a nutmeg into three-fourths of a cup of butter, and four cups of flour. Mix together until light, one and one-half cups of sugar and three eggs, add the flour and butter. Flour the board, roll out the mixture very thin and cut into rounds with the cutter.

CORN-STARCH CAKE.

One-half pound of corn-starch, one-half pound of flour, one-half pound of butter, one pound of sugar, six eggs, one-half teaspoonful of soda, one teaspoonful of cream tartar, one small cup of milk. Dissolve soda in a little vinegar, mix butter and sugar together until light, then add the yolks well beaten, then the milk, then the flour, then the corn-starch; put the cream of tartar into the flour, then add the soda, lastly fold in the whites, which should be very light.

CRULLERS.

Four eggs beaten separately, one cup of milk or cream, one cup of butter, two cups of sugar; mix the butter and sugar together, put one teaspoonful of soda in the milk and two of cream of tartar in the flour. Use flour sufficient to roll out one-third of an inch in thickness. Fry in hot, deep lard.

SOUR CREAM CAKE.

One cup sour cream, one and one-half cups sugar, three cups flour, one small teaspoonful of soda, three eggs; mix all together quickly and bake.

DELICATE CAKE.

Two cups powdered sugar, one-half cup butter, three cups flour, three-fourths cup milk, two teapoonfuls baking powder, six eggs—whites only. Cream the butter and sugar together, then add the milk, then the flour, in which put the baking powder, lastly the eggs; flavor with either lemon or almond extract.

DEVIL CAKE.

One cup of grated chocolate, two-thirds cup of dark brown sugar, one-half a cup of sweet milk, one egg—yolk only; mix these together and cook in the saucepan until thick, then cool and add one teaspoonful of vanilla. Take one cup of brown sugar, one-half a cup of milk, one-half a cup of butter, two eggs, two cups of flour, one spoonful of soda, dissolved in the milk; beat butter and sugar together, add the milk, eggs and flour, then add the cream mixture (when it is cool), and bake in square shallow tins; when baked, ice it with an icing made as follows: Two cups of coffee sugar, one-fourth cake of chocolate, one cup of boiling water, one-half a tablespoonful of butter; boil these together until the mixture thickens a little, then remove from the stove and stir until it is thick enough to spread nicely over the cakes; place the two layers together.

SOFT GINGER BREAD.

One and one-half teacupfuls of molasses, one-half teacupful of brown sugar, one-half teacupful of sour cream, one-half teacupful of sour milk, one-half teaspoonful of salt, two teaspoonfuls of soda, one teaspoonful of ginger, one teaspoonful of cinnamon, one egg, beaten well, flour enough to make a batter, not a stiff batter. Mix all well together and bake in shallow tins.

GINGER SNAPS.

Let one cup of molasses come to a boil, then add one teaspoonful of soda, let this cool. Mix one cup of butter, three-fourths cup of sugar, two eggs, well beaten together; add the molasses and two tablespoonfuls of water, one teaspoonful of cinnamon, two tablespoonfuls of ginger, one-half teaspoonful of cloves, one-half teaspoonful of allspice, add enough flour to the mixture so that it can be rolled out very thin; cut into rounds with cutter.

GOLD CAKE.

One cup of sugar, three-fourths cup of butter, two cups flour, one-fourth cup of milk, one teaspoonful of baking powder, eight eggs—yolks only. Beat sugar and butter together, add the yolks, then the milk, then the flour, in which sift the baking powder and a little nutmeg.

DROP CAKES.

One pound of flour, take out three tablespoonfuls, one pound of sugar, one-fourth pound of butter, one-fourth pound currants, two gills of sweet milk, one and one-half teaspoonfuls of baking powder, five eggs. Cream the butter and sugar, add one-half the milk, the yolks beat well, then the rest of the milk, then the flour in which the baking powder should be sifted, then the whites of the eggs, a little salt. Butter a large pan, drop the batter on in teaspoonfuls, sprinkle some currants on each one and bake; as these little cakes run together, they must be broken apart when taken from the oven. The batter for these cakes will keep a week in a cool place.

DOUGHNUTS.

One scant cup of butter, one and one-half cups of sugar, beat these together until light, then add two cups of milk, two eggs beaten light, and half of a yeast cake dissolved in a little water, half a nutmeg grated and flour enough to make a dough. Let the dough rise; it must be as soft as it can be handled. When light, roll it out to half an inch in thickness, cut into small balls; let these rise, then fry in deep, hot fat.

FEDERAL CAKE.

One pound of flour, one pound of sugar, one-half pound butter, one pound of fruit, one cup of sour milk, one teaspoonful of soda, one gill of wine, one gill of brandy, four eggs, one nutmeg; one pound of blanched almonds can be used in place of fruit. Mix butter and sugar together, add the milk, the flour, the eggs, spiced wine, soda, dissolved in a little warm water, then the flour.

FIG CAKE.

Two cups of sugar, one cup of butter, one cup of sweet milk, three cups of flour, one pound of sliced figs, two teaspoonfuls of baking powder, eight eggs (whites only); flavor with vanilla, a little salt. Take some of the flour to sprinkle over the figs. Mix butter and sugar together, add the milk, then the flour, in which sift the baking powder, then the whites beaten stiff, then the figs and vanilla.

FRIED CAKES.

Two well beaten eggs, one small tablespoonful of melted butter or lard, one cup of sugar, one pint of sweet milk, one quart of flour, three teaspoonfuls of baking powder. Mix the butter and sugar together, add the eggs, the milk, the flour, in which the baking powder is to be sifted; fry in very hot lard.

WHITE FRUIT CAKE.

Cream one pound of butter and one pound of powdered sugar together; add the beaten yolks of ten eggs and one pound of sifted flour with two teaspoonfuls of baking powder. Slice one and one-half pounds of citron; let it stand in a warm room for several hours. Blanch a pound of almonds and grate one cocoanut; add to the batter, with the stiffly beaten whites of the eggs. Line a cake pan with greased paper, turn in the mixture and set in a moderate oven. Bake slowly for two hours; when cold, ice with cocoanut frosting.

IMPERIAL FILLING FOR WHITE, CUP OR POUND CAKE, BAKED IN LAYERS.

One cup sour cream, half cup of powdered sugar, one teaspoonful of vanilla, or sherry, one pound of blanched almonds chopped fine. Whip the cream and the sugar, a little at a time, add the flavoring; put this mixture between the cake layers.

HICKORY NUT CAKE.

One and one-half cups of sugar, one-half cup of butter, three-fourths cup of milk, two cups of flour, whites of four eggs, two teaspoonfuls of baking powder, one cup of hickory nuts. Beat butter and sugar together until light, then add the milk; then the flour, in which sift the baking powder; then add the whites beaten until stiff, last the hickory nuts; bake in two shallow pans.

HERMITS.

One and one-half cups of sugar, one cup of butter. Sugar and butter stirred to a cream, three eggs well beaten together, one-half cup New Orleans molasses, one teaspoonful of soda, dissolved in two teaspoonfuls of cold water, one cup of seeded and chopped raisins, one cup of currants, one teaspoonful of mixed spices, cinnamon, nutmeg. Bake in small cakes by dropping in spoonfuls on a buttered tin.

SOFT ICING.

One-half pound of powdered, sifted sugar, one tablespoonful of boiling water, one tablespoonful of fruit juice. Must spread at once on cake.

ICING FOR CAKE.

White of an egg, one tablespoonful of lemon juice, one tablespoonful of vanilla, one cup of powdered sugar. Mix together and spread on the cake.

BOILED ICING.

One cup of granulated sugar, one-half cup of boiling water, boil from five to ten minutes or until the sugar spins; beat the white of one egg very light, add the boiling sugar slowly, and keep beating for at least five minutes to insure smoothness.

LEMON ICING.

The juice of one lemon, stir into it powdered sugar enough to form a soft paste. Spread on the cake.

JUMBLES.

One-half pound of butter, one pound of sugar, three eggs, a little salt, flour enough to make a paste that will roll out very thin. Beat butter and sugar together until light, then add the eggs, salt and flour. Cut with cutter with a hollow center.

JELLY CAKE.

One cup melted butter, three cups of sugar, one cup sweet milk, four and one-half cups flour, six eggs. Stir butter and sugar together, add the milk, then the yolks well beaten, then the flour, then the whites. Bake in tins, and when the layers are cold spread each layer with jelly.

LAYER CAKE.

One-half cup of butter, two cups of sugar, one cup of sweet milk, three scant cups of flour, three eggs, three teaspoonfuls of baking powder; bake in four layers. Put whipped cream on each layer. Beat the butter and sugar together until very light, then add the yolks well beaten, then the milk, in which dissolve the soda, then the flour, in which sift the cream of tartar; lastly, add the whites well beaten and the lemon juice.

LADY FINGERS

One pound of sugar, ten eggs, one-half pound of flour, one lemon; beat the yolks of the eggs and the sugar together until the mixture looks foamy and creamy, then add one-half of the whites beaten very stiffly; then add the flour, then the balance of the whites, then the lemon juice. Bake in quick oven. For the lady fingers, pour the above mixture into a pastry boat, or on brown paper, three inches apart; dust with granulated sugar. To remove, wet the back of the paper.

LADY CAKE.

One pound of sugar, three-fourths pound of flour, six ounces of butter, fourteen eggs, (whites only,) almond flavoring. Mix butter and sugar together until light, add one-half of the whites beaten very light, then the flour, then balance of whites and flavoring.

LITTLE CAKES.

One-half cup of butter, one and three-fourths cups of sugar; cream together. Two eggs, one-half cup of milk, about two cups of flour, or enough to make good cake batter, two teaspoonfuls of baking powder, nutmeg and one cup of currants. This makes eighteen little cakes.

FROSTING FOR LITTLE CAKES.

One cup of sugar and one-half cup of water boiled together until it strings; beat while hot into the white of of one egg beaten stiff.

LOAF CAKE.

One quart of flour sifted before measuring, one pint of sugar (A is best); one-half pound of butter, three eggs, two gills of cold water, one-half a grated nutmeg, three teaspoonfuls of baking powder; cream the butter and sugar together, add the yolks well beaten, then the cold water and nutmeg. Sift the baking powder into the flour, add to the mixture, and lastly add the whites well beaten. Bake in two well greased tins; have a good quick oven. Be careful not to jar the cake while it is baking; bake for thirty minutes; test with a broom whisp. You can ice the cake or use it plain.

MAPLE SUGAR CAKE.

Prepare the batter the same as for chocolate cake.

MAPLE SUGAR FILLING FOR CAKE.

One and one-half pounds of maple sugar, two eggs, (whites), one tablespoonful of water; boil the sugar and water together until it threads or spins, then stir into the well beaten whites slowly.

MACAROONS.

One-half pound of almond paste, four whites of eggs, three-fourths pound of sugar. Mix eggs and paste gradually, add sugar, beat well till very light. Butter a pan, drop on the paste in spoonfuls, sift sugar on. Bake in a moderate oven twenty minutes. First sugar, then paste and a little egg.

MADELAINES.

One-half pound of butter, one-half pound of sugar, one-half pound of flour, four eggs. Beat the butter and sugar together until light, add the yolks well beaten, then the flour; lastly, the whites beaten until stiff. Bake in small tins.

NUT CAKES.

One cup of butter, two cups of sugar, three cups of flour, three-fourths cup of milk, one-half cup of wine, five eggs, spices, two teaspoonfuls of baking powder, one cup of raisins, one cup of nuts (chopped). Mix the raisins and nuts and dredge with one-half cup of flour.

ORANGE CAKE.

Two cups of sugar, one half cup of water, five egg yolks, and whites of three, juice and rind of two oranges, two cups of flour, one teaspoonful baking powder, a little salt. Bake on jelly cake tins, and put between and on the top of each layer when baked, a frosting made of the whites of two eggs beaten very stiff, and the juice of one orange, and two cups of sugar.

PORK CAKE.

One pound of fresh or salt fat pork, chopped very fine, one pound of raisins, stoned; one pound of currants, one-half pound of citron, chopped fine; one quart flour, one pint of brown sugar, one pint of boiling water, one-half pint of New Orleans molasses, two teaspoonfuls of nutmeg, one teaspoonful of mace, two teaspoonfuls of cinnamon, one teaspoonful of cloves, one lemon, juice and rind; one tablespoonful of soda dissolved in two teaspoonfuls of boiling water. Pour the boiling water on the pork, stir until it is melted, then strain it through a sieve: add the sugar, molasses, spices and one-half of the flour, reserving a little to mix with the fruit; then add the soda, then the rest of the flour and the fruit. Have your pans greased and lined with paper, the paper needs no grease. Bake in three loaves; after three-fourths of an hour try with a clean broom straw, if done the straw will come out dry.

A PLAIN CAKE, TO BE EATEN WARM OR WHILE FRESH.

One cup of sugar, one-half cup of butter, one and one-half cups of flour, two-thirds of a cup of milk, one egg, one and one-half teaspoonfuls of baking powder, one saltspoonful of salt, one cup of stoned raisins or currants. Beat butter and sugar together, then add the egg well beaten, then the milk and the flour in which sift the baking powder, then the fruit. Bake in one loaf.

POUND CAKE.

One pound of butter, one pound of sugar, one pound of flour, ten eggs, one nutmeg, if liked. Cream the butter and sugar, add the yolks well beaten, then part of the flour, then part of the whites beaten stiff, then the rest of the flour and the whites. This batter by beating for thirty minutes, after it is all well mixed, will keep for several days or even weeks if kept covered and in a dry, cool place; only when it is required do not even stir it, but just bake as it is—in little tins or in large ones.

SOFT CAKES.

Two cups of sugar, one and one-half cups of butter, three cups of flour, one teaspoonful of soda, two teaspoonfuls of cream of tartar, eight eggs. Beat the whites and yolks separately; beat the butter and sugar together; to this add the yolks; stir in part of the flour with cream of tartar, and add the whites. Dissolve the soda in a little warm water, and add. Bake in small tins.

SPICE CAKE.

One pound of brown sugar, one pound of flour, one-half pound of butter, four eggs, one teacupful of sweet milk, one-half teaspoonful of soda, one teaspoonful of cream tartar, one teaspoonful of cloves, one teaspoonful of cinnamon, one half nutmeg.

SPONGE CAKE—1.

One pound of sugar, one-half pound of flour, ten eggs, one lemon, juice and rind. Grate the lemon, beat the whites very stiff; beat yolks and sugar together, add half of the flour, then half of the whites, then the flour, then the whites and lemon. Bake very quickly.

SPONGE CAKE—2.

Four eggs, two cups sugar, two cups flour, two teaspoonfuls baking powder, one-half cup cold water, juice of one lemon; add the water after the flour, a little salt. Beat the eggs and sugar together, add the flour with the baking powder, then the water, lastly the lemon.

ENGLISH PLUM CAKE.
(SHROPSHIRE.)

One pint of milk, one teacup of sugar, four ounces of butter, flour enough to make a soft sponge, as for bread, with one-half cake of yeast. Put the sugar dry into the flour, melt the butter, pour in the milk and set sponge to rise. In the morning add any fruit you wish—one full cup, Currants washed and dried, one cup of raisins, one-half cup of cut citron, a little cloves and cinnamon. Knead it up as stiff as for bread; when light, bake in slow oven. When done, wrap in a damp cloth; keep a damp napkin under the loaf.

QUEEN CAKE.

One pound of flour, one pound of sugar, three-fourths pound of butter, five eggs, one teaspoonful of baking powder; simmer together one half a nutmeg, one wine glass of wine, one wine glass of brandy, one wine glass of cream. Beat the butter and sugar together until light, add the yolks beaten light, then one-half of the flour, in which sift the baking powder, one pound of raisins stoned, one pound of currants, then the remaining flour and the brandy, cream and sherry mixed together, which should be cool, then the whites beaten very light. Bake in two tins lined with buttered paper.

FRENCH SANDWICH.

One-half pound of butter, one-half pound of sugar, one-half pound of flour, five eggs. Beat butter and sugar and yolks well together and the flour, and then the whites beaten very stiff; this makes a very soft mixture. Bake in tins with straight sides, and the cakes must be left in the tins until needed. Spread a thin layer of the cake mixture on the bottom of the baking tin, which must be well greased; on this put a layer about an inch thick of stoned raisins and currants, chopped figs and citron all well mixed together, then pour the remaining cake batter over this as evenly as possible; the larger part of the batter should be put on top, as it runs into the fruit; bake in a moderately hot oven. This cake is so rich that it cannot be handled for twenty-four hours, and then should be put on a flat board or a flat surface. Cut into squares like a sandwich.

SUNSHINE CAKE.

Whites of eleven eggs, yolks of six eggs, one and one-half cups of powdered sugar, measured after sifting; one cup of flour one teaspoonful of cream tartar. Beat whites until light, add the sugar, then the yolks well beaten, then add the flour. Bake like angel cake.

SPANISH BUNS.

One pound of flour, one-half pound of butter, one-half pound of sugar, four eggs, one pint of milk, one-half nutmeg one glass of wine, one cup of yeast or one cake of compressed yeast, one cup of currants, a little soda. Put the flour in a bowl, stir in the milk in which the butter has been melted, add the sugar, the eggs well beaten, the nutmeg, wine, the soda dissolved in a little water, the currants, lastly the yeast. Mix all well together and set to rise in the pans before baking; the pans must be shallow ones.

VELVET SPONGE CAKE.

Two cups of sugar, five eggs, one cup of boiling hot water, two and one-half cups of flour, one tablespoonful of baking powder. Beat the yolks a little, then add sugar and beat fifteen minutes, then put in the whites very firmly beaten, then add the boiling water, then the flour.

WASHINGTON CAKE.

One cup of sugar, one cup of flour, butter the size of an egg, four eggs, one teaspoonful of baking powder. Mix the sugar and butter together, add the flour and eggs. Bake in jelly cake tins and spread when cold with this custard : Juice of one lemon, one cup of sugar, one egg beaten very light, two grated apples, cooked together.

WHITE MOUNTAIN CAKE.

One pound of sugar, one pound of flour, one-half pound of butter, six eggs, one teaspoonful of soda, two teaspoonfuls of cream tartar, one cup of sweet milk, lemon. Bake like jelly cake. Spread frosting on each layer and pile. Beat butter and sugar together until light, add yolks well beaten, then the milk, in which dissolve the soda ; then the flour, in which mix the cream tartar, then the whites.

PLUNKETS.

One pound of butter, one pound of sugar, twelve eggs, three-fourths pound of corn-starch, one-half pound of flour, one tablespoonful of vanilla sugar. Beat sugar and butter together until light, add the yolks beaten, then the flour, then the whites well beaten, then the vanilla sugar. Bake in small tins.

SILVER CAKE.

Two cups of sugar, one-half cup of butter, eight eggs (whites only), two and one-half cups of flour, one and one-half teaspoonfuls of baking powder, three-fourths cup of sweet milk, one lemon (juice). Beat sugar and butter together until light, add the milk, then the flour, in which sift the baking powder, then the lemon juice, lastly, the whites beaten very stiff.

PRINCE OF WALES CAKE.

One cup of brown sugar, one-half cup of butter, two and one-half cups of flour, three eggs (yolks); use the whites for frosting ; one cup of sour milk, two tablespoonfuls of molasses, one-half teaspoonful of cinnamon, one-half teaspoonful of cloves, one-half nutmeg, one teaspoonful of soda, one-half pound of raisins chopped fine, one-fourth pound of citron cut fine. Mix the butter and sugar together until light, add the yolks well beaten, then the sour milk, then the flour, then molasses, then the soda dissolved in a little warm water, then the spices, lastly the fruit. Bake like jelly cake and then put together with boiled frosting.

SAND TARTS—BERMUDA.

One pound of sugar, one pound of flour, one-half pound of butter, one-half cup of sweet milk, one teaspoonful of baking powder sifted with the flour, two eggs, leave out the whites. Stir butter and sugar, add flour, milk and yolks; work until smooth. Roll out a little of the dough at a time quite thin, cut with a knife in squares. Mix one-half pound of blanched almonds, one-half cup of granulated sugar, one-half cup of cinnamon; wash the cakes with this mixture and the whites well beaten. Bake quickly.

ROYAL ICING.

Use the best confectioner's sugar, sift it until perfectly fine. Take the whites of two eggs, beat them slightly, then add the sugar gradually, adding a little lemon juice from time to time. A very little corn-starch improves this icing. When the icing is perfectly smooth and will spread on the cake without running, it is ready for use, and should be used at once. Place a lump on the center of the cake and spread it over the cake with a palette knife; dip the knife every now and then into cold water, then ice the sides of the cake, commencing at the bottom.

ALMOND ICING.

Grind fine one pound of blanched almonds and one pound of fine sugar; pound both together on a mortar; add enough white of egg to make all into a soft paste. Beat well, add one-half teaspoonful of almond flavoring, then spread on the cake and cover all with a royal icing.

FONDANT.

To make a small quantity, which is better to do at first, take one-half pound of loaf sugar, two tablespoonfuls of cold water, one-half teaspoonful of cream tartar; place in a perfectly clean sauce pan and let all dissolve gradually, stirring it all the time; then place the sauce pan on the hot fire and boil very fast; do not stir it, however; have a cup of cold water aften ten minutes' fast boiling, drop into it a little of the syrup, if it will roll into a soft ball between your thumb and finger it is done, take from the fire and let the syrup cool. When cool, beat it hard with a wooden spoon until it is a soft, creamy mass. Should the fondant bcome sugary, return it to the fire and add a few spoonfuls of cold water and proceed as before. Keep the fondant in a jar until required. When needed, place the jar in a sauce pan half filled with boiling water and stir the fondant until it is soft, then spread or pour it over the cake or cakes. The fondant can be made any desired color by the colorings sold for the purpose, and flavored as desired.

ICE CREAM, ICES, MOUSSE.

Always have the mixture to be frozen, cold before putting into the freezer; the ice crushed fine and one-third as much salt as ice; when the freezer is well packed in salt and ice, pour in a pint of water—this fills in the spaces left by the ice and salt, and helps the melting of the ice. Salt water at the freezing point is colder than fresh water at the same point. A mistake is often made in turning the dasher too rapidly; the cream will not freeze until the ice around begins to melt; use plenty of rock salt, turn the crank slowly, and the cream will be frozen in about twenty minutes.

APRICOT ICE CREAM.

Stew two-thirds of a pound of dried apricots in one quart of water until perfectly soft, then add three cups of sugar; cook until the fruit and syrup look clear, then strain through a fine sieve and put on the ice to cool. Mix one quart of cream and one pint of milk together and whip for fifteen minutes; be sure that the cream is very cold; then add slowly the apricots; when well mixed place the mixture on the ice for three hours to ripen One-half hour before required, freeze.

BANANA CREAM.

Peel six bananas and pound them to a pulp; add the juice of two lemons and one glass of curacoa, strain and add one pint of whipped cream and one-half pound of sugar; freeze.

CAFE PARFAIT.

One cup of strong coffee, two cups of sugar, one pint of cream; melt the sugar on the stove with a little water—about one-half cupful—until it is a rich syrup, then pour in the cream; when hot stir in the yolks of four well-beaten eggs. As soon as the mixture thickens, remove from the fire; when cool, add one pint of whipped cream, and freeze.

FROZEN EGG NOG.

Two quarts of thin cream, two teacups of sugar, five eggs, one nutmeg, two wine glasses of rum, one wine glass of brandy. Beat the yolks with one cup of sugar until light, add the grated nutmeg; beat the whites with the remaining cup of sugar; mix together; pour into the freezer; when partly frozen put in the brandy and rum very slowly and beat the mixture well, then add the whites beaten stiff.

MARASCHINO ICE CREAM.

To one pint of cream add four wine glasses full of maraschino, the juice of one lemon and one-half pound of sugar. Mix well together and freeze.

PEACH ICE CREAM.

One quart of rich cream, two dozen ripe peaches, cut into small pieces, sugar the peaches well and let them stand for one-half hour, then add them to the cream, and freeze.

PINEAPPLE ICE CREAM.

One pineapple grated fine, one cup of sugar, one quart of cream, scald one-half of the cream and the sugar; when cold, stir in the pineapple and the other half of the cream, which must be whipped; then put into the freezer. See general directions for freezing. Preserved pineapple is very nice; if used omit the sugar.

VANILLA ICE CREAM.

One pint of cream, one-fourth pound of sugar, four yolks of eggs. Put the cream in a double boiler and let it come to a boil, then pour it on the sugar and beaten eggs and mix well together; return to the fire and stir until it thickens, then strain and let it cool; add one teaspoonful of vanilla and freeze. A half pint of whipped cream stirred into the freezer when the mixture is half frozen may be added. The eggs may be omitted.

WHITE GRAPE ICE CREAM.

One pint of cream, one pint of milk, four eggs, separating the whites and yolks; two cups of sugar; beat whites. Add the other things together, stir in whites and one cup of brandied cherries and white grapes seeded, when cream is partly frozen.

APRICOT ICE.

One can of apricots, one pint of cream, one pint of water, two cups of sugar. Mix fruit, sugar and water; stir the cream in, when in freezer.

CURRANT FRUIT ICE.

Rub one quart of ripe currants through a fine sieve, add one cupful of water made very sweet; mix with this the unbeaten whites of three eggs and freeze, stirring constantly.

STRAWBERRY ICE.

One pint of strawberry juice, one pint of water, one pint of sugar, two lemons (juice only), two tablespoonfuls of gelatine dissolved. Freeze all together.

WIESBADEN ICE.

One quart of milk, one pint of cream, four eggs; beat yolks into the cream, add three-fourths pound of sugar; freeze partly, then add one can of Wiesbaden or any other strawberries, and the whites of eggs well beaten.

MOUSSE.

A mousse is made with whipped cream, and is frozen by being simply packed into a tin, this tin or mold surrounded by cracked ice and salt; it takes about four pints of coarse salt to freeze a two-quart mold. Put the mold into the ice and salt, then turn into it the preparation; stir all the time, then cover and let it remain for four or five hours undisturbed.

APRICOT MOUSSE.

Cook one half pound of California dried apricots until they are soft, then put them through the sieve; when cool, add to them the following ingredients: Beat together one and one-half cups of sugar and the yolks of four eggs, place on the fire and cook until smooth like custard, carefully stirring; when cooked, remove from the stove and cool, then add one pint of whipped cream, and freeze the mixture.

MAPLE MOUSSE.

One pint of cream, one small cup of maple sugar, four eggs. Put the sugar and beaten yolks of the eggs in a bowl and stir together until well mixed; set this on the stove and beat until it looks like custard. Whip the cream until stiff; mix all together. Have the ice ready packed around the freezer and stir while pouring in the mixture; let stand for four hours.

PEACH MOUSSE.

Take one quart of very ripe peaches or canned ones, rub them through a sieve, add one pint of sugar, mix these together until smooth, then add one quart of whipped cream, one wine glass of sherry may be added. Fill the mold after it has been packed in the ice and salt, and let it stand for four or five hours.

MOUSSE WITH STRAWBERRIES.

One quart of strawberries, press them through a sieve, then add one-half pound of powdered sugar, beat these together until smooth, then add one quart of whipped cream. Fill the mold, cover it closely, so as to prevent any salt from getting in; put the mold in a pail filled with ice and salt for at least two hours. When ready to serve, remove the mold, wash off in cold water or remove the salt water; remove the cover and serve.

ROMAN PUNCH.

Three-fourths of a quart of cold water, one pound of sugar, juice of three lemons, rind of one lemon. Cook these together, then cool; when cold put into the freezer and freeze. Twenty minutes before serving add one cup of rum and one-half cup of champagne or maraschino; serve in cups with whipped cream.

NESSELRODE PUDDING.

Take twenty Italian chestnuts, peel them and boil for five minutes; peel off the second skin and then cook them slowly with one cup of sugar, until they are tender, then drain and press them through a fine sieve. Put four eggs, yolks only, in a stew-pan with one-fourth of a pound of sugar and one pint of boiled cream; stir this mixture over the fire, but not allowing it to boil until it thickens, then put in the chestnut puree and strain all into a basin and add one tablespoonful of maraschino; cook together one small cup of stoned raisins, one small cup of currants and one-half cup of sugar and one tablespoonful of water; when cooked, drain and let them cool. Pour the chestnut cream into the freezer, partly freeze it, then add one-half a pint of whipped cream, the raisins and currants; close the freezer carefully and put it into the ice and salt for two hours, to finish freezing the cream. Make the sauce with one-half a pint of boiled cream, four eggs (yolks), one small cup of sugar; stir over the fire until it thickens, strain and add one tablespoonful of maraschino. Turn the pudding from the mold and pour the sauce around it.

ICE CREAM WITH CHOCOLATE SAUCE.

Make vanilla ice cream, and when serving pour over each portion some hot chocolate. Make this with any fine chocolate, the same as for a beverage, only let it be very thick and hot.

PASTRY, PIES, AND PUDDINGS.

Pastry can be made with any good flour, though "pastry flour" is more apt to be successful.

A VERY GOOD PASTRY.

One and one-half cup of flour, one-fourth cup of lard, one-fourth cup of butter, one-half teaspoonful of salt, ice water. Wash the butter, dry in a clean napkin, pat into a circular piece, add the salt to the flour, then rub into the flour the lard. It is better to cut the lard into the flour with a knife, moisten the flour to a thick dough with the ice-water, place the paste on the board, which sprinkle very lightly with flour, roll out the paste, then place on the butter and roll it out, fold the paste over, so as to make three layers; turn for three half rounds, pat again, roll out; repeat this three times. To place the butter, put it on the lower half of the paste, fold over, press the edges together with finger, so as to keep in the air; turn one side over the butter, then the other under. Always roll out from you.

PUFF PASTE—1.

Puff paste should be made in a cool place always. Take equal quantities of pastry flour and butter. Wash the butter well in ice water, work it into smooth ball. Mix into the flour one teaspoonful of salt to a pound of flour. Make a paste with ice water, work until perfectly smooth and stiff, let it rest five minutes. Roll the paste out, put the butter on it, fold the paste about the butter and roll it out to one-half an inch in thickness, then fold over twice, it will then be in four thicknesses; repeat this five times; let the paste rest each time, five minutes between.

PUFF PASTE—2.

One pound of flour, one pound of butter, scant one-half pint of ice water, one saltspoonful of salt. Mix the flour into dough with the ice water and salt; reserve a little flour for the rolling out of the butter. Knead the dough well, and then make it into a ball, which pound with the rolling-pin until it is full of blisters, then put the dough on the ice for fifteen minutes. Wash the butter in cold water, wring it out in a clean napkin until dry, then put it on the ice for fifteen minutes. Take the dough, roll it out to one-half an inch in thickness; take one-fourth of the butter, spread it on one-half of the dough, sprinkle just a little flour on it to prevent the rolling-pin from sticking to it, fold over the other half and roll it; fold four times, using all the butter—let the paste rest fifteen minutes between each rolling, then put the paste on the ice to become very cold. In winter this is accomplished quickly and well by putting the paste out of doors covered; when the paste is required, handle it as little as possible, roll it to the required thickness at once; the paste will be lighter and more delicate if this is observed; bear as lightly as possible on the rolling-pin.

BEEF DRIPPING PASTRY.

Take one pound of flour and one-half pound of beef dripping, prepared as directed; one-half pint of cold water. Mix the flour and water into a smooth paste, add one teaspoonful of salt; roll it out three times, each time place on the paste one-third of the dripping in small pieces, roll the dripping lightly into the paste—if desired for a fruit pie crust, add two tablespoonfuls of sugar.

BEEF SUET PASTRY.

One-half pound of beef suet, one pound of flour, one-half pint of cold water; take all the skin and shreds from the suet, chop it very fine, and rub it well into the flour with one teaspoonful of salt, work it all to a smooth paste with the water; roll it out to the thickness desired and it is ready to use.

FLEAD PASTRY.

One pound of flour, three-fourths pound of fresh flead, one-half pint of water, one saltspoonful of salt. Take off the skin from the flead, cut the flead into thin flakes, rub it into the flour, add the salt and water, work all into a smooth paste, fold it three times, then beat it well with the rolling-pin, roll it out and it is ready for use. This crust is very light and makes and excellent crust for apple pies, or small tarts.

A FINE PIE CRUST.

One pound of flour, one-half pound of butter; rub the flour and butter together while dry—add enough ice water to make a dough; do not knead the dough, but roll it out with the rolling-pin four times. Let it stand two hours at least before baking. This will be crust enough for four pies with top crusts.

PIE CRUST FOR ONE PIE.

One coffeecup of sifted flour, one-half coffeecup of lard or drippings, rubbed together with one-half teaspoonful of salt; cold water to moisten; do not make the paste wet; roll out quickly.

APPLE CHEESE PIES.

Mix together one-half pound of stewed apples, one-half pound of sugar, a little salt, juice of one lemon, four eggs. Line a pie plate with pastry and fill with the mixture, bake until brown.

APPLE MERINGUE.

Stew some apples until soft, add one cup of sugar, a little salt and a little nutmeg, strain through a colander; when cold, fill the pie tins, which must be lined with pastry, and bake; as soon as the pie crust is baked, remove from oven. Whip the whites of three eggs until stiff, add three tablespoonfuls of sugar and put over the pie; bake for a few moments, or until the meringue is firm.

APPLE PIE—1.

Slice the apples in thin slices, cover the pie tin or plate with a crust, which rub over with the unbeaten white of an egg. Put the apples on the crust, with one-half a cup of sugar, one-half saltspoonful of salt, a few bits of butter, one teaspoonful of flour and one teaspoonful of ground cinnamon; then put on the upper crust, bake about forty minutes.

APPLE PIE—2.

Line a deep pie dish with pastry, cut the apples in thin slices, sprinkle them well with sugar, a little nutmeg, saltspoonful of salt, and one tablespoonful of butter broken into bits; fill the dish and cover with pastry and bake slowly.

COCOANUT PATTIES.

Make some good puff paste; line some patty tins, grate one cocoanut; to one-half pound of the cocoanut add one-half pound of sugar, two tablespoonfuls of water or the milk from the nut, if it is absolutely fresh and sweet; stew the cocoanut for an hour or until it is tender, then cool it; when it is cool, add one teaspoonful of brandy, three eggs well beaten, and the rind and juice of one lemon. Fill the patty tins with the mixture and bake for fifteen minutes.

CUSTARD PIE.

Four eggs, one quart of milk, four tablespoonfuls of sugar, one-half teaspoonful of nutmeg, a little salt. Beat the yolks and sugar together, then add the milk, then the whites well beaten, the nutmeg and salt. Have the pie tins lined with pastry, pour in the custard and bake.

CHERRY PIE—1.

Line a pie plate with a good pie crust, fill the plate with ripe cherries stoned; sprinkle over them a cupful of sugar, a few bits of butter and a teaspoonful of flour. Cover with the upper crust, and bake.

CHERRY PIE—2.

Fill a deep pie dish with cherries which have not been stoned, sprinkle thickly with sugar and little bits of butter. Cover with a good pastry, and bake.

CHERRY ROLY POLY.

Make a good baking powder biscuit dough, roll it out to one-half inch in thickness, spread it with stoned cherries which have been well rolled in sugar, dust over a little flour, roll over and over, fasten well the ends, and steam for one hour and a half. Serve with sugar and cream.

CREAM PIE—1.

One pint of cream brought to the boiling point, two tablespoonfuls of cornstarch mixed with one-half cup of cream, stir this mixture into the boiling cream, stir until it thickens, then remove from the fire and let it cool; when it is cooled add the whites of three eggs beaten very light, with three tablespoonfuls of sugar, and one teaspoonful of vanilla; when thoroughly mixed, line two pie tins with pastry and bake; when baked, fill with the cream mixture and bake until brown or until the custard is set.

CREAM PIE—2.

One pint of milk, bring to a boil, add one egg well beaten, one-half cup of sugar, three tablespoonfuls of flour, wet with a little cold milk, stir this into the boiling milk and continue stirring until it boils; when cold, flavor with vanilla and spread on the pie-crust layers. Make layers of paste very thin and short.

CREAM PIE—3.

One pint of milk, boil; when boiling, add two full teaspoonfuls of flour, moistened with a little cold milk or water; beat the yolks of two eggs light, with one-half cup of sugar, add these to the milk, with one-half tablespoonful of butter; stir together until thick, then add one-half teaspoonful of vanilla. Cover the pie-tin with a crust, in which prick several little holes, bake; when done, pour in the cream mixture; when cold, beat the whites of the eggs very stiff with half cup of sugar spread over the pie, and slightly brown in the oven.

CHEESE CAKES.

One pound of mashed potatoes, one-half pound of butter, one pound of sugar, one pound of currants, the juice of one lemon and the grated rind, six yolks of eggs and three whites, one wine glass of brandy, a little salt, a little nutmeg, one-half teacup of almonds cut in pieces. Line little tins with pastry and fill with the mixture and bake.

LEMON PIE.

The grated rind and juice of two lemons, two tablespoonfuls of flour mixed to a smooth, soft paste with a little cold water; pour this into two teacupfuls of boiling water, stir until smooth on the fire and then place the mixture on a cool part of the stove; add five eggs and two cupfuls of sugar well beaten together; let the mixture cool; when cool, add the rind and juice of the lemons. Line three pie tins with pastry, fill with the lemon mixture, and bake; spread over each pie when baked a meringue made with one egg (white only), beaten until light with one tablespoonful of fine sugar; put back into the oven for a few minutes until the meringue becomes slightly brown.

LEMON CHEESE CAKES.

One-fourth of a pound of butter, one pound of sugar, six eggs, the rind and juice of two lemons, and the juice of one lemon more. Put all the ingredients into a stewpan, carefully grating the lemon rind and strain the juice; keep stirring the mixture over the fire until the sugar is dissolved and it begins to thicken; when it is thick and clear like honey it is done. Put it in little jars and keep in a dry place. When ready for use, line some little tins with pastry and fill them with the mixture and bake; add some pounded almonds on the top of each.

MINCE MEAT—1.

Eight pounds of beef cooked and chopped fine, sixteen pounds of chopped apples, one pound of suet, three pounds of raisins, three pounds of currants, three-fourths pound of citron, seven pounds of sugar, one-half pound of powdered cinnamon, two ounces of cloves, two ounces of allspice, one ounce of nutmegs, one saltspoonful of cayenne, one-half ounce of mace, two quarts of boiled cider, one quart of brandy, one quart of sherry, one glass of currant jelly; mix. Mince meat is improved by age.

MINCE MEAT—2.

Eleven pints of meat and tongue (one fresh tongue and six pounds of beef), seven pints of suet, fifteen pints of apples chopped, sixteen pints of raisins (eight ground and eight whole), eleven pints of currants, four pints of brown sugar, two pounds of citron ground, one and one fourth pounds of candied orange peel, two jars of orange marmalade, juice of four oranges and grated rind of two, two cupfuls of mixed spices, salt to taste, ten pints of French cooking brandy, seven pints of boiled cider, one tablespoonful each of ginger, cinnamon, cloves, allspice, mace, ground. More ginger, cinnamon and cloves than of the others. Add one saltspoonful of cayenne.

LITTLE MINCE PIES.

Line little, plain patty-pies with puff paste or any good pastry, fill them with mince meat, wet the edges of the paste and cover the mince meat with more paste and bake. Take from the pans before serving.

ORANGE PIE.

Made in the same manner as lemon pie, only substitute oranges for lemons.

ORANGE SHORTCAKE.

Same as peach short cake, only substituting the oranges cut in slices for the peaches.

PATTIES OR TARTS.

For twelve tarts or patties cut twenty four rounds of pastry with the large cutter; cut twelve into rings by cutting them with the smaller cutter quite through, then moisten these with a little cold water on one side and lay these on the rounds of pastry; bake from ten to twelve minutes; fill with preserves.

SWEET PATTIES.

Fill the patty-cases with sweetened, whipped cream, or with preserves with cream on top, or with rich preserves alone.

PEACH PIE.

Line a deep pie dish with good pastry; peel the peaches leaving them whole, add a little water and one cup of sugar, a little salt; cover the dish with pastry and bake.

PEACH SHORTCAKE.

Make a baking powder biscuit dough, only add to it one tablespoonful more butter; roll one layer of dough to about one-half inch in thickness, spread it lightly with melted butter, then roll the remaining half of the dough to the same thickness, place over the first and bake; the two layers will come apart when baked. If fresh peaches are used, take one quart of peaches, peel and cut fine, and one cup of sugar; let the fruit stand in the sugar for an hour before using, then spread the fruit on the crust, placing the upper crust on the peaches and keep warm. Serve with cream. If canned peaches are used, the syrup will make a sauce for the shortcake; if it is not sweet enough, boil the syrup with one-half cup of sugar and serve.

POTATO PIE.

One pint of mashed potatoes, three eggs, one pint of sugar, one-half cup of butter, one-half teacup of cream, one lemon, one tablespoonful of brandy. Mix together and bake. Have pie tins lined with good pastry.

PATTIES.

One of the most convenient articles of food to keep on hand to help out at any meal is patty shells. A filling may be made for them of cold fish, fowl, oysters, lobsters or almost any kind of cooked light meat, cut into small pieces and stirred into a nicely seasoned hot white sauce.

PUMPKIN PIE.

One quart of strained pumpkin, two eggs, two tablespoonfuls of butter, one-half cup of cream, one cup of milk, one cup of brown sugar, one teaspoonful of ginger, one-half teaspoonful of cinnamon. Line the pans with good pastry and fill with the mixture.

SQUASH PIE.

One pint of cream, one pint of cooked squash, one tablespoonful of butter, one-half cup of brandy, two cups of brown sugar, one teaspoonful of cinnamon, a little salt. Line the pie tin with pastry.

WASHINGTON PIE.

One cup of sugar, three eggs, two tablespoonfuls of cold water, a very little salt, one cup of flour, one full teaspoonful of baking powder. Separate the eggs, beat the yolks, add to them gradually the sugar, then add the flour, in which sift the baking powder; lastly, add the stiffly beaten whites. Bake in two deep jelly cake tins: when cold, split each layer in half, and spread on each a custard made as follows; One pint of hot milk, three eggs leaving out one white, three tablespoonfule of sugar, one tablespoonful of flour dissolved in a little cold milk. Beat the eggs slightly, strain into the hot milk, then the sugar and flour; stir in the double boiler until the mixture is thick; remove from fire; when cold, add one teaspoonful of vanilla extract or a few drops of almond extract, spread on the cake layers, pile them one on the other, and with the unused white of egg make a frosting with it and two tablespoonfuls of sugar.

STRAWBERRY SHORTCAKE—1.

The real old fashioned strawberry shortcake is made as follows: Chop three tablespoonsfuls of butter into a quart of flour; add one egg beaten up with a large cup of sour cream or rich lobbered milk, a teaspoonful of soda, dissolved in hot water and a little salt. Handle as lightly as possible, mixing with a knife; roll lightly and quickly into two sheets, lay one smoothly upon the other with a few bits of butter between them, and when done pull apart, waiting till they have slightly cooled. Cover the lower layer with a thick coating of strawberries and sprinkle liberally with powdered sugar; lay on the upper crust and send to table whole, to be eaten with thick, rich, sweetened cream.

STRAWBERRY SHORTCAKE—2.

Make the crust the same as for peach shortcake. Hull the berries. For one quart add one cup of sugar, crush the berries and let them stand in the sugar for an hour; just before spreading the fruit on the shortcake, add one-half teacup of cream to the berries; if another layer is liked on the top of the shortcake, use for this layer the berries without any cream mixed with them.

Stewed prunes, apricots and apples all make a very good shortcake, made in the same manner as peach shortcake.

VOL-AU-VENT.

Make some puff paste with one pound of flour, one pound of butter, one-fourth teaspoonful of salt. See directions for making puff paste. Roll out the pastry to one inch in thickness; cut in the size of the plate in which the vol-au-vent is to be served; brush over the top with beaten egg; make a circular incision one-fourth of an inch deep, one inch from the edge of the pastry. Bake the pastry; when cooked, remove the cover which will have risen during the baking; fill the vol-au-vent with creamed chicken, sweetbreads, lobsters, stewed fruit, whipped cream, or other articles desired.

VOL-AU-VENT OR PATTY CASES.

Have two round pastry cutters, one a little more than half the size of the other—these cutters can be purchased in sets. Roll out the puff paste to one-half inch in thickness; with the largest cutter, cut the number of patties required, then with the small cutter, cut the same number of cases; put these on top of the large ones, then cut with the smaller cutter nearly through one-half of the patties, put them together; when baked, remove this round of crust—it will come easily; and fill the cases and place the little cover over.

ALBERRY PUDDING.

Peel four bananas, slice them; peel six oranges, cut the pulp out free from the white part. Put these in layers in a glass dish and sprinkle over lemon juice. Boil together one and a half cup of sugar and one-half cup of water until a rich syrup is made. While hot, pour this syrup over the fruit, place on ice to become very cold before serving.

AMBROSIA.

Six large oranges, one cocoanut, one pint powdered sugar; peel and slice the oranges, remove the seeds, grate the cocoanut; put in layers in a glass dish—sprinkle sugar on each layer. Make a few hours before using.

APPLE FLOAT.

Three eggs (whites only) beaten very stiff, one quart of stewed apples sweetened to taste, have the apples very cold, and beat into the eggs until the mixture is stiff. Serve with cream.

APPLE PUDDING—GERMAN.

Fill a pudding dish with twelve apples, peel and core them, fill the cavity of each apple with sugar, cinnamon and raisins cut fine, pour over them a little wine and bake until soft; then make a batter with the yolks of five eggs, one cup of grated almonds, one cup of sugar and the whites of the eggs beaten until stiff; pour this over the apples and bake for five or six minutes.

APPLE FRITTERS.

Pare three apples; slice them half an inch thick, remove the cores, and lay the slices for an hour in the following mixture, turning them over every fifteen minutes. Mix together two tablespoonfuls of sugar, one teaspoonful of ground spice, one glass of wine, and pour upon the apples. At the end of an hour dip the slices into a batter. (See recipe for frying batter.) Lift each one out on a fork, and fry the fritters a golden brown in smoking hot fat, laying them for a minute on brown paper to free them from grease. Arrange them on a dish in a circle, and dust them with powdered sugar.

APPLE DUMPLING.

Same as Damson Plum—only substituing apples for plums.

APRICOT EGGS.

One sponge cake, baked in a round tin, cut it into slices about one-half an inch thick, cut these into rounds with a biscuit cutter. Spread over each round of cake a little apricot jam, and cover them with stiffly whipped cream, flavor the cream with a little vanilla or lemon juice. In the center of the cream place the half of a cooked apricot, dust over some fine sugar. These eggs are rapidly made, look pretty, and though an old-fashioned dessert are quite good.

APRICOT MUSCOVITE.

One pound of apricot jam or apricot preserves, made very smooth by passing through a sieve, if not sweet enough add some sugar. Make a custard with the yolks of four eggs and one scant pint of fresh milk; boil the milk, stir in the eggs and one cup of sugar. When thick, remove from fire and add one-half ounce of gelatine, which should have been soaked in warm water and strained. Whip these together, and as soon as the mixture sets add one-half pint of stiffly whipped cream and one small glass of either noyeau or apricot brandy or plain brandy. Place the mixture in a mold, put it into a pail, cover with ice and salt, and let remain for two hours. Any jam can be used in place of apricot.

APRICOT SHORTCAKE.

Same as for Strawberry Shortcake—substituting the apricots.

APPLE AND TAPIOCA.

One coffee cup of tapioca soaked for some hours in cold water; eight apples pared and cut in pieces, one cup of sugar. Put a layer of apples, then a layer of tapioca, sugar and the juice of one lemon, until the dish is full, then put in as much water as the dish will hold; bake for an hour; if the mixture seems too stiff add more water; it should look clear and brown when done. Serve with cream.

BAVARIAN CREAM.

One quart of cream, five ounces of sugar, one ounce gelatine, two teaspoonfuls vanilla, four eggs (yolks), a little pinch of salt. Make a custard by taking one pint of the cream, and the sugar and salt; when boiling hot, stir in the eggs well beaten; stir constantly to prevent curdling. As soon as the custard is thick, remove from fire and the hot saucepan; stir in the dissolved gelatine, then whip the other pint of cream and stir it into the custard when it is perfectly cold; pour into a mold and set on the ice for some hours.

BOILED BATTER PUDDING.

Three eggs, one-half tablespoonful of melted butter, one pint of milk, three tablespoonfuls of flour, a pinch of salt. Put the flour into a basin, add enough milk to moisten it; carefully rub down all the lumps, stir in the melted butter, keep beating the mixture hard, add the eggs beaten together; then add the salt. Butter a pudding mold, fill with the batter, tie down the cover tightly, put it into boiling water, move the mold a few times at first to prevent the pudding from settling, then boil for one hour and fifteen minutes. Serve at once when removed from the fire and serve with the pudding a fruit sauce or sugar and cream.

BREAD PUDDING—1.

Boil one teacup of bread crumbs in one pint of milk with a slice of lemon peel and one teaspoonful of butter; boil for ten minutes, then mash through a sieve, add two well beaten eggs, one teacup of powdered sugar, one saltspoonful of salt and one half pint of milk; mix well together, pour into a buttered dish; bake until the top is a rich brown; serve with cream.

BREAD PUDDING—2.

Put three-quarters of a pound of bread crumbs into a bowl with six ounces or six tablespoonfuls of sugar, two of butter, a saltspoonful of salt, and a pint of boiling milk, and let them stand for ten minutes; then add the yolks of six eggs beaten to a cream and the whites whipped to a froth; pour the pudding into a buttered mold, and steam it it one hour in a large saucepan containing boiling water enough to reach half way to the top of the mold. Turn the pudding from the mold and serve it with cream sauce.

BREAD AND BUTTER PUDDING.

Fill the pudding dish with slices of thinly cut bread, buttered, and strew over each slice some currants. Make a custard of one pint of milk, two tablespoonfuls of sugar, three eggs well beaten, a little salt and one-fourth teaspoonful of nutmeg. Mix these well together and pour over the bread and butter, and bake in a moderate oven for thirty minutes.

BREAD TARTS.

Cut slices of bread, one quarter of an inch thick; cut these with the biscuit cutter into circles; moisten them with a little milk, then spread over some jam or preserves; put the circles together as sandwiches, and then fry them in a little butter on each side until they are browned. Serve with cream or with a pudding sauce or without any sauce.

BRIGHTON PUDDING.

One pint of milk, three eggs, one-half teacup of butter, one cup of flour, one lemon. Beat eggs and sugar together, stir into the milk, then add the melted butter. Put into a buttered pudding mold and boil one hour; serve with cream or wine sauce.

BROWN BETTY.

Take eight large sour apples, peel and slice them. Butter a pudding dish or tin bread pan thoroughly and sprinkle over the bottom and sides fine fresh bread crumbs, then a put a good layer of brown sugar and bits of butter, then a thick layer of the apples with a sprinkle of cinnamon; repeat these layers until the dish or pan is full; do not be sparing of the butter; let the top layer be of bread crumbs, sugar, butter and cinnamon mixed. Bake for forty-five minutes in a moderate oven. Serve with sweet cream or a "hard sauce."

BROWN BREAD PUDDING.

One cup of brown bread crumbs, one cup of brown sugar, one teaspoonful of salt, one cup of currants, four eggs, spices. Mix; boil two hours in mold.

LITTLE BREAD PUDDING.

Pour over one cup of fine bread crumbs one quart of boiling milk, add one-half cup of sugar, two tablespoonfuls of butter, one saltspoonful of salt, a little grated lemon rind. When this mixture is cool, add two eggs beaten separately until very light. Put into small cups and bake eight minutes; serve hot with cream or fruit sauce.

CARROT PUDDING.

One-half pound of grated carrots, one-half pound of grated potatoes, one-half teaspoonful of salt, one pound of flour, one pound of raisins stoned, one pound of currants, eight tablespoonfuls of molasses. Mix well together and put into pudding mold and boil four hours. Serve with a wine sauce.

COCOANUT CREAM PUDDING.

Grate a fresh cocoanut, having first peeled, washed and wiped it dry. Mix with two tablespoonfuls of sugar, melt in one tablespoonful of water three-quarters of an ounce of gelatine; while this is melting take the whites of three eggs, mix them with one-half a pint of milk, stir over the fire until the custard thickens, then add four tablespoonfuls of sugar; then add the gelatine with the grated cocoanut and the milk from the cocoanut; whip half a pint of cream until very stiff and stir it into the cocoanut mixture; when nearly cold, add a little vanilla or lemon flavoring; put into a mold, and place on the ice.

CARAMEL PUDDING.

Beat four eggs a little, stir them into one pint of milk with one half cup of sugar, a few drops of vanilla. Put into a small tin, one cup of sugar and two tablespoonfuls of of water, let these cook together until very brown and thick, then pour the mixture into a mold; see that every part of the mold is covered with a part of the caramel; it is well after this to stand the mold in cold water for a moment to harden the caramel, then pour in the custard and bake until the custard is firm; turn out of the mold and serve either hot or cold.

CHARLOTTE RUSSE—1.

One-half pint of milk, put into the double boiler, when just at the boiling point stir in the yolks of four eggs, previously well-beaten, and three tablespoonfuls of sugar. Stir all carefully until the mixture thickens (but not too thick); take from the fire and add one-fourth of a box of gelatine which has been previously dissolved in a little milk and placed on the range to warm; let the custard cool and then add three tablespoonfuls of sherry wine; when nearly cold, add one quart of whipped cream, stir the cream in carefully. Line a Charlotte Russe mold with lady fingers, or slices of sponge cake and pour in the mixture. Set on the ice to cool.

CHARLOTTE RUSSE—2.

One ounce of gelatine dissolved in one-half pint of milk, three pints of cream, eleven ounces of sugar, four eggs beaten separately; whip cream until very light, add flavoring of lemon or vanilla; beat the eggs light, add sugar to the yolks, add the gelatine strained to the cream, then add the whites, beating well. Line the dish with sponge cake or lady fingers and fill with the mixture.

CREAM PUDDING.

Stir together one-half pint of cream and one tablespoonful of sugar, the yolks of three eggs, beaten well, a little nutmeg, then add the whites well beaten, pour into a pie dish which has been greased and sprinkled with bread crumbs about half an inch thick; sprinkle a layer of fine bread crumbs on top and bake about twenty minutes.

CORNMEAL PUDDING.

Two quarts of milk, four eggs, one cup of sugar, one cup of cornmeal, one cup of molasses, two teaspoonfuls of ginger, one-half cup of butter, one-half pound of seeded raisins. Put one quart of milk on to boil. Stir into one quart of cold milk the cornmeal, then stir this into the scalding milk with the butter and sugar; when the mush is cooked, let it become cool and then add the eggs and raisins. Put into pudding dish and bake for two hours, stirring occasionally.

BAKED CUSTARD.

One pint of milk, three eggs, one tablespoonful of sugar; beat the eggs and sugar together and stir into the milk; fill the custard cups nearly to the top, place them in a pan containing hot water which reaches to two-thirds of the top of the cups; bake twenty minutes; as soon as the custard is set, it is done; otherwise the whey will separate.

CHOCOLATE PUDDING.

Three eggs, (yolks only) beaten light, and one cup of sugar added gradually; three tablespoonfuls of sweet milk, one small cup of chocolate melted in hot water; stir these well together, add one cup of flour with two teaspoonfuls of baking powder and beat until smooth; add a little salt, then add the whites beaten stiff; put large spoonfuls of the pudding into greased cups, and steam for twenty minutes. Serve with the following sauce:

One cup of powdered sugar and one-half cup of butter beaten together until creamy, add one teaspoonful of vanilla, and then stir gradually into this one-half cup of milk; put the mixture in a bowl over a basin of boiling water; stir until it is smooth and creamy, no longer,

CHOCOLATE CUSTARD.

One-fourth pound of chocolate, one-fourth pound of sugar sifted. one and one-half pints of milk, four eggs, six drops of vanilla. Take a clean saucepan, put in it the crushed chocolate and sugar, pour the milk over by degrees, thoroughly stirring all the time; let it boil up, still stirring; move it to the side of fire to simmer for twenty minutes. Break four eggs separately (to be sure they are quite good); take the yolks of four and the whites of three and mix them with the cream, being careful it is not too hot; strain the whole through a fine strainer into the double boiler and keep stirring the same way until the custard thickens; it will take about twenty minutes after the water in the pan boils; when it is thick enough, take out of the hot water and leave it in the boiler till it is cold; stir a teaspoonfull of vanilla into the cream. Serve when required, in a glass dish or in custard cups.

FRIED CUSTARD.

Two eggs, (yolks), one teaspoonful of flour, one-half pint of milk or cream, one saltspoonful of salt, one tablespoonful of sugar, a little nutmeg; beat the eggs and flour together with a little of the milk, then add the rest of the milk warmed; beat the sugar, salt and nutmeg well into this mixture. Bake in a small dish until firm, then let it cool. Make a batter with one-half pint of milk, one egg, two tablespoonfuls of flour; mix the batter until very smooth add the whites left from the custard, add a little grated lemon rind and a little salt. Cut the custard into pieces, dip each piece in the batter and fry in deep, boiling fat for two minutes, then serve with a little powdered sugar over them.

CORN-STARCH PUDDING.

Dissolve two large tablespoonfuls of corn-starch in a little cold milk; stir this into one pint of boiling milk; stir constantly until the mixture thickens, then add four tablespoonfuls of sugar, then add the well beaten whites of three eggs, and cook for a minute or two to cook the eggs, add one-half saltspoonful of salt and one-half teaspoonful of vanilla or lemon; take from the fire and put into a mold; when cold, serve with cream or a fruit sauce.

BOILED CUSTARD.

One pint of milk, three eggs, (yolks), one tablespoonful of sugar. Beat the yolks and sugar together, the milk warmed and added, the whole cooked in a double boiler. Stir the mixture constantly and as soon as it is as thick as good cream, remove at once; when cold, add the three whites beaten very stiff and serve; this custard must not stand long after the whites are added.

DAMSON DUMPLING.

One quart of Damson or German plums, one-half pound of sugar. Make a good soda biscuit dough or suet crust. Roll it out thin, line a buttered pudding mold with it, fill the center with the plums, add the sugar, pinch the edges of the crust together so that the juice will not escape, tie over all a floured cloth. Put the pudding into boiling water and boil for two hours. Serve with a sauce made of a portion of the plums and one cup of sugar stewed together or with sugar and cream.

DIPLOMATIC PUDDING.

One pint of thick cream two tablespoonfuls of white sugar, one-half a lemon, one wine glass of brandy, one ounce of gelatine. Put the cream into a basin and whip it to a stiff froth with the sugar, add the brandy and juice of the half lemon, next the gelatine, which has been melted. Divide the cream, color half with a few drops of carmine or with fruit rubbed through a sieve; pour the white part into a mold first and let it set, then the colored half; put it on ice till required. Turn out, and serve.

FRIAR'S OMELETTE.

Pare and core ten large apples, stew them until tender, then add two tablespoonfuls of butter and one-half pound of sugar, one-half saltspoonful of salt, rub through the sieve and add one egg well beaten. Butter thoroughly a plain mold or dish; strew fine bread crumbs over the sides and bottom, fill it with the stewed apples; put on the top another layer of bread crumbs and bake for one-half hour, turn from the mold and sprinkle fine sugar over and serve hot.

A PLAIN FIG PUDDING.

One-fourth pound of bread crumbs, one-fourth pound of flour, one-fourth pound of suet chopped fine, six ounces chopped figs; mix these together and add two eggs; boil for four hours in a well greased bowl. Serve with cream and sugar.

FRUIT FARINA.

Sprinkle three tablespoonfuls of farina into one quart of boiling milk, using a saucepan set into a kettle of boiling water in order to prevent burning; flavor and sweeten to taste and boil for half an hour, stirring occasionally; then add one pint of any ripe berries or sliced apples, and boil until the fruit is cooked (about twenty minutes); the pudding may be boiled in a mold or cloth. It should be served with powdered sugar.

FIGS IN CREAM.

Pull the figs apart and pour over them enough cold water to cover them; let the figs remain in the water over night, the next morning simmer the figs in this water until they are plump and tender. To each pound of figs add one-half teacup of sugar and the juice of one lemon; simmer together ten minutes; then place the figs on the ice, and when required, serve them covered with whipped cream.

GERMAN ICE PUDDING.

Line a mold with a clear jelly, then take six sponge cakes, six macaroons and soak them in sherry and brandy; add one-half pint of cream and one-half ounce of gelatine dissolved in a little milk. Stir all well together in a basin and when nearly cold add some preserved fruits (cut up). Put into the mold and keep in a cool place till wanted. Serve with a rich cream custard around the dish. Flavor the custard with brandy. The gelatine must be dissolved in boiling milk and the cream must be whipped before adding to sponge cakes.

HOLLANDAISE FRITTERS.

Four cupfuls of cold, boiled rice; two eggs well beaten, one-half cupful of grated cheese, one tablespoonful of cream, a little salt and pepper. Mix well together and make into small flat cakes; have some hot fat in the pan, not a deep fat; brown the cakes in this, cooking slowly; turn and brown on the other side. Serve hot with either lamb chops or steak.

ITALIAN CREAM.

One-half pint of sweet cream, six sheets of white sheet gelatine, one-half stick of vanilla, the yolks of four or five eggs. The above is to be well cooked over a slow fire, then stir in one-fourth pound of Sultana raisins; when cold, stir in one-eighth pint of whipped cream just before serving; and place on the ice in a mold for a few minutes.

KISS PUDDING.

One quart of sweet milk. When boiling, stir into it four tablespoonfuls of corn starch which has been dissolved in a little cold milk; when the milk thickens, add the yolks of four eggs well beaten; put into a pudding dish. Beat to a stiff froth the four whites, add one teacup of powdered sugar, one teaspoonful of vanilla, spread this over the milk mixture, brown quickly in hot oven. Sprinkle on the top some grated cocoanut; serve cold. The sweet liquid which settles at the bottom, serves as a sauce.

MARMALADE PUDDING.

The weight of four eggs in butter, the weight of four eggs in sugar, the weight of four eggs in flour. Mix the butter and sugar together, then add the eggs well beaten (whites and yolks separately); then add one teaspoonful of soda dissolved in a little warm water; lastly, add one generous tablespoonful of orange marmalade. Grease the pudding mold, fill with the mixture only a little more than half full, as the pudding rises to twice its bulk; steam for two hours; keep up a steady boiling under the steamer; when cooked turn on to a dish and serve with whipped cream. This pudding is attractive looking as well as very good.

MOUNTAIN PUDDING.

One-half pint of milk, one egg, one tablespoonful of butter, one tablespoonful of sugar, two teaspoonfuls of baking powder, a little salt and nutmeg. Beat the butter and sugar together, add the egg well beaten; stir in the milk, then the flour, in which sift the baking powder; mix together quickly; bake in one cake and serve with sauce either of wine or sugar and cream.

FRIED PANCAKES.

One pint of sour milk, two pints of flour, two eggs, one saltspoonful of salt, one-half teaspoonful of soda, the grated rind of one lemon. Mix the flour and milk together until smooth, add the soda dissolved in a little warm water, then add the salt and lemon; lastly, the eggs beaten until light. Have the lard in the frying kettle deep and hot, drop the batter by spoonfuls into the hot fat and fry for one minute; serve with sifted sugar over them.

PLUM PUDDING—1.

One pound of beef suet chopped fine, one-half pound of bread crumbs, one-half pound of flour, two pounds of currants, two pounds of raisins stoned, one pound of Sultana raisins, one-half pound of sugar, one pound of citron cut fine, one-half pound of orange peel chopped fine, one-half pound of lemon peel chopped fine, one wine glass of wine, one wine glass of brandy, one teaspoonful of cinnamon, one teaspoonful of nutmeg, one-half teaspoonful of cloves, one-half teaspoonful of allspice, twelve eggs. Mix the suet, bread crumbs, flour, sugar, yolks together, then the spices, brandy and wine, then the fruit; lastly, the whites of the eggs beaten light. Have quart bowls buttered; fill these with the mixture nearly to the top; have a cloth wet in hot water wrung out and floured, tie this over the bowls, plunge all the puddings into a large deep pot with boiling water to cover them; keep them covered and boiling for six hours. It is better to make the recipe into several small puddings, though it can be boiled in one large bowl if desired. The puddings will keep for a year if kept dry and cool; when one is desired, plunge into boiling water one hour before serving, boil steadily, then remove the cloth and turn the pudding on a platter and serve with wine sauce or whipped cream.

PLUM PUDDING—2.

One and one-half pounds of raisins, one pound of currants, one-half pound of Sultanas, six ounces of citron, six ounces of orange peel, six ounces of lemon peel, six ounces of bread crumbs, six ounces of flour, one pound of beef suet, three-fourths pound of sugar, three-fourths ounce of spice, nine eggs, one-half pint of brandy, one-fourth pint Noyeau, peel and juice of one lemon, some bitter almonds. This quantity makes five puddings of moderate size, not large; boil two and one-half hours when made and two and one-half hours more when needed. Mix all the ingredients well together, butter the bowls and fill nearly to the top with the mixture, tie the bowls in cloths, which have been dipped in hot water and then floured.

CANNED PEACHES.

One can of peaches, drain off all the juice; one-half box of gelatine, to which add one-half pint of cold water; let this stand for two hours, then add one-half pint of boiling water to dissolve the gelatine, then add the juice from the peaches; let this mixture just come to boiling point on the stove. Place in the mold the peaches, first dipping the mold into cold water, then pour the gelatine over the fruit. This mixture must stand over night to become very cold. Served covered with whipped cream.

PINEAPPLE BAVARIAN CREAM.

One pint of pineapple, one-half cup of sugar, one half package of gelatine, one large cup of whipped cream or the whites of four eggs. Soak the gelatine in one cup of cold water; when dissolved, strain it into the juice of the pineapple, add the sugar and let all come to the boiling point on the stove; remove from fire; when it is cool and commences to thicken add the whipped cream, or if you use the eggs. add them and then the pineapple, which must be chopped fine; beat the mixture until very light, pour into a pudding or jelly mold and set in the ice box to harden. Serve with whipped cream. Strawberry cream is very nice made in the same way, only rather more sugar must be used.

PRUNE PUDDING.

About fifteen large prunes; wash, soak in cold water; stew them until quite tender, cool, stone and chop them very fine; mix one-half cup powdered sugar, one-half teaspoonful cream tartar, pinch of salt; beat five whites of eggs until almost stiff, beat in the sugar mixture carefully and lightly, a little at a time; add the prunes, turn all into a charlotte mold holding two and one-half pints; set the mold in a pan and pour around it hot water; bake in a moderate oven about twenty-five minutes. Serve with whipped cream, or make a custard sauce with the yolks.

POTATO PUDDING.

Boil six potatoes until tender, mash them while hot, and add to one pint of mashed potatoes three-fourths pint of sugar, three-fourths pint of butter, six eggs, one grated nutmeg, the juice of one lemon, one wine glass of brandy. Bake in pudding dish about one-half hour.

PLUM CHARLOTTE.

One quart of ripe plums stoned, one pound of sugar; cook these together, butter some thin slices of bread, lay them on the bottom and the sides of a pudding dish, pour the plums on boiling hot; cover the dish, and when quite cold serve with cream.

QUEEN OF PUDDINGS.

One quart of milk, one pint of bread crumbs, yolks of four eggs, one tablespoonful of melted butter, a little salt Mix these together, place in greased pudding dish and bake one-half hour; when the pudding is cold spread on the top a layer of good jam, and on top of the jam the whites well beaten with one teacup of sugar. Serve with cream.

RICE PUDDING.

One-fourth of a pound of rice, washed in several waters; then put into the stew-pan with one and one-half pints of milk and stew gently until tender, then add one tablespoonful of butter and two tablespoonfuls of sugar; stir well and remove from the fire; when cool add three well beaten eggs, a very little salt and one-fourth teaspoonful of nutmeg; then put the mixture into the pudding dish and bake for twenty minutes.

ICED RICE PUDDING.

Wash one pound of rice, put it into one quart of milk and cook until quite soft, add two vanilla sticks and three-fourths pound of sugar, a little salt. Let all simmer until the rice grains are almost dissolved, take from fire, add the beaten yolks of four eggs; when cold add one pint of cream and freeze, when partly frozen add some chopped raisins and the whites well beaten. Serve with sweet meats or compote of fruits.

RICE PUDDING WITH FRUIT.

One pound of rice, four ounces prunes, apples and raisins; quarter the apples, boil the prunes in an open stew-pan; wash the rice well. Dip a clean cloth in hot water, squeeze out, place it in a deep basin, spread out, then lay the rice around, the fruit in the middle and a little salt sprinkled in and the peel of a lemon chopped fine, a little cinnamon and cloves, one ounce of powdered sugar; cover the fruit with rice, tie up the cloth rather loosely to allow room for the swelling of the rice. Place an old plate in the bottom of the stew-pan, have the water boiling and plunge the pudding in for two hours. This can be served with roast meat, and is very good.

PLAIN RICE PUDDING.

Two tablespoonfuls of rice, washed; one quart of milk, two tablespoonfuls of sugar, one-half cup of stoned raisins. Bake slowly for an hour or a little longer. Serve cold. Wash the rice carefully, place in dish and cover with the milk and one-half saltspoonful of salt; cook slowly for one half hour, then add the sugar; add more hot milk; stir the pudding carefully under the skin which forms of the milk; keep adding milk until the whole mixture is very soft and creamy; the raisins can be added if desired; the pudding may have a little nutmeg flavoring or a little lemon.

ROLY-POLY PUDDING.

One-half pound of beef suet chopped fine, one-half pound of flour. Mix suet and flour together, add one teaspoonful of salt; when the suet and flour are mixed make into a stiff paste with a little cold water; roll out once one-half inch thick; on this spread raspberry or blackberry jam, not quite to the edge of the pastry; wet the edge, roll up the pastry and pinch the edges together, then dip a clean pudding cloth into hot water, wring it out, flour one side and lay the pudding into it; tie each end of the cloth and pin the center, plunge into boiling water and boil steadily for one and and one-fourth hours.

SOUFFLE.

For the baking of a souffle, the oven should be moderately hot; the dish in which it is baked should always be well greased.

SOUFFLE PUDDING—1.

Three eggs; beat the whites and yolks separately until very light, add one tablespoonful of corn starch, two tablespoonfuls of flour, one saltspoonful of salt and enough milk to make a batter. Butter a pudding dish and pour the mixture into it and bake in a quick oven for fifteen minutes. Serve with a wine sauce.

SOUFFLE PUDDING—2.

One fourth of a box of gelatine soaked for one hour in a little cold water, one cup of milk, two eggs, one-half cup of sugar, three tablespoonfuls of cornstarch. Put milk into the double boiler with the two yolks, the sugar and the cornstarch, which must be first mixed with a little cold milk; let the mixture come to a boil, then take from the fire and add to it the gelatine; beat all well together with one teaspoonful of vanilla and the beaten whites, then let it cool; when it is cool beat into the mixture one-half pint of whipped cream. Put into a mold and serve with a whipped cream.

SAVARIN WITH RUM.

One pound of sifted flour, one-fourth pound of sugar, one-half pound of butter, eight eggs, one cake of yeast dissolved in one-half pint of warm milk; strain the yeast and put into it as much of the flour as will produce a soft dough; roll this into a ball; place the remainder of the flour in a deep basin, lay the ball of dough on it, cover it up and leave it in a warm place until the ball of dough has risen; then add the sugar, the butter slightly melted, the eggs, a pinch of salt, and mix the mixture with the fingers until a smooth paste is obtained. Butter well a large, plain mold; put on the bottom and sides some fine chopped almonds and fill with the cake mixture, which should not more than fill two-thirds of the tin. Cover the tin and place it in a warm place to rise; when well risen, bake in a moderate oven for one and one-half hours. Before turning the cake out stab the top with a knife in several places and pour over it a syrup of two parts old rum and one part very sweet syrup, then turn on to a dish and serve either hot or cold.

SPONGE PUDDING.

One pint of sweet milk, six eggs, four tablespoonfuls of flour, butter the size of an egg. Boil the milk, when boiling, add the butter, stir in the flour mixed to a soft paste with a little of the cold milk; when the sauce is thick remove from the fire and let it cool; when cold add the yolks of the eggs well beaten, then the whites beaten stiff; mix all well together. Butter a two quart pudding-dish, pour in the mixture, place the dish in a pan of boiling water two inches deep; bake in a hot oven for thirty-five minutes. Serve with wine sauce. Serve as soon as baked.

SPANISH CREAM.

One quart of milk, one-half box of gelatine, four eggs beaten separately, two teaspoonfuls of vanilla, one cupful of sugar. Soak the gelatine in the milk for one-half hour, then put it on the fire in a double boiler; beat the yolks light, add to them the sugar, stir well together; as soon as the milk boils, stir in the eggs and sugar until the mixture thickens, then take from the fire to cool. Beat the whites until they are stiff, add the vanilla, beat the whites into the custard and put into a mold. Serve cold.

SNOW CUSTARD.

One-half box of gelatine, the juice and grated rind of two lemons; pour over it one-half pint of cold water, and when the gelatine is well soaked, add one-half pint of sugar and a pint of boiling water; strain through a cloth; when cold, beat the whites of three eggs stiff and mix them in the gelatine well. Let them rise to the top and put the mixture in a cool place to harden. Take the yolks of three eggs and make a custard and flavor it with vanilla; this custard is poured around the jelly, after it is put in the saucers or dishes.

STRAWBERRIES WITH RUM.

To have the full flavor of the berry and yet avoid all fear of indigestion, try eating them with rum. Hull the berries, place them in a glass bowl, sprinkle them well with powdered sugar, and to each quart of the fruit add one-half pint of Jamaica rum and water—one-third rum, two-thirds water. Stand the bowl on the ice for a half hour before serving.

SPANISH PUFFS.

One-half a cup of cold water, one teaspoonful of butter, four eggs, one saltspoonful of salt; put the water and butter into a stewpan; when it boils, add sufficient flour to form a paste that will leave the sides of the pan; it must be very stiff. Let this cool, then add the yolks of the eggs, one at a time. Have some deep, boiling lard and drop the mixture, a teaspoonful at a time, into it and cook for two minutes. Serve with wine and a little melted butter mixed together and poured over the fritters.

SPONGE BATTER PUDDING.

On cup of milk ; make boiling hot and stir into it one-half cup of flour carefully stirred into one cup of cold milk ; cook these together for five minutes, stirring frequently ; three eggs beaten separately ; add to the hot mixture two tablespoonfuls of butter, then add the yolks and two tablespoonfuls of sugar ; lastly, the beaten whites. Bake for thirty minutes in a pan ; set into a pan of hot water ; serve with cream.

SUET PUDDING—1.

One cup of molasses, one cup of suet chopped fine, one cup of milk, one cup of stoned raisins, one teaspoonful of soda, four cups of flour, one teaspoonful of salt. Mix all together, put in buttered pudding mold ; boil for three hours.

Sauce for same : One cup of sugar (powdered is best ; one-half cup of butter ; rub together until creamy, then add one-half cup of hot wine.

SUET PUDDING—2.

One cup of suet chopped fine, one cup of sweet milk, one cup of molasses, one cup of raisins, three cups of flour, one teaspoonful of ginger, one-half teaspoonful of cinnamon, one-half teaspoonful of cloves, one-half nutmeg, one teaspoonful of soda, mixed with the last cup of flour ; chop the raisins. Add if you like one cup of currants. Steam three hours. Serve with hot or cold sauce.

SAUCE FOR THE PUDDING.

One whole egg beaten with two-thirds cup of sugar, three tablespoonfuls of milk. Scald the milk and stir together briskly.

SWEDISH PANCAKES.

Three eggs, yolks only ; nine tablespoonfuls of sweet milk, one tablespoonful of flour, one tablespoonful of sugar, a little salt. Beat all together until very light ; bake on hot griddle; do not turn them but roll with a knife; beat the whites very stiff, add a little sugar and pour over the pancakes, or else whip one-half pint of cream and pour it over instead of the whites.

TOOTHSOME PUDDING.

One quart of milk; when boiling, stir in two tablespoonfuls of farina, then three eggs beaten together until light, one-half cup of sugar, two tablespoonfuls of melted butter. Mix well together. Bake one-half hour.

TRANSPARENT PUDDING.

Eight eggs well beaten, one-half pound of butter, one-half pound of sugar, one-half nutmeg grated. Put into the saucepan and keep constantly stirring till mixture thickens. Cover the pie plates with good puff paste; fill with the mixture after it is cool, bake in a moderate oven. Slices of citron and candied orange can be added if desired.

VENETIAN FRITTERS.

Two tablespoonfuls of rice; wash it, dry and then add one pint of cold milk, and let the milk and rice simmer slowly; stir it frequently until thick and dry; add one tablespoonful of sugar, one tablespoonful of butter, a little salt and the grated rind of one lemon, then let the mixture cool; when cool, add two tablespoonfuls of currants, three tablespoonfuls of apples chopped fine, one tablespoonful of flour and three well beaten eggs; beat these well together, then drop from a spoon into deep hot fat; fry quickly, and serve with sugar sprinkled over them on the dish.

VENOISE PUDDING.

Five ounces of stale bread cut into dice, three ounces of Sultana raisins, two ounces of chopped candied lemon peel, three ounces of sugar, rind of one lemon grated, one-half pint of milk, one-fourth pint of cream, four yolks of eggs, one-half wine glass of sherry, one ounce of butter. Cook the loaf sugar in an old saucepan till it gets black; add the milk, cream, yolks of eggs, the bread, raisins, peel, rind of lemon, sugar and sherry. Mix well together. Butter a china mold, put in the mixture and steam two and one-half hours with a buttered paper over it; turn out and serve with German sauce poured round it.

YORKSHIRE PUDDING.

Three eggs well beaten, one pint of milk, small teaspoon salt, two-thirds of a cup of flour Mix the eggs and milk, take one cup of the mixture and pour over the flour and stir until smooth, then add the remainder and beat well. Bake in hot gem tins forty-five minutes; baste with the drippings from the beef; serve around the beef on the platter.

PRESERVES, ETC.

All preserves and canned fruits should be kept in a cool dark, dry place. Always add a little salt to apples when cooking them, salt improves and brings out the flavor of the apples and not so much sugar is required.

BAKED APPLES WITH BUTTER.

Pare eight good cooking apples and remove the cores—it is better to take out the core of an apple before peeling it; fill the cavities with butter, place the apples in a pan; sprinkle over the apples one cup of sugar, and one teaspoonful of cinnamon; put two tablespoonfuls of water in the pan, and bake the apples in a slow oven until they are tender, then remove from the oven, put them in the dish in which they are to be served; strain the syrup over them.

FRIED APPLES.

Slice the apples; have the frying pan hot; put in one tablespoonful of butter, then the apples, sprinkle a little sugar among the apples; fry slowly until a good brown.

APPLE JELLY.

Pare the apples, cut them in pieces, place in the preserving kettle with a very little cold water, boil slowly until the fruit is soft, skim, then strain through a jelly bag; weigh the juice and for each pound of juice allow three-fourths of a pound of sugar, unless the apples were very acid, then one pound of sugar will not be too much; boil for fifteen minutes, skim, and then stir the sugar into the juice; skim carefully; cook until the sugar is dissolved, or until the juice jellies upon the spoon; then pour into glasses; cover these the next day with papers wet in alcohol, and paste over these another paper. One tablespoonful of lemon juice may be added if desired.

APPLE MARMALADE.

Prepare in the same manner as peach marmalade, omitting the lemon juice.

APPLES STEWED.

Eight firm, large sour apples; pare, core and rub them over with lemon juice; then cook them in a syrup made with one cup of sugar, one pint of water, two cloves. Stew the apples very slowly so that they will retain their shape; when they are soft, put them into a glass dish and strain the syrup over them; to be served cold.

ASPIC OR SAVORY JELLY.

Two calf's feet, three pounds of the knuckle of veal, three-fourths of a pound of lean ham, two onions, three carrots, one bunch of herbs, one blade of mace, twelve pepper-corns, one bunch of sweet herbs, four quarts of water; boil these together until the liquor is reduced to two quarts; skim and strain; when cold skim off all the fat, put the jelly back into the stewpan, stir in the whites of two eggs well beaten, stir until the broth boils, then let it simmer slowly for fifteen minutes; strain through a jelly bag into a mold.

French cooks flavor with one tablespoonful of tarragon vinegar.

BLACKBERRY JAM.

Pick over the berries carefully; to every pint of berries allow three-fourths pint of sugar, mash together and then place in the preserving kettle and let all boil slowly until the syrup thickens; skim the jam and put into jars; the next day cover with papers wet in alcohol, and another cover of stiff paper pasted on with the white of egg slightly beaten.

BLACK CURRANT JELLY FOR GAME.

Mash the currants and boil them in a very little water, just enough to prevent their burning, then strain the juice, and to every pound of juice add one pound of sugar; boil the juice for ten minutes, skim and add the sugar, stir until dissolved. Pour into glasses and cover these when cold, with papers dipped in alcohol.

CURRANT JELLY.

Make the jelly when the fruit is just turning red—the jelly will be firmer and of a better color than it will be made from very ripe currants. Strip the currants from their stems, wash them and put into the preserving kettle, stir until the juice starts from them freely, then strain the juice through the jelly bag, weigh the juice and to every pound allow one pound of sugar, boil the juice for twenty minutes, skim carefully, then add the sugar, which should be hot; stir until the sugar is dissolved, skim and pour into jelly glasses, cover these next day with paper wet in alcohol, and an outside paper tied or pasted over. If the currants are not too ripe the jelly will be firm without longer boiling. Test the juice on a saucer; if it jellies quickly it is cooked enough.

WHIPPED CURRANT JELLY.

TO SERVE WITH GAME.

One hour before dinner take a glass of currant jelly and whip it with an egg; whip until it is all foamy. Whip the whites of two eggs until very stiff, add to them two tablespoonfuls of fine sugar, fold them into the jelly and heap on a glass dish, putting a little granulated sugar over. Any tart jelly can be used in this way.

WHIPPED CRANBERRY JELLY.

TO SERVE WITH ROAST TURKEY.

Prepare the cranberries, removing all skins as recipe given, and proceed as for whipped currant jelly.

PRESERVED SOUR CHERRIES.

A pound of sugar to a pound of cherries, stoned. Take one-half the weight of the sugar to make a syrup, scald that syrup and pour it over the cherries and let it stand until the next morning, continue to do this for eight mornings, the ninth morning put in the other half of the sugar and scald it; when boiling put in the cherries and let them scald, then seal in glass jars.

CRAB APPLE JELLY.

Put the crab-apples into the kettle with not quite enough water to cover them, let them simmer until soft; strain through a sieve. Take the pulp and strain it through a cheese cloth bag, then strain all the juice through a flannel bag. To the juice allow three pints of sugar to four pints of juice; boil the juice twenty minutes before adding the sugar; boil together until the juice will thicken on a spoon when tested. Fill the jelly glasses, dip them in warm water before filling. When the jelly is cold put a thin paper on the top of each glass, dipped in alcohol, and paste over the top of the glass a paper which can be pasted tightly over by using the beaten white of egg for the paste.

BRANDIED CHERRIES.

Pick the cherries on a dry, clear day; fill wide mouthed, glass jars with the fruit, and then pour in as much good, pale brandy as the jars will hold. Cover closely and place in a cool, dry place for four weeks. Then pour off the liquor; add to each pint three-quarters of a pound of white sugar; boil these together until a thick syrup is obtained, strain it and pour it over the cherries, then boil all together for five minutes; return to the bottles and cover tightly.

GRAPE JUICE.

Take only fresh ripe grapes, the Concord grapes make the richest juice, though other grapes may be used. Free the grapes from the stems, use no sugar; put on the fire; as soon as the grapes are soft strain them through a jelly bag of flannel or cheese cloth; when strained, put back on the fire, and when boiling once more, bottle and seal or put into glass jars and seal.

FRUIT JAM.

Mix strawberries and pineapple. To every bowlful of strawberries put one-half a bowlful of pineapple shredded fine,—to each pound of mixed fruit put three-fourth pounds of sugar. Boil for two hours and seal while hot.

PEAR PRESERVES.

Four pounds of hard pears, four pounds of sugar, one-fourth pound of preserved ginger, four lemons, one pint of water. Pare and cut the pears into very thin slices, chop the ginger fine. Place pears, ginger, sugar, lemon peel and water into the preserving kettle and boil until the fruit is transparent, adding the lemon juice at the end. Seal while hot.

DAMSON PLUM JAM.

Stone the plums, which should be fresh and ripe, boil them for forty minutes in the preserving kettle, skim carefully, then add three-fourths of a pound of sugar to every pound of plums, boil for fifteen minutes, then put into small glasses or jam pots; cover when cold with papers dipped in alcohol, and outside of these paste a stiff paper.

Green gage plums are prepared in the same way.

BRANDY PLUMS.

Ten quarts of plums, seven pounds of sugar, to every pound a half pint of water; when melted, put in the plums, having stuck them all with a pin. Throw them into cold water, then back into the syrup and let them stand until tender (do not boil). Strain the syrup, then let cool, when cold put your plums into jars, and to every half pint of syrup put one-half pint of brandy; bottle.

PEACH MARMALADE.

Pare, cut in pieces and weigh the peaches; for every pound of fruit allow a pound of sugar. Cook the peaches in a very little water for three-fourths of an hour, skim carefully and then add the sugar; crack a number of the stones and put the kernels into the marmalade, add one tablespoonful of lemon juice; boil all together for ten minutes, then put into small glasses; cover the next day with papers dipped in alcohol, and paste an outside paper over. It is an improvement, after the peaches are tender and before the sugar is added, if the fruit is pressed through a sieve and then returned to the fire.

PLUM MARMALADE.

Prepare in the same manner as peach marmalade, only omitting the lemon juice.

PINEAPPLE MARMALADE.

Peel the pineapples, carefully removing all the dark specks, then grate the fruit on a coarse grater, and put it into the preserving kettle, allowing to each pound of fruit a scant pound of sugar. Boil sugar and fruit together until the fruit is clear, skim and then put into small glasses or jam pots. Cover when cold with papers dipped in alcohol, and over this paste stiff white paper.

QUINCE AND APPLE MARMALADE.

Peel, cut in pieces, equal quantities of apples and quinces, and follow the directions for peach marmalade, omitting the lemon juice; add one-half teaspoonful of salt. Be careful to remove the hard parts of the quince around the cores, and cook the quinces first in water until tender before adding the apples.

CANNED PEACHES.

Peel the peaches, remove the stones, then weigh the fruit; to every pound of peaches put one-fourth pound of sugar, place all in the preserving kettle with a little water; let the fruit boil for ten minutes, skim carefully. Place in jars, and fill the jars very full. Screw on the covers as soon as the fruit is put in the jars.

PRESERVED PEACHES.

Peel the peaches, cut in halves, remove the stones, weigh the peaches. For every pound of fruit allow one pound of sugar; place the sugar and peaches in the preserving kettle with just a little water; crack some of the stones and put the meats with the fruit; stew slowly and skim often; when the peaches are clear remove them to a platter; let the syrup boil until thick, then strain it over the peaches; when cold, place in glasses or jars, and cover with papers dipped in alcohol.

BAKED PIE PLANT.

Cut the pie plant into pieces about an inch long, put in a baking dish with an equal weight of sugar, cover closely and bake about one hour.

QUINCE JELLY.

Quarter and core the ripe quinces, throw them into cold water until all are prepared; weigh, and allow one pint of water to each pound of fruit, simmer the fruit until it is very soft, be careful it does not burn, then strain through a jelly bag, do not squeese the bag; weigh the juice, put it in a preserving kettle, and boil rapidly for twenty minutes; skim, then stir into it one pound of sugar to each pound of juice. If the fruit is very sweet three-fourths of a pound will answer. Boil for twenty or thirty minutes, stir constantly and skim carefully until the juice jellies in falling from the spoon; then pour into jelly glasses, cover the next day with paper wet in alcohol, and then paper pasted over the tops.

QUINCES PRESERVED IN SLICES.

Pare and core and cut into thin slices the ripe quinces; throw the slices into cold water until all are prepared. For every pound of fruit allow three-quarters of a pound of white sugar. Put the quince slices into the preserving kettle with a very little water, cook the fruit for ten minutes, then add the sugar, which has been dissolved in as little water as possible. Cook together until the slices of fruit are soft and clear. When clear, put into glasses and the next day cover with papers wet in alcohol and covered with dry papers.

EAST INDIA PRESERVES.

One-half bushel of green tomatoes; after washing and slicing them into round, rather thick slices, put them into a porcelain kettle and boil until they are a light, transparent green color. Drain off the water and measure the tomatoes; take to each pound of tomatoes, one pound of sugar, three lemons cut into slices, five cents' worth of ginger root broken into small pieces; boil all these well together until the mixture is very thick—but the pieces should keep their forms—remove from the fire. In four days boil the mixture again if it is not thick enough. This preserve need not be sealed in jars.

SPICED TUTTI-FRUTTI PRESERVES.

Scald twelve pounds of currants, rub them through a sieve to remove all seeds and stems; after this add to the currants three pounds of seeded raisins, twelve oranges cut in pieces and all seeds removed, and the grated rind of two oranges; add ten pounds of sugar, two teaspoonfuls of powdered cinnamon, one-half teaspoonful of powdered mace. Stew slowly until quite thick.

GRAPE JELLY.

Pick the grapes from the stems, wash and mash them, cook until they are soft, then strain; then boil this juice for for five minutes, then strain and add to one pint of juice one pound of sugar. Boil together for fifteen minutes.

LEMON JELLY.

One box of gelatine, soak in one pint of cold water for one-half hour; add one quart of boiling water, one quart of sugar, the juice of eight lemons. Strain into a jelly mold.

PRUNE JELLY.

One pound of prunes, one-fourth pound of sugar, one-half a lemon, one ounce of gelatine, one-half pint of cream. Put the prunes into a saucepan with sufficient water to cover them, add the sugar and the peel of the lemon, stew gently two hours, pass through a wire sieve, add the gelatine, having previously soaked it in water. Crack the prune stones and put the kernels into the jelly; boil all together for a few minutes and pour into a china mold which is the shape of a ring. Whip the cream and heap it up high in the center of the mold, and serve.

WINE JELLY—1.

One box of gelatine, soak this in one pint of cold water for two hours, then add one quart of boiling water, one and three-fourths pounds of sugar, the juice of two lemons and one pint of sherry.

WINE JELLY—2.

One package of gelatine, soak for two hours or more in one cup of cold water, then add the juice of one lemon and a little of the grated rind, two cups of granulated sugar, two cups of boiling water, two cups of Catawba or sherry wine; let all soak together for an hour, then add the water and strain through a flannel bag; when all is strained put the liquid into a jelly mold and set on the ice to harden. If desired to serve with cream, put the jelly into a mold which has an open center; this center can be filled with whipped cream when ready to serve.

RASPBERRY JELLY.

To each pound of raspberry juice add one pound of sugar. Prepare the juice in the same manner as for currant jelly.

RASPBERRY JAM.

Select ripe, fresh fruit; to each pound of fruit allow one pound of sugar; mash the raspberries, add the sugar, and boil together until the jam is clear, thick, and smooth—remove all the scum as it rises. When cooked put into jelly glasses; cover when cold with papers dipped in alcohol, and on the outside put papers either pasted or tied down.

STRAWBERRY JAM.

Prepare in the same way as for raspberry jam.

STRAWBERRY PRESERVES.

Take the hulls from the berries; if possible avoid washing the berries—if it is necessary to do so be as expiditious as possible. Take one pound of sugar to each pound of fruit; place the berries in preserving kettle, let them come to the boiling point slowly; boil for fifteen minutes, carefully skim them, then place in small jars or tumblers; the next day cover with a paper wet in alcohol, and outside of this a white paper pasted down over the tops with a paste made of the white of an egg slightly beaten.

TO STERILIZE FRESH FRUITS.

Fill the jars with the fruit, which must be freshly gathered and fully ripe. Sprinkle white sugar over the fruit. Place the filled jars in a fish boiler, fill it half full of warm water; place a little straw between the jars. Bring the water to boiling and keep it at this point for fifty minutes, keeping the boiler almost closed; scald the covers of the jars, place them on the jars as quickly as possible while the fruit is hot.

STRAWBERRIES PRESERVED IN THE SUN.

Select fine, large berries, remove the hulls. To each pound of berries put three-quarters of a pound of white sugar, let the sugar remain over the berries for three hours, then place all in the preserving kettle and boil for ten minutes. At the end of that time carefully remove the berries from the syrup with a skimmer and place them on platters and put them in the sun. Cook the syrup until it is thick, then pour it over the berries. The next day pour off the syrup, re-heat it, pour it over the berries and put all in the sun. Keep the berries in the sun until all the syrup is absorbed, then put into glass jars and cover with papers wet in alcohol, and with dry papers pasted over.

VEGETABLE MARROW PRESERVE.
BOSTON SQUASH.

Peel and remove the pulp and seeds, then cut into inch cubes, let no water be added, the juice of the marrow being sufficient moisture for the syrup—two pounds of marrow, two pounds of sugar, the juice of one lemon, the peel cut fine, three-fourths of an ounce of root ginger, one saltspoonful of cayenne pepper; boil gently one and one-half hours; when the syrup is transparent, add one-half of a wine glass of sherry, brandy or whiskey; place in glasses and cover with papers wet in alcohol and an outer paper pasted over. Be careful to rub the marrow, not to wash it, should any earth adhere.

WATERMELON PRESERVES.

Sixteen pounds of watermelon; remove the green rind and the seeds, cut the melon into two-inch squares. Take one-half pound of sugar to every pound of fruit, place in kettle one layer of fruit, one layer of sugar, then let these stand over night; next morning boil for four hours steadily, then add six lemons cut up into very small pieces and a little ginger root; boil one-half hour longer.

SYRUP.

To every pound of white sugar allow one-half pint of water and one-half the white of an egg. Beat the egg until light, then put it, the sugar and water, into a clean saucepan, but let the sugar dissolve before putting on the fire. When the syrup boils, add one teacup of cold water, but do not stir it at all. Carefully remove all the scum as it rises, and when the syrup is clear it is ready for use. Put into glass jars and cover. It will keep for a long time.

ORANGE SUGAR.

Cut off the thin yellow rind of oranges, and dry it. When it is dry (it will take two days to dry) put into the mortar with one cupful of granulated sugar. Pound the mixture until it is a powder, then rub it through a very fine seive. The rind of twelve oranges will require two cupfuls of sugar. When very finely powdered, put into tight glass jars. One tablespoonful of this mixture is required for flavoring a custard or cake.

Lemon Sugar can be prepared in the same manner as orange sugar.

VANILLA SUGAR.

One pound of powdered sugar, one ounce of Vanilla bean, split the bean, remove the seeds, pound well together with the sugar until fine, then bottle for use.

FRIED APPLES.

Slice the apples; have the frying pan hot; put in one tablespoonful of butter, then the apples; sprinkle a little sugar among the apples; fry slowly until a good brown.

SALTED NUTS AND CANDY.

SALTED ALMONDS—1.

Blanch one pound of freshly-shelled Jordan almonds by pouring boiling water over them. When they have stood covered for five minutes rub off the skins of the nuts, one by one, with the finger and thumb. This process of removing the skin of the almond, called blanching, is easily accomplished if the water is actually boiling, not merely warm, when it is poured over them. For this purpose the nuts should be placed in a tin pan and left a moment on the stove after the boiling water is poured over them. They should all be covered in order that the skins of all shall be "started," so they will rub off easily with the finger and thumb. Dry the blanched nuts with coarse towels, so as to absorb any moisture about them, and measure them by the pint. Allow two tablespoonfuls of the best olive oil or the same amount of melted butter to each pint. Toss the nuts, a pint at a time, until they are evenly or thoroughly coated with the oil, or melted butter, if you prefer it. Let the nuts stand closely covered in the closet, under the oven or in some such warm place for about an hour, until they have partly absorbed the oil about them. Dredge two tablespoonfuls of salt over them, and stir in order to distribute the salt evenly. Spread the almonds on tin biscuit-pans, or better still, on sheets of tin that fit the oven, and let them bake in the oven bottom until they are slightly colored or begin to be crisp. If the oven is hot, it will not take over ten or twelve minutes. It must not be too hot or they will burn.

Salted almonds are served at dinner, with the cheese and crackers, or at an afternoon tea. They are sometimes chopped and put on chocolate loaf-cake.

SALTED ALMONDS—2.

Shell the nuts and blanch them by covering them with boiling water for a moment, then throw them into cold water in order to remove the skins. To one pint of nuts take one tablespoonful of olive oil or melted butter; let the nuts stand in this for an hour, stir them occasionally, then drain and sprinkle the nuts with two tablespoonfuls of salt. Put into a moderate oven and bake until they are all a delicate brown.

You can prepare peanuts and pine nuts in the same manner.

SALTED HICKORY NUTS.

Proceed as for salted almonds—without blanching them.

PECAN NUTS.

Proceed as for salted almonds—without blanching them.

NUT LOAF.

Chop very fine one-half pound of nuts—almonds, pecan or hickory nuts, add one pound of bread crumbs, one-quarter of a pound of butter. Stir these into one pint of boiling water, add one egg well beaten, a little salt, pepper and a pinch of sage or any sweet herb. Mix well together. Butter a baking dish, pour in the mixture, sprinkle some fine crumbs and bits of butter on the top and bake for one hour in a moderate oven, then turn the loaf on a platter and garnish with celery tops or parsley.

CARAMEL.

One and one-half pounds of brown sugar, one-fourth pound of butter, one-fourth pound of chocolate (Baker's), one teacupful of milk. Boil twenty minutes, stir all the time, then add one tablespoonful of vanilla. Pour on buttered plates.

CARAMELS.

Two pounds of brown sugar, one cup of milk, piece of butter the size of an egg, one-half pound of chocolate. Boil between twenty and thirty minutes; on taking off pour in the white of one egg well beaten; flavor with vanilla; beat six minutes, then cool.

CHOCOLATE CARAMELS.

One-third of a cake of Baker's chocolate, two cups of granulated sugar, one-half cup of sweet milk, one piece of butter the size of an egg; flavor when done with vanilla, using about one tablespoonful. After boiling the chocolate, sugar and butter for about fifteen minutes, the sides of the kettle become sugary, then pour in the vanilla, take off the fire put on two buttered cake pans; cut before it is hard into squares.

FOOD FOR INVALIDS.

To provide a sick person with nutritious food, of the proper quantity and quality, is one of the most important requirements of good nursing. It is well known that drugs alone cannot take the place of food. In the often long convalescent stage of illness resources are taxed to the utmost to prepare the proper food which shall be at the same time nourishing and tempting.

The tray becomes a source of weariness and the question: "What shall I give the invalid?" a constantly recurring one. Milk is now given so generally that it is absolutely necessary to be able to prepare it in many different ways, for of no food will a patient weary sooner. Let the tray always present an inviting appearance, every napkin and dish be perfectly clean, the food arranged in an inviting manner. Special care should be given that any diet ordered to be served hot is really hot, and any diet to be served cold, is cold.

The food should never wait in the sick room before being served, and the tray and contents be at once removed after the patient is fed. Attention to little details, trivial perhaps in themselves when one is well, but of great consequence to an invalid, will aid greatly towards the recovery of the patient.

BEEF BROTH—1.

A good beef broth is really much more nourishing than beef tea. To make the broth take a piece from the neck, chop it and the bone quite fine, have more beef than bone. Take one pound of beef and one-third of a pound of bone, put one quart of cold water over the meat and bone, cover the pan and let it simmer for four hours; remove all fat, put with the broth two stalks of celery and a little salt; strain and serve a small cupful at a time.

BEEF BROTH—2.

Take one pound of the leg of beef, trim off all fat and pound the meat well, then put into the stew-pan with one quart of cold water, one small carrot cut fine, one onion sliced, a little salt, one blade of mace; stir the broth until it boils, then skim carefully; place on the back of the stove and let it simmer for two hours; strain and serve. If put away to keep, be sure to remove all fat before warming it again. This should be done to all broths.

The extracts of beef are nearly always made from the least nutritious part of the fresh meat, so that there is little left in it, but the flavoring matter and the salts, these serve to give an agreeable flavor and rich color, but no solid nourishment.

BEEF ESSENCE.

This is much better for an invalid than beef tea. Take a good beefsteak from the round, say two pounds, cut it in small pieces, put into a Mason jar and set in the oven, in a pan of hot water; as the juice runs from the meat take it away at intervals and slightly salt it. One teaspoonful of this liquor is worth a pint of the ordinary beef tea.

BEEF JUICE.

Heat on the broiler a thick piece of steak, about one pound; when hot, squeeze out the juice; serve at once.

RAW BEEF SANDWICH.

Scrape the tender meat with a sharp knife, spread it on thin slices of buttered bread, season with a little salt; cut off the crusts and cut the sandwich from corner to corner, so as to make two small, three-cornered pieces.

CLAM BROTH.

Take twelve clams, boil them in their own liquor for fifteen minutes, strain the liquor and serve.

CHICKEN BROTH.

Take an old chicken, cut it in pieces and put it in the saucepan with three pints of cold water, one tablespoonful of rice; let the soup simmer slowly; when the chicken is thoroughly cooked, take from the fire, skim every bit of fat from the soup before serving; season with salt and pepper.

EGG BROTH.

Beat an egg until it is frothy, stir into it a pint of boiling hot meat broth, free from fat, season it with a saltspoonful of salt, and eat it hot, with thin slices of dry toast; it may be given to assist the patient in gaining strength.

MEAT BROTH.

One pound of mutton, one pound of veal, one-half a chicken, one calf's foot, two quarts of water, one teaspoonful of salt, a little pepper; simmer for four hours, strain and put in a mold and keep on the ice until needed. Serve hot.

MUTTON BROTH.

One and one-half pounds of mutton, free from gristle, one quart of cold water, two tablespoonfuls of rice, one-half teaspoonful of salt; simmer for four hours, strain and serve a small quantity at a time to the patient; serve very hot.

BROTH MADE FROM THE SHEEP "TROTTERS."

Take eight trotters with just a little of the lower part of the meat from the leg; put them into four quarts of cold water and one cupful of rice; let them simmer slowly for eight hours, add a little salt and take from the fire and strain. The next day take off every particle of fat and heat a little of the broth; it should be given in small quantities and frequently. This is a very excellent broth for a weak stomach. A patient can retain it when all other broths or foods have failed.

VEAL BROTH.

Two pounds of perfectly lean veal, one-fourth pound of pearl barley; cut the meat into thin, small pieces; boil it and the barley together for three hours, boil slowly; then strain through a sieve and add one-half teaspoonful of salt. This broth is light and nourishing, and easy of digestion.

HAMBURG STEAK.

Take one-half pound of good beef; scrape all the pulp from the fiber, season with a little salt and pepper, make into a small steak and broil over a clear fire, or cook on the skillet, which should be very hot before the meat is put on it. Three minutes will cook the steak. Place a small piece of butter on the steak, garnish with a little bit of parsley, and serve very hot.

MILK OF EGGS.

Beat the yolks of two fresh eggs with one-half tablespoonful of sugar and one teaspoonful of orange flower water; stir these into one-half pint of boiling milk or water. This must be taken hot, and is most soothing for a cold or cough.

EGG AND PORT WINE.

One fresh egg mixed with one tablespoonful of cold water. then add one wine glass of Port wine, a little grated nutmeg. Put a teaspoonful of sugar into the sauce-pan and when hot, stir in the egg mixture and stir carefully. The mixture is then poured into a glass and served with a cracker.

POACHED EGGS.

Have the water in the sauce-pan boiling, add a little salt and one tablespoonful of vinegar. Break the eggs separately into a saucer, slip them into the water carefully; do not let the water boil again. Pour some of the hot water over each egg with a spoon, so as to make a thin white film over them. Take carefully from the fire; place each egg on a piece of hot toast. Serve hot.

EGGS POACHED IN BROTH.

Have the broth hot in the sauce-pan, break very gently the eggs into it, cook three minutes, remove and put each egg on a slice of hot toast; if the gravy is desired, thicken it with a little flour, add one teaspoonful of butter, strain around the egg.

POACHED EGGS IN MILK.

Have the milk boiling hot, add a little salt, drop in the eggs carefully, one by one; remove as soon as they are set; place on hot toast, and serve at once.

EGG-NOG.

One egg beaten very light, one tablespoonful of sugar beaten into the egg, then add slowly one tablespoonful of brandy and one-half a cup of milk—cream may be substituted for the milk.

BREAD JELLY.

Remove the crust from the roll, slice the crumb and toast it; put the slices in one quart of water, and set it over the fire to simmer until it jellies; then strain it through a cloth, sweeten it, and flavor it with lemon juice; put it into a mold and cool it upon the ice before using.

CURRANT JELLY-WATER,

Dissolve one teaspoonful of currant jelly in a glass of cold water.

CHICKEN JELLY.

See chapter on Chicken.

LEMON JELLY.

Three lemons—juice only, one pound of white sugar, three pints of boiling water, one ounce of gelatine dissolved in the boiling water, then add the juice and sugar and strain into small molds.

RESTORATIVE JELLY.

One half box of gelatine, one tablespoonful of granulated gum-arabic, three tablespoonfuls of sugar, two tablespoonfuls of lemon juice, two cloves, one-half a pint of port—soak all these together for two hours; keep the basin covered; then put into a sauce-pan and cook, stirring constantly until everything is dissolved, then strain and place on the ice. This jelly is excellent where the patient is unable to swallow solid food or even liquid, for it melts slowly in the mouth. A tablespoonful of beef juice can be added when the jelly is taken from the fire, if a stimulent is desired.

STRENGTHENING JELLY.

One pint of port wine, one package of gelatine, three-fourths of an ounce of gum arabic, one-fourth pound of rock candy. Place all in a basin and let the mixture stand all night; the next morning put the basin in one of boiling water, stir constantly until the ingredients are dissolved, then strain through a jelly bag into a mold.

SAGO JELLY.

One cupful of sago soaked over night in cold water. Boil it in a double boiler for one hour, then uncover and let the water boil away; add two cupfuls of sugar and the juice of one lemon; pour into the dish in which it is to be served to cool. Serve rich cream with jelly.

TAPIOCA JELLY.

Wash one ounce of tapioca, soak it over night in cold water, and then simmer it with a bit of lemon peel until it is thoroughly dissolved. Sweeten it to taste, and let it cool before using.

EGG PUDDING.

One egg beaten until light, and one teaspoonful of flour which has been mixed smoothly into one tablespoonful of milk, add a saltspoonful of salt (be careful with the salt as many invalids dislike salt), strain into a buttered cup, and set into boiling water to simmer for twenty minutes.

EGG TEA—1

Beat the yolk of an egg in a cup of tea, and let the sick person drink it warm; the yolk is more readily digested than the white, and has a better flavor; and the tea is a powerful respiratory excitant, while it promotes perspiration, and aids the assimilation of more nourishing foods.

EGG TEA—2

The white of one egg beaten into a stiff froth; the yolk beaten light with one teaspoonful of sugar. Mix together and pour into a half cupful of hot milk, stir all the time; add a little grated nutmeg and a wee pinch of salt.

BARLEY GRUEL.

Three tablespoonfuls of pearl barley, wash in several waters, then drop it into one pint of boiling water for five minutes. Pour off this water and add one quart of fresh boiling water; put on back of stove and let it simmer for three hours, then strain and season with a little salt or sugar. Equal quantities of barley gruel and milk make a nourishing drink.

EGG GRUEL—1.

Beat well one egg, add a very little salt, one sprig of parsley; stir this into one cup of boiling water, strain over small slices of hot toast.

EGG GRUEL—2.

Boil two eggs until perfectly hard, when cold, mash the yolks smooth and stir gradually into the yolks one cup of hot milk, and a little salt and serve in bowl.

FARINA GRUEL.

Stir two tablespoonfuls of farina into three tablespoonfuls of milk; pour this into one pint of boiling water, boil it until thoroughly cooked; stir frequently. Take from the fire, add one saltspoonful of salt and two tablespoonfuls of cream.

FLOUR GRUEL.

Put into a strong cotton cloth, one pint of flour, tie it up into a ball, boil for four hours, keep it well covered with water. When needed to use, have one pint of milk boiling in the double boiler, stir into it one tablespoonful of the flour-ball, (you scrape the ball and mix a little water with the flour), add one saltspoonful of salt and a little sugar if liked. This is an excellent remedy in cases of summer complaint. The ball will keep for months, if kept dry and cool.

GRAHAM GRUEL.

One tablespoonful of graham flour mixed with four tablespoonfuls of water: stir this into one pint of boiling water, cook for thirty minutes, add one saltspoonful of salt, and strain into one cup of cream. Serve hot.

INDIAN MEAL GRUEL.

One quart of boiling water. Mix two tablespoonfuls of meal with two tablespoonfuls of cold water, stir this into the boiling water; when it boils, put it on the back of the stove and simmer for two hours, then add one-half teaspoonful of salt, simmer for one-half hour, then put some of the gruel into a cup and add one tablespoonful of cream and serve hot.

OATMEAL GRUEL.

Mix two tablespoonfuls of oatmeal with three tablespoonfuls of cold water: put this into one pint of boiling water, pour in gradually and boil five minutes, stirring constantly; add one teaspoonful of salt, skim and strain through a hair sieve. One tablespoonful of cream improves the gruel, if it is permitted by the physician.

OATS AND CREAM GRUEL.

Take one tablespoonful of rolled oats and cook them in one pint of water; when soft, strain through a sieve; add to this one cup of cream, one saltspoonful of salt; let this mixture come to the boiling point, then remove from the fire and add the whites of two eggs, beaten stiffly. Add a little sugar and a little grated nutmeg.

SAGO GRUEL.

Soak one ounce of sago, after washing it well, in a pint of tepid water for two hours; then simmer it in the same water for fifteen minutes, stirring it occasionally; then sweeten and flavor it to taste, and use at once.

PEA SOUP.

One pint of fresh, green peas; boil until tender, then drain and mash them through a sieve, return to the stewpan and add one pint of thin cream, one teaspoonful of sugar, one saltspoonful of salt, a little pepper, one-half tablespoonful of butter; let the soup become hot, and serve with crackers. This is a nutritious soup for an invalid.

TAPIOCA SOUP WITH CREAM.

Boil with one pint of white stock, one tablespoonful of prepared tapioca; let in simmer until the tapioca is clear. Mix the yolks of two eggs with two tablespoonfuls of cream, a little salt and pepper. Let the soup cool; when cool, stir in the egg and cream mixture, after which beat together, but do not boil or the eggs will curdle.

TAPIOCA CREAM.

One cupful of tapioca; soak this over night in one cupful of milk; the next morning cook the tapioca and milk until soft, then add the yolks of three eggs and one cupful of sugar. Take one quart of milk; when boiling, stir in the tapioca mixture and cook until it thickens, then take from the fire and stir in the whites of the eggs, beaten very stiff, and any flavoring that is liked; pour into a mold and let it cool, or it can be served hot.

TAPIOCA PORRIDGE.

One teacup of tapioca soaked in two teacupfuls of cold water for several hours, then add one and one-half pints of milk and cook for several hours in the double boiler; add a pinch of salt and one glass of wine. One-half cup of sugar if desired sweet.

PANADA—1.

Steep one cupful of bread crumbs in hot water until they have absorbed all the water, then add a little more water and mash through a sieve. Make a custard with one cup of milk and one egg; when thick, add it to the panada, add a little salt. Serve either hot or cold.

PANADA—2.

One ounce of grated bread or crackers, add one-half a pint of boiling water, boil for five minutes, then add one tablespoonful of grated nutmeg.

EGGS AND ORANGE JUICE.

A palatable, nourishing drink for a person with weak digestion is made with the whites of two eggs beaten but not frothed, and the juice of one orange; place on the ice until very cold. The white of an egg, beaten, slightly sweetened and flavored with orange juice or a little vanilla, is also a good drink for an invalid; all should be served very cold.

WINE WHEY.

Take one cup of new milk and boil, adding a cup of sherry. Then strain through a cheese cloth.

MILK PREPARATIONS.

Milk is of special value as a food for invalids; it is easily taken, easily digested, and the diet is more under the control of the physician than other foods. Life can be supported for a long time on milk alone.

"Milk contains all of the ingredients needed for nourishment; it furnishes the materials needed which build up the body and keep it in repair, and also those which supply it with fuel to keep it warm and to furnish the animal machine with the necessary power to do its work. Skim milk has great value as a food when used in cooking or when taken with bread. Milk comes nearest to being a perfect food."

BAKED MILK.

Put the milk into a jar; cover the top with white paper; bake the milk in a moderate oven until thick as cream. This preparation of milk can be taken by the most delicate stomach.

CLABBERED MILK.

Fill a glass dish with milk, cover and let it stand until it is smooth and jelly like—in winter this may take three or four days, in summer, two generally. When the milk is clabbered, put the dish on the ice for an hour to chill it, do not disturb it. Serve with sweet cream and a little grated nutmeg.

MILK WITH CHOCOLATE.

Grate one ounce of chocolate; mix it into a paste with a little cold milk, then stir it into one pint of boiling milk, add a little salt, one teaspoonful of sugar, and the well-beaten yolks of two eggs. Serve hot.

CHICKEN MILK.

Cut a chicken into small pieces, see that it is well cleaned in a careful manner, take off the skin, put the chicken into a sauce-pan which is either granite-ware or China-lined, add a tablespoonful of celery cut fine, a little sprig of parsley, four pepper-corns, one-half saltspoonful of salt; cover the meat with cold water and let it simmer until the meat is all in rags, then strain into a bowl; when cold, it should be a firm jelly. When needed, carefully wipe off every bit of fat from the top of the jelly. Take equal quantities of jelly and fresh milk, boil them together, strain into a cup—one teacupful is sufficient at a time. It can be used hot or allowed to again become cold and formed into jelly. A small strip of toast can be served with it if desired.

CITRONIZED MILK JELLY.

One quart of milk, three-fourths of a pound of powdered sugar, four lemons, one ounce of gelatine. Boil the milk, sugar and gelatine together with some of the lemon rind cut very thin, then put the mixture into a basin to cool; add the juice of the lemon and stir until the milk is curdled, then pour into a mold and let the jelly set. The casein rises to the top; when the jelly is turned out it occupies the base and the jelly the top.

DIGESTED MILK.

One pint of milk added while boiling hot, to one pint of cold milk, then add thirty grains of carbonate of soda, then one and one-half teaspoonfuls of Liquid Pancreaticus; mix and let stand for three hours in an even temperature. This preparation can be used when Koumiss is not obtainable. Take a large wine glassful at a time.

HOT MILK.

Hot milk is one of the most nourishing things that can be given to a weak or exhausted patient, or to any one suffering from a severe chill. If it is absolutely necessary to add any other stimulant, add it after the milk is taken from the fire. The milk should never boil for hot milk.

JUNKET.

One pint of fresh milk, warm the milk slightly, then stir into it one teaspoonful of rennet liquor, or one teaspoonful of Prepared Pepsin—use only the best for preparing Junket. Stir the rennet liquor or the pepsin only enough to mingle it with the milk; the milk will thicken in a few minutes; place on the ice or in a cold place. Serve with sweet cream and sugar or with cream and a little nutmeg.

LABAN.

One quart of new milk, one tablespoonful of yeast; stir the yeast into the milk and let it stand for twenty-four hours—it will then be hard. Take a tablespoonful of this and stir into a quart of new milk and put it away to harden—this is Laban. To keep a supply, if needed, reserve a tablespoonful each day for the next preparation. Eat with sugar and cream.

MILK SOUP.

One quart of milk, one egg, one-half tablespoonful of flour, a little salt, one-half teaspoonful of sugar, a little lemon peel or a bit of cinnamon stick. Boil these together; as soon as the mixture boils, remove from the fire and stir in the white of egg beaten very stiff.

THICK MILK.

Put into the stew-pan one tablespoonful of flour, one tablespoonful of sugar, a saltspoonful of salt. Mix together until a smooth paste with one pint of milk; stir with a wooden spoon; if too thick add more milk. Boil for fifteen minutes. The soup should be thick enough to coat the spoon. Add a little nutmeg if liked and serve. It is a digestible soup for young children.

MILK WITH WHITE OF EGG.

One cup of milk; beat well with the milk the white of an egg; put into a glass and serve; add the milk slowly to the egg. The addition of a tablespoonful of clear coffee is sometimes relished by the patient—or the milk slightly salted.

MILK SHAKE.

Fill up a large glass two-thirds full of sweet milk, sweeten with syrup, or with the strained juice from any rich preserve, a few drops of vanilla can be added or a teaspoonful of orange juice. Fill up the glass with pounded ice, place the mixture in the shaker and shake well, or pour from one glass to another until well mixed.

BARLEY WATER.

Wash two ounces of pearl barley in cold water until it does not cloud the water; boil it for five minutes in half a pint of water; drain that off, put the barley into two quarts of clean water, and boil it down to one quart. Cool, strain, and use. Pearl barley largely contains starch and mucilage, and makes an excellent soothing and refreshing draught in fevers and gastric inflamations.

CRUST COFFEE.

Toast two slices of bread until very brown, break into small pieces, put one-half pint of the pieces into a pitcher and pour over them one and one-half pints of boiling water; cover the pitcher, let it stand for ten minutes, then strain. Serve either hot or cold—a little milk can be added if liked, or the coffee can be made with boiling hot milk instead of water.

FLAXSEED LEMONADE—1.

Put two tablespoonfuls of flaxseed into a pitcher, pour over it one pint of boiling water; let this steep for three hours on the back of the stove, then strain and add the juice of one lemon and one tablespoonful of sugar or more if desired; if the lemonade is too thick, add more water. This is soothing for colds and fever.

FLAXSEED LEMONADE—2.

Pour one quart of boiling water over four tablespoonfuls of whole flaxseed, and steep three hours, covered. Then sweeten to taste, and add the juice of two lemons, using a little more water if the liquid seems too thick to be palatable. This beverage is very soothing to the irritated membranes in cases of severe cold.

KOUMISS.

Two quarts of milk slightly warmed, add two tablespoonfuls of sugar and one-half of a two-cent cake of compressed yeast. Blend ingredients thoroughly, bottle and cork and tie corks down; put in warm place for six hours and then in ice box for two days before using.

ICELAND MOSS CHOCOLATE.

Dissolve one ounce of Iceland moss in one pint of boiling milk; boil one ounce of chocolate for five minutes in one pint of boiling water; thoroughly mix the two, and give it to the invalid night and morning. This is a highly nutrative drink for convalescents.

DRY TOAST.

In making toast there is apt to be great carelessness and ignorance shown; the bread is generally cut too thick and the slices are unevenly colored. Cut the slices thin and even; it is a good plan to dry the slices before toasting, then place them on the toaster over a clear fire, and turn constantly so that the slices are well browned; always serve toast hot,

CREAM TOAST—1.

Toast a slice of bread evenly and quickly; dip it into boiling water, then sprinkle a little salt on it, and cover with rich hot cream.

CREAM TOAST—2.

Prepare as for dry toast; pour over a little hot water, which must be drained off in a few minutes; then spread some butter and a little salt on the slices, and pour over some good rich cream; place in a hot oven for a few minutes and serve at once.

MARROW-BONE TOAST.

Take two beef marrow-bones, cover each end with dough made with flour and water mixed together, boil the bones for an hour, then remove the dough, take out the marrow, spread on hot toast and season with salt and cayenne, and serve hot.

OYSTER TOAST.

Chop very fine fifteen good oysters, add a little salt and pepper and a little nutmeg; beat two eggs with one tablespoonful of cream, heat and stir in the oysters, simmer together for five minutes, then pour the mixture over slices of hot, buttered toast.

WATER TOAST.

When the toast is ready, place in hot plate, pour over a little boiling water, spread a little butter evenly on top and a little fine salt, cover tightly for a few minutes to soak up the water, and serve immediately.

OATMEAL WAFERS.

Sift the oatmeal flour several times that it may be very fine; take one quart of flour, mix it into a dough with cold water, add a little salt, work the dough until smooth, then roll it out very thin; cut into squares or bake in one large sheet in a very cool oven.

CHICKEN CREAM.

Pound the breast of a cooked chicken to a smooth paste in the mortar; add some of the broth, one saltspoon of salt and a little pepper; keep on the ice; when required to use, heat a portion over hot water and add two tablespoonfuls of cream.

CAUDLE.

Put one-half a wine glass of wine into any plain gruel, flour or cracker; stir it in while the gruel is hot, but not on the fire.

CRACKERS AND MARMALADE.

Toast three soda crackers, dip them for one minute in boiling water, spread them with a little sweet butter, and put between them layers of orange marmalade, or any other preserve or jelly; put plenty upon the top cracker and set them in the oven for two or three minutes before serving. This makes a delicate and inviting lunch for convalescents.

CUSTARD SAVORY.

Mix the yolks of two eggs and the whites of one in a gill of white stock, put into a small jam pot, tie a piece of buttered paper over it and boil for one-fourth hour in a bain-marie. Serve either hot or cold with buttered toast.

CUSTARD FOR AN INVALID.

Three tablespoonfuls of milk, one egg beaten into the milk and one dessert-spoonful of flour, which has been warmed and dried; when the ingredients are thoroughly blended, strain into a buttered cup, place the cup in a pan containing hot water, cover the top of the cup with a wet cloth. Bake slowly for twenty minutes, then turn it on to a small dish—be careful not to break the custard—put a nice bit of butter on top, and a little fine sugar.

CRACKERS AND CREAM.

Pour boiling water over one large cracker, sprinkle a little salt over and cover the cracker a few minutes, then pour over some cream and serve.

SOAKED CRACKERS.

Cover a hard pilot biscuit with cold water, when the water is all absorbed, cover the cracker again with cold water and place in the oven; when thoroughly heated, put a little salt on it and two tablespoonfuls of sweet cream.

CUSTARD BROTH.

Four fresh eggs, beat them until smooth, then pour them into three teacupfuls of broth, either of chicken, veal or beef; strain and then fill four cups with the custard, place them in a pan of boiling water, which should come within one-half inch of the tops of the cups—the water must not boil. Bake until the custard is firm, no longer; let the custards cool in water. They may be eaten either hot or cold.

SANDWICHES.

HOW TO MAKE.

Sandwiches may be made of white, brown or Graham bread. The bread should be at least twelve hours old and close grained. Spread each slice lightly and evenly with butter or mayonnaise dressing, as may be required, before cutting from the loaf; lay the slice on a flat surface to be spread with the sandwich mixture; over this place another spread slice of bread and press them together with a broad-bladed knife. They may be cut into various shapes, the square, triangular or diamond form being the most in use. Round sandwiches are made by using a large sized biscuit cutter. Slices cut into squares large enough to roll make another variety.

SARDINE.

Sandwiches in any form are always welcomed. The following are a little different from the regulation sandwiches. Remove the skin and bones from some sardines and chop them and add a small strip of cooked ham chopped very fine. Mix with these some paprika and mustard, a little tomato or walnut catsup to give it a flavor, and just enough vinegar to make the mixture into a thick paste. Spread a thin slice of bread with butter and with a layer of the mixture. Lay another slice of buttered bread upon this and again cover with the mixture. Repeat with three or four slices of bread, then take off all the crust and cut the bread down into thick slices as you would jelly cake.

BROILED SANDWICH.

A broiled sandwich is unusual and is exceedingly good, as well as being a nice mode of using underdone beef. Spread thin slices of Graham or white bread with butter and place between the slices rare beef chopped fine and seasoned with salt and paprika. Place the sandwiches in a double broiler and brown the bread over a clear fire slowly. so that the meat shall have time to become heated. Lay the sandwiches upon a heated dish and brush the tops with hot butter. A horseradish sauce is often served with these sandwiches.

CHEESE SANDWICH TO SERVE WITH SALAD.

Cut slices of bread thinly in finger lengths; butter them and cut thin slices of Swiss cheese and place them between the slices; season the cheese with a little cayenne; dip the sandwiches in melted butter, place in the oven for a few minutes or until the bread is brown. Serve hot.

POTTED CHEESE SANDWICHES.

Pound together one-half pound of Cheshire cheese and five ounces of butter, a pinch of sugar. Stir into a stiff paste with a little white wine and spread evenly on hot toast.

CAVIARE SANDWICHES—1.

Spread caviare on bread and butter, squeeze lemon over it, and add a trifle of cayenne pepper.

CAVIARE SANDWICHES—2.

Take a small box of caviare, turn it into a shallow dish and beat into it alternately, a little at a time, lemon juice and olive oil, and stir until you have a thick, white paste. Spread it thickly on bread. Over this scatter some finely chopped olives.

CREAM CHEESE SANDWICH.

Delicious sandwiches may be made with one cup of English walnut meats chopped very fine and mixed with enough Philadelphia cream cheese to make a paste. Add a little salt and spread on very thin bread.

CELERY SANDWICHES.

Boil two eggs fifteen minutes, throw them into cold water, remove the shells and rub the eggs through a course seive, add to them a cup of finely chopped celery and enough mayonnaise dressing to season it and make a paste. Spread on buttered toast.

CHERRY SANDWICH.

Another sandwich to serve with punch or lemonade is made of candied cherries chopped fine and moistened with a little wine. Spread the mixture between water thin biscuits.

CHICKEN SANDWICHES.

Chop the white meat of cold boiled chicken very fine, and mix with it enough highly seasoned mayonnaise dressing to make a paste, add to this a few chopped olives and spread between buttered slices of bread. Another chicken filling is made by chopping the chicken fine with half as many blanched almonds as you have meat; season with salt and a dash of cayenne pepper. Moisten with a little cream until it is thin enough to spread nicely. This is excellent on brown bread.

HOT CHEESE SANDWICHES.

To prepare them slice the bread very thin and cut it round with a large sized biscuit cutter. Put a thick layer of grated cheese between the two circles of bread, sprinkle the cheese with salt and cayenne pepper and press circles of bread together. Fry them in a spider in equal parts of hot lard and butter. Brown them on each side and serve hot.

FISH SANDWICHES.

Graham bread is especially good for fish sandwiches. To make a sardine sandwich take three sardines and remove the skin and bones. Put them in a bowl with one teaspoonful of anchovy paste, the yolks of three boiled eggs, two tablespoonfuls of olive oil and the juice of half a lemon. With the back of a spoon rub this mixture to a paste and spread on bread.

FRIED SANDWICH.

A delicious fried sandwich is made with stale bread and a bit of dry cheese—two things that can usually be found in one's larder; cut the bread thin and spread it with French mustard; cover this with a thick layer of grated cheese and sprinkle with salt and a dash of cayenne. Press the slices of bread well together and cut them into any shape desired.

Have equal parts of lard and butter heated to boiling point in a frying pan; put in the bread sandwiches and cook both sides brown and serve very hot. These sandwiches may be varied by scattering a little minced ham or chopped parsley over the cheese.

HOT SANDWICH.

Here is another mode of utilizing stale bread. Graham or white can be used; cut it into rather thick slices and lightly toast them, cutting them into any fancy shape. To three-quarters of a cup of chopped ham or tongue add a little grated cheese, some chopped parsley, a tablespoonful of cream and the yolk of a beaten egg. Mix these ingredients well together and spread thickly upon the toasted bread and sprinkle a little grated cheese over the top. Place the pieces in a baking pan, put them into a hot oven and brown well.

HAM SANDWICHES.

One can of deviled ham, soften with rich cream and one glass of sherry. Spread on thin bread and butter.

LETTUCE SANDWICH.

Cut the bread very thin and stamp round with a biscuit cutter; spread thickly with mayonnaise dressing, and lay white crisp lettuce leaves on the dressing between the slices, letting the lettuce leaves come beyond the slices; press the upper piece of bread over the lettuce and trim the leaves with sharp scissors to make them even on all sides. Watercress may be used in the same way.

OLIVE SANDWICH.

Chopped olives mixed with a little mayonnaise dressing are a popular filling for sandwiches at five o'clock teas, as well as brown or white bread cut very thin, and buttered and spread with almonds, walnuts or Pecan nut meats pounded to a paste with a little salt.

RAISIN SANDWICHES.

Raisin sandwiches are excellent to serve with lemonade. With a pair of sharp scissors cut large raisins in two, lengthwise, and remove the seeds. Lay the fruit closely together between thin buttered bread and cut into fancy shapes.

MAYONNAISE WITH OLIVES.

Cut with the pastry cutter some rounds of thin, white bread; spread with mayonnaise sauce, in which mix chopped olives.

COLD ROAST BEEF SANDWICH.

A hearty sandwich that most men are fond of is made thus: Chop very fine cold rare roast beef, and to one cupful of meat add one-fourth of a teaspoonful of salt, one teaspoonful of tomato catsup, and the same amount of Worcestershire sauce and of melted butter, stir until well blended and spread on thin slices of bread. Or thus: To half a cupful of thick mayonnaise add two spoonfuls of whipped cream, a dessertspoonful of grated horseradish, and two of chopped cucumbers. Spread the bread with this mixture, and then with a thin layer of finely chopped rare beef and cover with more dressing and bread.

SPANISH SANDWICHES.

Butter some slices of fresh brown bread, and sprinkle on each slice a little cayenne, then put some boned anchovies, laying them flat, and sprinkle over all the yolk of an egg cooked hard and rubbed through a sieve, some finely minced cold chicken, and a little chopped parsley; place the other slices of bread over, press them well together, cut into rounds and serve garnished with sprigs of parsley.

LEBERWURST SANDWICHES.

Spread the leberwurst on slices of rye bread, do not use butter. Leberwurst is a German sausage made of goose's livers, truffles, etc. Scoop out of the sausage skin.

TOMATO SANDWICH.

Cut thin slices of bread and butter evenly, then cut them into rounds with a biscuit cutter, lay on one slice of the bread a slice of ripe tomato, sprinkle the other slice with grated cheese, season with salt and pepper; press the two slices together.

FISH SANDWICH.

Use any cooked fish, free from bones, spread the slices of bread with butter; mix the fish with finely chopped pickle and mayonnaise, and spread on the bread.

SAUSAGE SANDWICHES.

Take the small link sausage, split them lengthwise and broil on each side. When they become cool, cover buttered bread with delicate lettuce leaves and lay the sausage upon them; then the thinnest possible slices of cucumber pickles, and lastly a piece of buttered bread. Cut them into small squares.

It may well be said of sandwiches that their name is legion.

BEVERAGES.

APPLE TODDY.

Two tumblers of boiling waters, two tumblers of white loaf sugar, one tumbler of best brandy, one-half tumbler of peach brandy, one-half tumbler of Jamaica rum. Remove the cores from ten apples, bake them. Mix the sugar well in the boiling water first, and then add the other liquors, then the apples; this is better made the day before it is to be used.

BONUM.

Three-fourths quart of whiskey, one gill of Vermouth, one-third wine glass of orange bitters, thirty drops of Angostora bitters, one wine glass of Benedictine, one wine glass of Curacoa, one glass of rock candy syrup.

COCKTAIL A LA SHERRY.

Equal portions of Old Tom gin and Vermouth, small portion of orange bitters, a dash of Marischino.

CHOCOLATE.

"Time and experience, those two great masters, have proved that, when properly prepared, chocolate is wholesome, nourishing and easily digested; and also that it is most suitable for those who have much brain work—for clergymen, lawyers, literary men, and, above all, for travelers."—Brillat-Savarin.

ARABIAN CHOCOLATE.

One-half pound of French chocolate, one pound of rice flour, one-fourth pound of arrowroot, one-half pound of loaf sugar pounded fine. These should be well mixed together; a tablespoonful may be slightly wet with milk or water, then stirred into one pint of boiling milk and boiled for five minutes. It can be served either hot or cold.

CHOCOLATE.

To one quart of boiling milk take four ounces of chocolate; put the chocolate into a small pan on the fire, add three tablespoonfuls of cold water; stir together until the chocolate is thick and smooth, then stir it into the boiling milk; add three tablespoonfuls of sugar. Stir for five minutes and serve hot. If desired, put on the top of each cup one spoonful of whipped cream. One teaspoonful of sherry to each cup greatly improves the chocolate.

FILTERED COFFEE.

Allow one and one-half tablespoonfuls of ground coffee to each person. Put the coffee into the filter and pour over the boiling water slowly, allowing one cup of water for each person; after all the water has gone through the coffee pour it all through the second time.

COFFEE FOR FIVE PERSONS.

One cup of coffee before being ground, half egg, two quarts of boiling water. Beat one egg with two tablespoonfuls of cold water. Grind the coffee, put one-half the egg on the grounds, then wet it thoroughly with cold water so that every grain will be wet. Pour the boiling water on, boil about ten minutes after it comes to a boil. The other half of the egg will answer for the next coffee.

Note.—Put all the water on the coffee that is required, as it spoils the coffee to add water after. The water should be perfectly fresh, and the coffee should be used as soon as it has boiled.

The coffee should be placed on the hottest part of the range, or gas stove, so that it will boil as quickly as possible, watching it constantly that it may not boil over.

The coffee pot should never be washed with soap, or a dish cloth, simply rinse it out thoroughly with cold water, then with boiling water; turn the pot upside down to dry. Never use a towel to dry it.

Use a wooden spoon or ladle, and never use anything else; rinse and dry as soon as you are through with it. Never let the coffee pot stand with coffee in it.

COCOA.

Full directions come with all the various preparations offered in the leading grocery houses.

"VERY BEST EGG-NOG."

Eighteen eggs; beat the yolks until very smooth with enough sugar to make the mixture sweet, add very slowly in a thin thread stream one pint of brandy and one pint of Jamaica rum; then add two quarts of rich cream, then the whites of the eggs beaten until stiff, with enough sugar to make them sweet; put the whites on top of the mixture and serve.

EGG-NOG.

One pound of sugar, twelve eggs, one quart of whipped cream, one nutmeg grated, one pint of brandy. Beat the yolks and sugar together until very light, then add the whites beaten stiff, then add the whipped cream, and lastly add the brandy drop by drop as oil is used in making mayonnaise dressing; this way of adding the brandy will be found a great improvement over the old way of pouring it into the mixture.

EGG LEMONADE.

Break one egg into glass, rub two lumps of sugar on the rind of a lemon, put into the glass; squeeze the lemon juice over the sugar, half fill the glass with powdered ice, fill to the top with cold water, shake vigorously with a shaker, then grate a little nutmeg on the top.

FISH HOUSE PUNCH.

One quart of brandy, two quarts of Jamaica rum, one gill of peach brandy, one quart of lemon juice, five pounds of loaf sugar (dissolved); add the lemon juice to the sugar and then pour in the mixture of spirits; nine pounds of water and ice. For forty people.

FRUIT PUNCH.

This punch is served in small glasses either before a luncheon or during the dinner after the roast. Any fresh fruits can be used—strawberries mixed with raspberries, cherries, pineapple cut in small slices, white grapes cut in halves with the seeds removed. Boil together a cupful of rum and two cupfuls of sugar. As soon as the syrup boils, pour it over the fruits and let all become cold, then fill the glasses and place on the ice—or place in a can and pack in ice and salt. Serve very cold.

"GOOD LEMONADE."

For a quart of good lemonade take the juice of three lemons, using the rind of one. Peel the rind very thin, getting just the yellow outside; cut this into pieces and put with the juice and powdered sugar, of which use two ounces to the quart, in a jug or jar with a cover; when the water is just at the boiling point pour it over the lemon and sugar, cover at once and let it get cold.

CALCUTTA LEMONADE.

This lemonade is almost equal to liquor in richness. Pare thinly two dozen lemons and squeeze the juice on the peel; let this remain twelve hours, then add two pounds of granulated sugar, a quart of sherry wine, three quarts of boiling milk. Let it strain through a flannel jelly bag, and serve with chopped ice.

CHABLIS OR CLARET CUP.

One lemon; cut off the peel very thinly, twelve lumps of sugar, two wine glasses of sherry, one quart of chablis or claret; stir these well together and then place on the ice; just before serving add two bottles of soda.

CREME DE MENTHE.

Fill a bottle with sprigs of fresh mint, add the juice of two lemons and one pint of brandy; let these stand for one week, then add a syrup made with three ounces of rock candy.

SHANDY GAFF.

One bottle of ale made very cold, with one bottle of ginger ale; mix together, serve cold and quickly.

GRAPE JUICE MEAD.

Two quarts of grape juice, twelve lemons, six oranges, one quart of American champagne, two quarts soda or Apollinaris, two cups of lump sugar; rub some of the lumps of the sugar over the lemons and oranges; mix the juice of the lemons, oranges and grape juice well together with the sugar, then strain through a jelly bag; just before serving add the champage or soda; put large lumps of ice in the pitcher and serve in glasses.

GINGER CORDIAL.

One ounce of green ginger, one ounce of rock candy; melt the candy, put with it tne ginger in small pieces, and add one quart of brandy; put into a bottle and let it stand for one month, then strain and bottle.

MILK PUNCH.

Eighteen lemons, cut off the rind and steep them for two days in one gallon of brandy or rum; then strain and add two nutmegs grated, three pounds of loaf sugar, two quarts of boiling milk, four quarts oi cold water and the juice of the lemons. Stir all these very well and strain through a flannel bag. Add the boiling milk last; bottle and cork tightly.

IMPERIAL PINEAPPLE PUNCH.

Slice a pineapple very thin, peel four large oranges, take off all white pulp and separate them into eights; put pineapple and oranges into a large bowl, add twelve ounces of sugar, eight ounces of lemon juice (the juice of four lemons), four drops each of essence of lemon, cinnamon and vanilla, pour over one quart of boiling water, let it stand until cool, then add one pint of jamaica rum, one-half pint arrack, one bottle hock, one wine glass chartreuse; add just before serving one bottle of champagne and one bottle of seltzer.

RUM PUNCH.

One quart of rum, one ounce of Young Hyson tea, two quarts of water, twelve lemons, juice and grated rind of nine, sweeten to taste; steep the tea, pour into the mixture and bottle; when needed pound a quantity of ice very fine, put into the punch bowl or into small glasses and pour the punch over. Replenish from the bottle; do not pour all into the punch bowl; make the mixture rather sweet.

VERY GOOD PUNCH.

Two pounds of loaf sugar, two cups of strong black tea, six wine glasses of brandy, six wine glasses of rum, four oranges, juice only, two bottles of champagne; mix well together; this amount makes two gallons of punch—add pounded ice, when ready to serve.

WASHAW PUNCH.

Twelve eggs, four pounds of sugar, two quarts of sherry, one pint of water, one stick of cinnamon in the wine; beat the eggs and sugar together; boil the wine and water, stir in the eggs and sugar quickly and serve.

WEST POINT PUNCH.

One goblet of brandy, one goblet of Jamaica rum, one teacup of green tea, eight tablespoonfuls of currant jelly mixed with the hot tea, one goblet of white sugar, the juice of four lemons, four lemons cut in thin slices, one pineapple cut in thin slices, two quarts of champagne, one teacup of Curacoa, plenty of pounded ice; mix well, let the punch ripen for an hour before adding the ice.

SIBERIAN PUNCH.

One quart of thick cream, one-half pint of fine sugar, two whites of eggs, one half tablespoonful of corn starch. Let cream come to boiling point; mix eggs, sugar and corn starch together, then stir all slowly into the boiling cream until cooked; then cool and add one quart of brandy when partly frozen. This will serve ten portions.

TO MAKE TEA.

The water must be freshly boiled. Pour some hot water into the teapot, then pour it out and put in one teaspoonful of tea for each cup and one over, pour over the boiling water, let the tea steep for five minutes. It must not boil. For afternoon tea served with lemon, Formosa Oolong is the best.

TEA.

In the place of the slices of lemons, a little bit of vanilla bean or a few drops of orange flower water may be added to the water.

TEA PUNCH—1

One quart of green tea, juice of twelve lemons, four oranges; one small bottle of imported orange-flower water, one quart of Santa Cruz rum, one small tumbler of Maraschino, twelve bottles of club soda, sugar to taste, slices of orange, lemons, and other fruits in season.

TEA PUNCH—2.

Two quarts of Jamaica rum, twelve lemons, three pounds of pulvarized sugar, two cups of green tea. Cut the rind of the lemons as thinly as possible, string all on long string and soak in the rum. Steep tea, pour it over the sugar and lemon juice, then add the rum. Just before serving, fill up the punch bowl with powdered ice and pour over the mixture.

TEA PUNCH—3.

One pound of loaf sugar, one cup of green tea, three wine glasses of brandy, three wine glasses of rum, three lemons, one bottle of champagne. Fill the glasses with powdered ice and pour over the punch.

PEACH BRANDY.

Put six large peaches sliced, in one quart of brandy, put the kernels from the peach stones; add three ounces of rock candy. let these stand for six weeks, then strain and bottle.

ORANGE BRANDY.

Two quarts of good brandy, three-quarters of a pint of fresh orange juice strained, one pound white sugar. Peel the rinds from the oranges very thinly, add them to the brandy, the orange juice and sugar; mix together and cover closely for five days, occassionaly stirring; then strain and bottle. This will keep for years.

LEMON BRANDY.

Prepare as for orange brandy.

USEFUL HINTS.

ECONOMY.

Never go in for that sort of seeming saving which consists in the use of cheap materials either in meats, groceries or fats; the best articles are the cheapest in the end. Economy is a good and a splendid quality, but it must be intelligent economy. The avoidance of waste in every department of the kitchen, larder and pantry is the only true economy. Never allow the least scrap to go to loss, but strive to turn even the scraps to some good use. Scrupulous cleanliness is indispensible. Clealiness in everything, vegetables carefully washed and rinsed, every utensil invitingly clean.

BROWNED FLOUR.

Put some sifted flour into a pan, place it on the stove and stir constantly from the bottom, whenever it begins to stick—do not let it burn, but when well browned, it is done. Put in a tin canister or glass jar to keep until needed.

TO CLEAN CURRANTS.

The best way is to sprinkle them with flour and rub them until the grit, stems and flour are removed; then put them in the strainer and let the water run through them until it is perfectly clear; then dry the currants on a coarse towel.

SWEET HERBS.

Many recipes call for "Sweet Herbs;" the proper mixture is: One part marjoram, two parts thyme, and three parts parsley. It is a wise precaution to dry bunches of these herbs carefully, sift them through a sieve, and mix in the above proportions and bottle ready for use.

Add a pinch of **salt** when whipping the **whites of eggs.**

A little **sugar** is a great improvement to **soups.**

Add a little **salt** to **sweet dishes.**

Beat the **yolks of eggs** until they are a light lemon color.

Put one teaspoonful of hot water always into the **yolk** of an egg when **used for breading,** with crumbs and eggs.

In making **hard sauce** add the powdered sugar slowly, a little at a time.

Always **fold in the whipped whites of eggs,** into cake batter or other batters, rather than to beat them in.

Always **strain any mixture of flour and milk or water** to avoid lumps and always add milk or water a little at a time in mixing any thickening.

MEAT.

Never place meat directly on the ice in the refrigerator; the water draws out the juices of meat.

Never allow meat to remain in the paper in which it is brought from the butcher, or in the hot kitchen; put it at once in a cool place.

All meat that has been hung long must be carefully scraped and washed off with vinegar and water before using—the outer skin may have acquired a stale taste.

All warmed-over meats, if fried, should either be breaded or else dipped into batter and fried. The batter, or egg and bread crumbs form a crust and keep the meat tender and juicy; if cold meat is fried without either, it is always hard and stringy.

Meat is cooked in "its own juice," by placing the piece in a stone jar with a cover, without any water, and letting it cook on the back of the stove slowly and gently.

All meats cooked at a low degree of heat are rendered tender and palatable.

In broiling either meats or fish, be sure that the gridiron is perfectly clean, and that it is rubbed with good fat, and is hot before using.

In broiling, no thin pieces should be broiled, only thick fleshy pieces. No forks should ever be stuck into them, nor should they be cut with a knife. You may sprinkle your steak or chop with a little pepper, but never add the salt till the meat is done.

Cold beef cut in slices, covered with vinegar over night, then dipped in egg well seasoned with salt and nutmeg, rolled in bread crumbs, fried, makes a very good lunch dish.

Always rub the broiler or gridiron with fat before using, and always have it hot before putting on the meat or fish to be broiled. Broiling requires a brisk fire, free from smoke.

A mixture for croquettes can be made and moulded and the croquettes kept in a cool place until needed, when they are easily cooked.

Always see that the oven is hot one hour before baking; meat is spoiled in a cool oven.

It is indispensible to good cooking that every **dish requiring to be served hot** should not wait in the kitchen, but should be served with promptness.

Remember that wine increases the taste of salt. For this reason where **wine is used for flavoring,** very little salt should be put in until after the wine has been used, when more may be added if necessary.

If the water is **hard water,** a little pinch of soda should be added to soften it for cooking purposes.

TO KEEP MEATS UNTAINTED.

Put a piece of charcoal inside of any poultry to be kept over night in summer; when meat has a close or slightly tainted smell wash it in water in which is dissolved a teaspoonful of soda, or in water and vinegar mixed.

Keep lemons in a crock filled with cold water.

Put oyster shells into a **stove that is clinkered.** Put in when the fire is hot.

EGG STAIN.

Salt will remove the stain on egg spoons.

TO THICKEN WITH CORNSTARCH.

Corn starch is used to thicken soups or sauces because it makes a smoother thickening, but it should be cooked for fifteen minutes—ordinary flour requires five minutes to cook.

MUSHROOM POWDER.

Mushroom powder can be successfully used in place of fresh mushrooms in scrambled eggs and omelettes.

TO REMOVE MORTAR AND PAINT.

Mortar and paint may be removed from window glass by washing the glass with strong, hot vinegar.

TO KEEP A CHEESE FRESH.

Wring out a cloth in cider vinegar, wrap it around the cheese, cover with a paper bag and keep the cheese in a dry, cool place. The cheese will retain its freshness and will not mold.

Serve **cream cheese** with figs.

Figs may be freshened by washing them thoroughly, drying and then heating them in the oven—take out and roll in powdered sugar.

TO KILL COCKROACHES.

Helebore sprinkled about on the floor of the rooms infested by cockroaches, will kill the pests; they eat it and will be poisened. Be sure to sweep the helebore up every morning.

TO REMOVE BLACK BEETLES.

Try fresh cucumber peelings where black beetles and cockroaches haunt.

TO FRY BREAD TO SERVE WITH SOUP.

Cut some slices one-fourth of an inch thick from a stale loaf, pare off the crust and divide the bread into small dice; put in the pan—for one-half pound of bread a tablespoonful of butter; when it is hot put in the bread, and fry until it is colored a pale brown; drain from the butter and keep warm until served.

FRIED BREAD FOR SOUP.

Cut stale bread into thin slices and moisten them with milk, then cut into dice, put in a pan and fry in butter until brown.

CROUTONS FOR SOUP.

Cut some slices of bread into small dice and fry in a little hot butter until of a light brown color.

BREADING AND RASPING—1.

For breading, use beaten eggs, oil and crumbs of either cracker or stale bread; if bread is used, rub the crumbs through a sieve, dry in the oven, and place in a tin box until ready to use. In breading, the eggs should be well beaten; for three eggs, add one tablespoonful of oil, one tablespoonful of water, a saltspoonful of salt and a pinch of pepper.

"Raspings" are made from crusts of bread baked to a bright golden color, then crushed with the rolling pin, passed throug a sieve, and put by for use—the coarse crumbs being used to sprinkle over roast birds, etc.

BREADING—2.

In preparing the crumbs for breading any articles, to successfully cover the articles, you must use a quantity of crumbs—there should be a quart or more of prepared crumbs on the board.

CRUMBS.

Mix crumbs with a little melted butter before putting on the top of any dish.

CRACKER CRUMBS.

Crackers should be made hot, then rolled and sifted, rolled and sifted again, until they are very fine; all crumbs for breading should be made very fine before using.

MUSH.

Put mush for frying into baking powder tins. You can slice the mush in round slices which will present a very appetizing appearance.

BREAD CRUMBS.

Save all pieces of bread. The large slices can be used for toast; small pieces be used in puddings or dried for crumbs. Use the white part and crusts separately, dry in oven, sift, then put away in glass mason jars.

CAKE CRUMBS.

Stale cake is useful in making various puddings.

TO CLEAN FRUIT.

The best way to remove sand and grit from small fruits, when washing them is necessary, is to lay the fruit loosely in a clean wire basket and dip the basket into fresh water several times, then let the fruit drain before using.

TO CHOP PARSLEY.

In chopping parsley, after it is very fine, wash it, then place in the corner of a napkin and wring it dry; the parsley will, after this, sprinkle easily over any dish for which it is required.

TO CLEAN IRON KETTLES.

A little vinegar and salt, boiled in an iron skillet or spider, will remove all burned and black spots.

TO PREPARE GELATINE.

Gelatine must be soaked in cold water first, then dissolved in hot water.

LEFT OVERS.

Never throw away any of the cereals left over from breakfast, they are improved by long cooking, and can be added to the supply for the next morning, or they can be sliced and fried.

Save all the vegetables left from dinner. They can be used to make a salad with either a French dressing or mayonnaise, or they can be used in the soup the next day. Save all the bits of meat which are trimmed from the roast or steak and all bones; use these for the soup stock. Clarify all bits of suet, and other fat bones to use for frying. Grate all the bits of cheese and put into a clean jar to serve on crackers or toasted bread, or to use with macaroni.

CHOPPING SUET.

Always add a little flour when chopping suet to prevent the suet from oiling and sticking together.

TO CLEAN SILVER.

Silver that has been laid away, and has become tarnished, can be cleaned quicker if the whiting used to clean with is moistened with sweet oil before applying to the silver. Afterwards, dry whiting can be used as usual.

Grease all pans and molds with butter, dripping or lard, using a small brush.

TO KEEP FOOD WARM.

When it is required to keep some dish already prepared warm for a time before serving, place in a pan of hot water.

TO CLEAN KETTLES.

When any KETTLE has become BLACK AND BURNED, boil in it a solution of sal soda for an hour or more. Use soda to soften the grease on pans, and scour with Sapolio.

TO CLEAN DRAINS.

Pour a solution of concentrated lye down the drain pipe of the kitchen sink at least twice a week, to prevent the grease stopping the pipe.

THE REFRIGERATOR.

See that the REFRIGERATOR is kept absolutely clean, the drain pipe kept open by washing the refrigerator out three times a week with cold water with soda or borax dissolved in it.

STEAMING VEGETABLES.

Many vegetables can be steamed or stewed in the oven when the top of the range is full. After preparing them, place them in an earthenware jar with a spoonful of water and a very little butter. Cover the jar and stand it in a sauce pan of water or the jar can stand in the oven. Green peas, beans, cauliflower, cabbage, all can be so cooked.

PUT AWAY UTENSILS.

In cooking, try to clear up all utensils used as you go on; do not allow all to accumulate. Wash and put each one back in its place. Neatness, order and method should be observed in every kitchen.

DRIED FRUITS.

Dried fruits are better stewed in a double boiler, or baked in an earthen jar in the oven, using as little water as possible, the fruit to be closely covered. Always carefully look over all dried fruits before cooking them, then soak them for two or three hours in cold water, or until they are soft and swollen to their full extent, when they should be stewed in the same water; add the sugar just before they are fully cooked.

Apple sauce is vastly improved by being baked in an oven instead of being stewed.

LIME WATER.

To make lime water, frequently needed for an invalid's or a child's use, put one pound of unslacked lime into a large bowl; pour over this three quarts of boiling water; let it stand for fifteen minutes, then stir it well with a stick. Place the bowl in a cool place for several hours; at the end of the time pour off the clear water and bottle it. A teaspoonful may be added to a glass of milk in case of an acid stomach, or to render the milk more easy of digestion.

BURNS.

In case of a burn, cover the place with bicarbonate of soda (salaratus) and bind over it a soft cloth; this will relieve by keeping the air from the burnt place. As soda is in all kitchens this is a convenient remedy. Lime water also is an excellent remedy. Wet cloths in it and place over the burn.

ORANGE SUGAR.

Cut off the thin yellow rind of oranges, and dry it. When it is dry (it will take two days to dry) put it in the mortar with one cupful of granulated sugar. Pound the mixture until it is a powder then rub it through a very fine sieve; the rind of twelve oranges will require two cupfuls of sugar; when very finely powdered put into tight glass jars. One tablespoonful of this mixture is required for flavoring a custard or cake.

LEMON SUGAR.

Lemon sugar can be prepared in the same manner as orange sugar.

VANILLA SUGAR.

One pound of powdered sugar, one ounce of vanilla bean; split the bean, remove the seeds, pound well together with the sugar until fine, then bottle.

MERINGUES.

In making a meringue, after beating the whites of the eggs until they are very stiff, add the sugar to the whites, beating it into the whites with a silver spoon, a little at a time; add the flavoring at the last; the white of one egg requires one tablespoonful of sugar. A meringue should be baked in a slow oven.

ONION JUICE.

When onion juice is required, pare the onion and cut it in four pieces if a large onion, and squeeze the pieces in a wooden lemon squeezer; keep the squeezer for this use only. Or the onion can be pressed against a coarse grater and the juice extracted.

TO KEEP MEATS.

Meat can be kept in summer for a longer time if it is thoroughly rubbed over with olive oil; steaks should be dipped in oil or melted butter or dripping, and then hung up.

Meat can be rubbed with ginger, every crevice filled, if desired to keep it for a few days.

When **sponges** have become **soft and sour** rub into them some lemon juice, then rinse several times in luke warm water and dry.

Wash **old glass jars** in hot water in which is dissolved a tablespoonful of baking soda; after, rinse well in cold water.

Flat irons that are rusty can be cleaned by rubbing them with wax tied in a cloth, the irons to be warm; then rub them well on a board strewn with salt.

Ink spots can be removed from the fingers by a little ammonia.

A little ammonia and alcohol mixed, rubbed on black silk will **remove the "shiny" look,** so often seen on seams of dresses.

TO WASH BLANKETS.

To each pailful of rain water use one tablespoonful of borax.

Fill the wash boiler with water; cut into small pieces two cakes of any good white soap. When this is dissolved and the water boiling, strain into the washtubs through cheese cloth.

Put in the blankets; do not mix the colored borders; put all of one color together; let the blankets remain in the water over night; cover the tubs. The water should be made tepid before the blankets are put into it, so cold rain water can be added to the hot water.

The next morning rinse the blankets up and down in the water by holding the ends and going all around the four sides; then have the wringer set very loosely and wring the blankets into another tub containing clean cold rain water. Rinse the blankets in this the same as in the first water; then wring into another tub of cold water; wring again into a third tub; from this water take the blankets— do not wring them; hang them on the lines dripping wet in the hot sun, changing them twice; that is, turning them upside down twice. The blankets will be beautifully soft and clean after they are dry.

FURNITURE POLISH.

A FAMOUS RECIPE FROM WARWICK, ENGLAND.

One ounce of white wax, one ounce of beeswax, one-half ounce of Castile soap, one-half ounce of soda, one-half ounce of camphor, one pint of turpentine, one pint of boiling water.

Cut the wax and soap into small pieces and dissolve

with the soda and camphor in the turpentine. Then add the boiling water and shake well together, until it looks white, and about the consistency of thick cream; bottle. When required, apply a little on a flannel cloth evenly and rub it off with a clean soft cloth. This preparation can be used on any kind of wood work, or on leather goods.

TO RESTORE THE "PILE" ON VELVET.

To restore the "pile" on velvet hold the velvet over boiling water the wrong side next to the steam, brush the velvet lightly as the steam goes through the fiber.

PAPER BAGS.

The large paper bags which are made for holding banana bunches are very nice for holding blankets and other woolens, which require to be put away from moths in summer.

CLEANING MIXTURE FOR BLACK GOODS.

One-half pint of alcohol, one-half pint of distilled water, one ounce of aqua ammonia. Mix and bottle.

FOR CLEANING CARPETS.

One bar of good soap, or electric soap; shave fine into one gallon of cold water, add four ounces of pulverized sal-soda, eight ounces of fine borax. Boil fifteen minutes. Put this into three gallons of cold water and one-half pint of alcohol. Rub on carpet with scrubbing brush, and wipe off carefully with a clean cloth.

CLEANING MIXTURE FOR CLOTHING.

One gallon of deodorized benzine, one-half ounce of ether, one-half ounce of chloroform, one ounce of alcohol. Mix well and bottle.

CLEANING MIXTURE FOR RUGS, ETC.

Two-thirds bar of ordinary kitchen soap, two quarts of water in which dissolve the soap, one tablespoonful each of borax, alum and washing soda. Mix and let all cool, then add two tablespoonfuls of ammonia and one tablespoonful of Fuller's earth.

CLEANSER FOR WOOLENS.

One-fourth pound of white castile soap, one-fourth pound of ammonia, one ounce of ether, one ounce of alcohol. Cut soap very find and dissolve thoroughly in warm water, one quart; add four quarts of soft water, then the other ingredients. Bottle at once.

COLD CREAM—1.

The woman who wishes to be sure that the ingredients of her cold cream are absolutely pure can make it herself with but little trouble.

The butcher's and not the druggist's is the place to seek for the basis. Secure from him some fine white tallow. Cut into bits, put it into a saucepan without any water; set the sauce-pan in a jar of boiling water and let all remain until the fat is thoroughly "tried" out of the tallow. Strain through a fine sieve and while still warm stir in a teaspoonful of the essence of camphor to every cup of tallow. Next a tablespoonful of your favorite perfume and stir until the whole is a sweet smelling liquid. Before it has had time to cool pour into a little toilet jar and set upon the ice over night. It will keep indefinitely and will be found a delicious remedy for all the ills that winds and weather bring to the feminine skin.

COLD CREAM—2.

Four ounces of oil of almonds, one and one-half ounces of white wax, one and one-half ounces of spermaceti, one and one-half ounces of rose water, one and one-half ounces of glycerine. Melt these together over a gentle heat; when blended, stir until the mixture is cold; place in small porcelain jars and cover.

PERFUMED BAGS FOR THE BATH.

Mix together five pounds of oatmeal, one-half pound of pure Castile soap powdered fine, one pound of powdered orris root. Make small cheese cloth bags and fill with the mixture; fill the bags loosely, and sew up one end; put in the bath and use in place of sponge.

FOR CHAPPED HANDS.

One-half ounce of gum benzoin, three and one-half ounces of rose water, one-fourth ounce of glycerine. Mix together and bottle. Or equal parts of glycerine, rose water and spirits of camphor. Rub a little on the hands after washing and before drying them.

TO CLEAN RUSTY METALS.

Clean with kerosine, which is better than oxalic acid for brass or copper ware. Kerosene is harmless, while oxalic acid is poisonous.

PASTE.

In making a paste either with flour or starch, add a little oil of cloves or of winter green, and the paste will not sour or mold.

A SPICE PLASTER FOR SEVERE PAIN.

One teaspoonful of ground cloves, one teaspoonful of ground cinnamon, one teaspoonful of ground ginger, one teaspoonful of mustard, one teaspoonful of ground allspice, one teaspoonful of wheat flour. Mix well together; pour over the mixture enough boiling water to moisten; stir until smooth and spread on cheese cloth, and apply as hot and as quickly as possible.

TO WASH FANCY WORK.

In all cases of embroidery on linen, the work should be carefully pressed when finished, and it is important for every embroiderer to know how this may be done in the simplest and safest manner. The proper way to press the finished work is to lay the embroidery face down on a clean cloth spread over an ironing blanket or two or three thicknesses of flannel; place a thin dampened cloth on the back of the article to be pressed, and then use a hot iron deftly on the wet surface until it is perfectly dry. A steaming process is thus engendered, whereby the embroidered linen is rendered smooth and the effectiveness of the work much enhanced.

TO SOFTEN SHOES.

Shoes that have become stiff and uncomfortable by being worn in the rain or that have been lying unused for some time, may be made soft and pliable by using vaseline well rubbed in with a cloth and rubbed off with a dry cloth.

TO REMOVE THE SMELL OF PAINT.

Put a pint of clean, cold water with a slice of lemon in it, in the newly painted room. Change the water every three or four hours and the unpleasant odor will be taken away.

A FEW LESSONS FOR THE COOK.

Teach your cook to have a place for everything and to put everything in its place.

Cleanliness, economy and punctuality are necessary.

Keep all dry stores, such as sugar, rice, etc., in clean, dry, covered tins.

Never pour the water in which greens or cabbage has been cooked, down the kitchen sink. Throw it outside; but if this is not possible, at once flush the sink with hot water in which some common washing soda has been dissolved. This prevents the odors from pervading the house.

Never bang the oven door when cake or bread is being baked.

Put in all soiled saucepans some hot water and a small lump of washing soda, until there is time to wash and dry them.

When gas stoves are used, insist that the burners are turned out as soon as a dish is cooked. A large saving of gas will be the result.

JARELLE WATER.

Remember never to use Jarelle water on anything colored; use only on white goods.

TO REMOVE A SCORCH MARK FROM LINEN.

Slice a large onion, pound it well, then add to the juice one ounce of white soap and one ounce Fuller's earth and one pint of vinegar. Boil these together, and spread the mixture on the scorched linen and leave it on until dry, when the article must be well washed in soap suds.

USES OF TURPENTINE.

Spirits of turpentine will restore the brilliancy to patent leather. Boots and bags look almost new under its influence.

Applied to a burn where the skin is not broken, it gives quick relief.

It sends down the skin of a blister and prevents soreness.

Workmen's white overalls and artists' working aprons should be steeped in turpentine for twenty-four hours before washing to loosen and remove paint.

A little added to the steeping water (a tablespoonful to a gallon) will make linen beautifully white.

A flannel dipped in hot water and sprinkled with turpentine will relieve hoarseness. This application is also often ordered for the relief of lumbago and rheumatism. It generally relieves neuralgia in the face.

A few drops in boxes and cupboards will prevent moths.

Soak rags in it, and then place near the holes of mice. Renew the oil from time to time. It effectually drives them away.

Add a few drops to starch to prevent the iron sticking.

For a paint mark on cloth that will not wash, put turpentine on with a small brush. Begin on the outside of the stain and work to the middle, in order to prevent it spreading.

Turpentine mixed with beeswax makes a well known polish for floors. A cloth wrung out of turpentine brightens up an oil cloth.

Two parts of sweet oil and one of turpentine make a reliable furniture polish. It instantly removes finger marks.

But do not forget that turpentine is highly inflammable, and that it should never be exposed to a flame of gas or fire.

ADDITIONAL RECIPES.

APRICOT EGGS.

One sponge cake (one baked in a round tin), cut it into slices one-half an inch thick with a round cutter about the size of a tumbler. Spread over each round a little apricot jam, and cover with whipped cream slightly flavored with either lemon or vanilla. In the center place half an apricot, a canned one is the better, dust it with powdered sugar. The eggs are easily and quickly made; they are pretty and good for a simple dessert.

APRICOT MUSCOVITE.

One pound of apricot jam, rub through a sieve, and, if not sweet enough, add some fine sugar. Make a custard with one scant pint of milk and the yolks of four eggs. When the custard is thick, let it cool and then add to it one-half an ounce of gelatine which has been dissolved in a little hot water, strained and cooled. Whip all well together, and as soon as the mixture begins to become firm add one-half a pint of stiffly whipped cream, one wine glass of either noyeau or apricot brandy. Pack into a mold and place in a pail, surrounded with broken ice and salt; let it remain in this for at least two hours. Any good fruit jam can be used in the place of apricot.

ARTICHOKES CREAMED.

Boil two pounds of Jerusalem artichokes in milk until soft enough to mash through a sieve. To the milk in which they were boiled, add enough more, one-half pint, add the yolks of four eggs slightly beaten, one saltspoonful of salt, one-half saltspoonful of pepper, and cook until thick, then add the artichokes and the white of one egg beaten very stiff. Put the mixture into a well buttered mold and steam for one hour, covering the mold on top with a white paper well buttered, then let it become very cold in the refrigerator. When required, turn from the mold and serve with a mayonnaise.

CUSTARD SOUFFLE.

Two scant tablespoonfuls of butter, two tablespoonfuls flour, beat these well together until light and smooth, then pour gradually over one cup of boiling milk, and cook all for eight minutes, stirring constantly. Beat together the yolks of four eggs and two tablespoonfuls of sugar, add to the cooked mixture and put away to cool. When cold, add the whites of the eggs beaten until stiff; put all into a buttered baking dish and bake for twenty minutes in a moderate oven.

SUMMER SQUASH—FRIED.

Cut the squash into slices one-fourth of an inch in thickness, dip these into flour well seasoned with salt and pepper, fry in hot butter or good fresh beef dripping until brown.

FONTAINBLEU CHEESE.

One quart of fresh milk, stir into it one teaspoonful of liquid rennet (the milk must be made just blood warm), only stir slightly. As soon as the milk is thick, stir to separate the curd from the whey, then drain and add two tablespoonsful of cream. Line some small wooden molds which have perforated bottoms, with cheese cloth; place in these the cheese; let it drain for two or three days, then remove from molds and serve with salt or sugar and cream.

GREEN PEPPERS AND CHICKEN.

Boil two green peppers for ten minutes, cut off the tops, remove the seeds, and chop very fine. Mix the minced peppers with two cupsful of finely chopped cold chicken, three tablespoonsful of butter, three tablespoonsful of flour, one and one-half cupsful of chicken broth. Mix well together, add a little salt, cook until very hot and serve on toast.

DUCHESS PUDDING.

Eight tablespoonsful of bread crumbs, pour over these one-half pint of boiling milk; cover, and when cold, add six tablespoonsful of crushed macaroons, eight tablespoonsful of finely chopped suet, one-half teaspoonful of salt, the rind of one lemon grated, six tablespoonsful of sugar, three eggs, beaten together; mix well and put into a buttered dish and bake for two hours in a moderate oven.

JAVELLE WATER.

One pound of sal soda, one quart of water, boil together until the soda is all dissolved. While this is being done, put one quarter of a pound of chloride of lime into one quart of water; let it settle, pour off all the clear liquid and add it to the liquid soda; bottle and keep for removing stains from linen.

JUGGED CHICKEN.

Cut the chicken, which may be an old fat one or a young one, into pieces the same as for fried chicken; for every pound of chicken take one tablespoonful of flour, which season well with salt and pepper; roll each piece of chicken in this flour, then pack the chicken closely into an earthenware crock and cover with cold water; cover the crock and bake for two hours, if a young chicken is used; three, if an old one, in a moderate but steady oven; the chicken requires no stirring.

For Boiling.

VEGETABLES :

Asparagus	Thirty Minutes
Beans, *to bake*	Five Hours
Brussell Sprouts	Fifteen Minutes
Cabbage	Forty to Sixty Minutes
Cauliflower	Thirty Minutes
Corn	Thirty Minutes
Lima Beans, if fresh	Thirty Minutes
Lima Beans, if old	Forty-five Minutes
Onions	Thirty to Forty-five Minutes
Parsnips	Forty Minutes
Peas, green	Thirty Minutes
Potatoes	Thirty Minutes
Spinach	Twenty Minutes
Squash, Summer	Twenty-five Minutes
Squash, Winter	Forty Minutes
String Beans	Thirty-five to Fifty Minutes

For Baking Fish.

Bass, Codfish, Haddock, Halibut, Salmon, Whitefish and all large fish, per pound................Fifteen Minutes

---

The following items of cook's measurement are worth remembering :

One pint of liquid equals one pound.
Two gills of liquid make one cupful.
Four teaspoonsful make one tablespoonful.
Two round tablespoonsful of flour weigh an ounce.
Half a pound of butter will make one cup.
Four cups of flour make one pound.
Two cups of granulated sugar make one pound, but of powdered sugar it will take two and one-half cups to make one pound.

www.ingramcontent.com/pod-product-compliance
Lightning Source LLC
Chambersburg PA
CBHW030300240426
43673CB00040B/1011